SHIELDS OF THE REPUBLIC

SHIELDS

OF THE

REPUBLIC

THE TRIUMPH AND PERIL OF

AMERICA'S ALLIANCES

Mira Rapp-Hooper

Harvard University Press

Cambridge, Massachusetts
London, England

First Harvard University Press paperback edition, 2023
First printing

Publication of this book has been supported through the generous
provisions of the Maurice and Lula Bradley Smith Memorial Fund.

Library of Congress Cataloging-in-Publication Data

Names: Rapp-Hooper, Mira, author.
Title: Shields of the republic : the triumph and peril of America's
alliances / Mira Rapp-Hooper.
Description: Cambridge, Massachusetts : Harvard University Press,
2020. | Includes bibliographical references and index.
Identifiers: LCCN 2019045224 | ISBN 9780674982956 (cloth) |
ISBN 9780674292161 (pbk.)
Subjects: LCSH: Alliances. | Cold War. | United States—Military
relations. | United States—Foreign relations—20th century. |
United States—Foreign relations—21st century.
Classification: LCC E183.7 .R27 2020 | DDC 327.73009/04—dc23
LC record available at https://lccn.loc.gov/2019045224

To Rayna Rapp, mother and mentor extraordinaire

CONTENTS

SHIELDS OF THE REPUBLIC

INTRODUCTION

All along the 2016 presidential campaign trail, American foreign policy orthodoxies fell in cascades. The party responsible was Donald Trump, the Republican nominee. American treaty allies were among his constant targets of criticism. He routinely called NATO "obsolete" and accused security partners of taking advantage of the United States economically.[1] He expressed casual disregard for the possibility that South Korea or Japan—both close allies—might suffer a North Korean nuclear attack. Foreign policy leaders the world over were aghast and yet hamstrung to respond. In the United States, Trump's critics struggled to explain why America has alliances, what they have accomplished, and why they remain valuable.

Trump's attacks on alliances did not win him the election, but they were not so transgressive as to disqualify him. Most Americans are highly supportive of alliances, but Trump's voters have embraced his position tightly. For the first time in modern history, our global partnerships are partisan objects. Democrats and independents favor them, while the president's core supporters stand opposed.[2]

Now, well into the Trump administration, campaign rhetoric is inextricable from US policy. The president has issued mafioso-like threats against allies, demanding that they spend more on defense. He has alienated them through the prospect of war with North Korea and Iran and pursued rapprochement with long-held adversaries while partners watch from the sidelines.[3] Congress has evinced some willingness to protect US alliances, but its small progress lays bare an uncomfortable truth. Most powers related to this longstanding tool of statecraft lie in the president's hands, which means the chief executive has near-unilateral ability to put alliances at risk.[4] For the moment America's seventy-year-old alliance structure remains intact. But it is absorbing such serious damage from within that full recovery cannot be guaranteed.

The president's alliance antipathy has taken root in part because it is not entirely unreasonable. To many voters, America's overseas military posture seems a grand expenditure that generates little or nothing in return. Why commit so much money to protect others, these voters ask. Why should the United States, the world's most powerful and most well-defended nation, take risks and make sacrifices for foreigners? Why devote taxpayer dollars and American troops to weaker allies who can give us so little in return?

But while this view is not totally baseless, it is also dangerously misguided. The system's original architects, survivors in some form of the Second World War, understood its value implicitly. After two global catastrophes in just twenty-five years, they were seared with reminders of why Washington should want to craft and fund security alliances. It was clear that alliances were necessary to deter and defend against the Soviet Union, to reassure war-torn partners in Europe and Asia, and to prevent further conflict. To younger generations, who have only known relative peace and prosperity, this calm may seem evidence that alliances are useless. At midcentury, however, Americans understood that alliance success would be measured in crises that never seized headlines and wars they were not called upon to fight.

With the passing of the alliance system's original architects and stewards, along with the everyday citizens who experienced the last century's wars, America lost its custodians of the counterfactual. Few can recall the dangers of a world in which the United States has no allies. Contemporary observers heavily discount an effective tool, in

no small part because they have been spared the world that neces-
sitated it.[5]

But America's alliance network is not only a victim of its own success. Since the end of the Cold War, the system has atrophied not
just in public esteem but also in the minds of policymakers, who have
lost sight of strategic goals. When the fall of the Soviet Union left
American power unrivaled in material and political terms, the
United States found itself with ample means and boundless ends, and
its foreign policy unconstrained. In this world of luxury, the alliance
system persisted but was unmoored from strategic purpose. Alliances were no longer clearly focused on defense and deterrence, and
scant effort was made to justify to the public their endurance. In the
years since, politicians and strategists have done little to change
course.

Influential scholars have abetted this alliance detachment. While
most foreign policy practitioners have consistently supported
alliances—albeit with perennial concerns about the balance of alliance responsibility—a vocal minority of international relations theorists have argued that US alliances are fundamentally dangerous.[6]
According to this view, allies draw the United States into conflicts it
could have avoided, and they drive its defense spending to unaccept-
ably high levels.[7] In place of the existing alliance structure, these
theorists support a grand strategy they call *restraint*. In journals,
books, and the *New York Times,* they call for the United States to
adopt a less ambitious foreign policy involving fewer overseas
commitments.[8]

Until the 2016 election, alliance skeptics received little pushback,
despite the fact that the restraint narrative can be misleading. For
example, in critiques theorists often conflate nonallies such as Saudi
Arabia with formal treaty partners, incorrectly suggesting that these
countries use the cover of US security guarantees—which they do
not enjoy—to behave recklessly.[9] Restraint proponents also rarely

consider the counterfactual: What would the last seventy years of US foreign policy have looked like without alliances? What risks would Americans assume if we end them? And while restraint arguments can be tested, they seldom are. Claims that allies pull the United States into unwanted wars or inflate its defense budgets are verifiable, yet, with a few exceptions, scholars have demurred.[10]

If these skeptical arguments have not been thoroughly examined, it is in part because so few scholars have investigated America's alliance successes. This most consequential of topics has slipped through the cracks of academia. Political scientists concern themselves with universal state behavior, as opposed to a single country's foreign policy choices, so they tend not to focus on whether a given state has achieved its strategic objectives. Instead they elucidate alliance patterns globally and throughout history.[11] Historians, for their part, have focused on specific alliances in discrete periods. They rarely seek to generalize their findings across time or space.[12] Academia has been both too broad and too narrow to answer a question of fundamental policy importance.

When candidate Trump emerged espousing reckless alliance views, academics and other policy experts supportive of alliances lacked the full accounting they might have used to persuade voters differently. Political leaders, retired military personnel, journalists, scholars, and others disputed Trump's position, but they struggled to engage directly with his instincts and explain the potential consequences of his views. Instead they merely asserted that the anti-alliance perspective was dangerous and out of step with recent history. They did not have the factual and theoretical ammunition to persuade members of the public whose placid life experience seemed to demonstrate that alliances were worse than useless—expensive, entangling, unnecessary for security.

In these pages I seek to provide the accounting that was missing in 2016. The balance of evidence suggests that America's alliances have been remarkably successful at protecting the United States. At the same time, no American ally has ever been the victim of a major attack, forcing the United States to come to its aid. There also is little evidence that allies entrap Washington in serious crises, wars, and stifling political commitments. And while the United States has maintained a healthy defense budget to support its troops and bases abroad, this spending has largely been devoted to Washington's preferred strategy of forward defense, not to America's allies per se.

Seventy years ago the US alliance system was designed to work in just this way. With the Axis Powers vanquished and most of Europe and Asia decimated, the United States was strong but exposed. Airpower and nuclear weapons had neutralized its fortuitous geography, and the Soviet Union offered a serious challenge. Instead of returning to foreign policy independence, Washington broke a long-standing tradition of eschewing standing alliances and extended a system of mutual security guarantees. The result was a genuine strategic innovation: a peacetime alliance system intended to neutralize threats before they reached the nation's shores, to protect partners, and to foster control over them. Maintaining this system has not been easy or cheap, but to assess its true value one must compare its burdens to the costs imposed by a world without allies. Understood in these terms, America's alliance network yielded immense Cold War political and security advantage at an acceptable price.

This remarkable alliance system, however, does not meet the trials of our time. Detached from its original goals, the system and its logics have not been updated for the contemporary world. In the immediate aftermath of the dissolution of the USSR, Cold War alliances in Europe and Asia were preserved despite the absence of a major adversary in either region. Abundant American power and resources kept US security guarantees alive, but this was a period of drift: alliances endured but ceased to be instruments of defense and deterrence, necessary to ensure American prosperity and security. Instead they were agents for America's global preponderance, used, for instance, to bolster liberal democracy in Eastern Europe. In the twenty-first century, the profound challenges posed by China's rise in Asia and the reemergence of Russian aggression in Europe demand that the alliance system recoup clear strategic purpose. The international system has changed twice over without concomitant alliance reform. In the meantime, the nature of competition itself has evolved. Adversaries are developing sophisticated military approaches to erode security guarantees and bypassing those guarantees altogether by acting in "subconventional" and nonmilitary domains. Information warfare, maritime assertiveness, hacking, and economic coercion are the terms of modern competition. More than the invective of any one president, complacency in the face of these transformations puts the alliance system at grave risk.

In spite of thirty years of drift, America's alliance system can be salvaged and its record of excellence extended for decades more. Its aims may be dated, but it is well positioned geographically, comprising the very states with which Washington should want to ally if it constructed a strategy from scratch today. The faulty alliance narrative, however, stands in the way; it must be corrected if the salvage operation is to succeed. Restoring the country's most successful tool of statecraft will not be possible if the American public and its leadership doubt the system which has kept the country safe.

Reevaluating America's alliances is a longstanding tradition. The United States has for generations reconceived the purpose of alliances as its role in the world has changed. This is because alliances are means with which to accomplish strategic ends, not objectives in themselves—they cannot usefully remain static as American strategy transforms. Today, as China rises and relative power shifts away from the United States, Washington should want to keep Beijing from establishing a closed sphere of influence in Asia and Moscow from infringing on Europe's political autonomy. This will only be possible with the help of alliances built for the challenges of the present.

If the United States recedes from the world or loses its allies through neglect, its security and prosperity will wilt. Instead the country might again embrace a new alliance logic. That would entail collaboration among allies for defense and deterrence in nonmilitary as well as conventional military domains, because the contours of conflict have changed since postwar security guarantees were formed. Allies must approach this task knowing that the era of boundless American power is in twilight, and that the United States faces ample domestic pressures, which may continue to stress its global partnerships. If the United States and its allies are able once more to recalibrate their collective-defense strategies, their security network will continue to reap strategic advantages. If they fail to re-inject this tool of statecraft with fundamental purpose, they risk losing the system altogether. Then the United States will likely pay a solemn price in blood and treasure.

Methods, Scope, and Definitions

This book reckons with America's alliance record, auditing its logics, costs, and benefits; explaining why the system has come under domestic and international duress; and contending that it can and must be saved. To this end, I draw upon history, international relations theory, and policy analysis. But this is not a traditional work of history or political science. I do not uncover documents or proffer a novel theory. Instead I rely on primary and secondary sources from multiple disciplines to make evidence-based arguments about America's alliance performance during the Cold War, explain the subsequent strategic drift, and make the case that policymakers must urgently set about to preserve and reform our alliances.

In a departure from most scholarly accounts, I assess all US alliances in Europe and Asia through present day, rather than focus on a single country or region. The book proceeds in approximate chronological order, commencing with an analysis of America's evolving alliance rationales from the country's inception. Two chapters are devoted to America's alliance record during the Cold War, after which I turn to the immediate post–Cold War period, and finally the present day.

The book's scope is, no doubt, ambitious. Nothing less is required to elucidate the dynamics of America's wholly uncommon foreign policy strategy. The long view illuminates the system's victories and its stumbles. Yet I find that the costs and risks of alliance have often presented themselves differently than we assume, with consequences far less grave than imagined.

Throughout the book, I rely on counterfactual analysis. Although this is a somewhat unusual approach, it is suited to the task at hand. That is because we cannot detect directly the nonevents that are the measure of alliance success. If alliances are serving their defensive, deterrence, and assurance purposes, wars and crises will never erupt, and allies will not defect. The challenge, then, is to isolate the role of alliances in achieving these results because other causal factors may be at play: peace and cooperation may prevail because an adversary lacks the will to attack or an ally the wherewithal to stray. If we are to credit alliances with propitious historical outcomes, we must parse a variety of forces that could explain the same results. With this in mind, I at times imagine how US foreign policy might have proceeded if Washington did not have alliances to rely upon. Of course, it is impossible to truly isolate one variable in a complex web of interconnected international political relationships linked across time and space, making counterfactual analysis an imperfect technique. Nevertheless, the difficulties surrounding alliance measurement call for its use. The method can help us to appreciate the strategic power that security guarantees have bestowed—and to recognize more clearly what we stand to lose without them.

A note on definitions is also warranted. This book is a study of formal alliances, which is to say, relationships that have been codified in mutual defense treaties. This does not include relationships of close alignment, which may have alliance-like features but lack a mutual defense treaty—say, the US-Israel relationship.[13] I also treat as distinct nontreaty relationships involving defense commitments.

The foremost example is the US pledge to Taiwan, which was once a treaty but was reduced to an act of Congress.

While relationships of alignment may be subject to some of the same principles I describe here, their reduced formality places them in a different analytic category. By electing to extend formal alliances to some states and not others, US policymakers give treaty allies a fundamentally distinct status. This is all the more true because, unlike its European counterparts, the United States had historically refused formal alliances before the early Cold War. If policymakers understood a need to dispense with this tradition and take on treaty allies as a separate class of partners, there was by definition something special about that group. It is only reasonable to assume, therefore, that the commitments extended to aligned but nonallied countries are qualitatively different than those of formal alliances, leading potentially to different results. For example, the loose security guarantee of nonallied partnership will typically have weaker deterrent effects. It would therefore be an analytic error to conflate formal alliances with informal alignments. There are volumes to be written on strategic use of informal alignments, but that task is not assumed here.

Finally, a word about terminology. I use the terms "alliance," "treaty alliance," and "security guarantee" interchangeably. Each refers to a formal treaty arrangement, in which a state pledges itself to aid an ally if the latter is attacked. In the case of the United States, the precise content of these pledges varies somewhat across alliances, as I detail in Chapter 1.

Book Outline

Chapter 1 argues that, throughout its history, the United States formed or abjured alliances based on a changing set of strategic goals. When it finally constructed its vast alliance system in the postwar years, it did so for reasons that were entirely novel.

From the post-revolutionary period through the First World War, the United States tended to avoid alliances for fear that entanglement with Europe would jeopardize its independence. The country preferred to rely instead on its favorable geography and an unencumbered foreign policy. With the close of the Second World War, however, American leaders recognized that an epochal strategic shift was taking place. The United States had ascended to superpower status, and the Soviet Union was its only peer. But while the United States was exceptionally strong, its geographic fortunes were reduced by long-range sea power, airpower, and nuclear weapons. Under these circumstances, the luxury of an independent foreign policy evaporated. Strategists felt urgently that the United States could not face this dawning world alone. If Western Europe or Asia fell to the Soviets militarily or economically, American officials supposed, the US economy and homeland could not endure. Allies would have to become the country's first line of defense. This was a novel idea in statecraft. Alliances had long been used to prosecute and win specific wars, but this ambitious system was intended to keep conflict from breaking out in the first place.

Chapter 2 examines the particular alliance commitments of America's early Cold War strategy. The United States formed a far-flung network involving twenty-three other countries. This was not altogether an intuitive scheme. Why should a major power have believed that pacts with small, faraway, war-ravaged states would guarantee its own survival? Yet, for reasons that I explore, this logic proved successful. Early Cold War planners hoped alliances would enable forward defense—that is, defense far from the homeland—and achieve deterrence. They also hoped that the allies would be reassured and more willing to accept US control. The pacts largely delivered on these objectives. The victories of the alliance system can be catalogued by the wars that did not occur and crises that did not escalate when Cold War politics suggested they otherwise might have. A case study of the 1961 Berlin Crisis contemplates how the United

States might have lost its Berlin foothold to the Soviet Union if not for its alliance strategy.

Chapter 3 examines the costs of the Cold War alliance-based strategy. It is hard to tabulate the costs of these guarantees for two simple reasons. First, we can never know what precise costs the United States would have accrued to maintain its security without alliances. Second, alliance costs can be measured in a number of ways, all of them imperfect. Alliance costs may be defined in terms of additional dollars spent on defense; wars fought in order to defend allies; or the political control and freedom of action relinquished when an ally abandons a treaty or entangles its benefactor.

By each of these admittedly flawed metrics, the Cold War alliance strategy was not nearly so costly to the United States as we might imagine. Indeed, the country faced few of the political costs that international relations scholarship would lead us to expect, and the financial costs were entirely tolerable. Without alliances, however, the United States would likely have confronted new and unaffordable forms of entrapment and abandonment—entering wars on unfavorable terms and without dependable partners—and would have lost out on the vast economic benefits that follow alliance treaties. The Cold War alliance strategy was almost certainly less costly than an alliance-free strategy would have been in a similar world.

Between 1989 and 1991, the target against which America had carefully arrayed its security guarantees disappeared. Chapter 4 investigates why and how US alliances in Asia and Europe survived the Cold War. In the 1990s Moscow seemed to be on the road to reform, and while China's economy was growing, there were no indications that the country was just two decades from becoming a power competitor. America was unrivaled. With material and political luxuries nearly unprecedented in human history, US policymakers sought to remake security guarantees under new logics in the hope of consolidating Cold War gains. The alliance structure was retained but its purposes recast. In Europe NATO became a tool for promoting regional security and liberal democracy. In Asia alliance renovations created two tiers of pacts, with the US-Japan and US-South Korea alliances updated for regional threats, while alliances in Southeast Asia atrophied. These post-Cold War changes ended up fostering some of the most substantial vulnerabilities US alliances now face, as detailed more extensively in Chapters 5 and 6.

The era of unrivaled American power would not last. Chapter 5 explores the reemergence of competition, from China and Russia. I argue that, because of their incomplete post-Cold War transition, US alliances are not presently equipped for either threat. Moscow and Beijing have each developed military and nonmilitary strategies that seek to undermine US alliances and Washington's role as a security guarantor. In distinct ways, each pursues its geopolitical aims asymmetrically and incrementally, using what I term *competitive coercion*. Competitive coercion seeks to diminish alliances' effectiveness and to exploit gaps in alliances by advancing adversary aims in ways that do not trigger treaty provisions. If either challenger succeeds in undermining US alliances—China has the better odds—it may fashion a closed sphere of influence in its region, shutting out American economic, political, and military power and jeopardizing US interests. Moreover, Chinese and Russian competition in cyberspace and via other new technologies further obviates America's geographic barriers. The United States finds itself less able than ever to keep itself secure by withdrawing to its borders. As a result its alliances have never been more important.

Chapter 6 turns inward. Contemporary challenges to American alliances are as much domestic as international. The 2016 election placed at the helm of American foreign policy a leader who has been antagonistic toward the alliance system for much of his public life. America's alliances are now routinely held at risk over longstanding issues of defense burden-sharing, and US alliance management is increasingly coercive. But America's alliance peril runs far deeper than the unorthodox views of a single president. The United States now faces fundamental questions about its role in the world, including whether the country can sustain a strategy reliant on security guarantees. Persistent domestic economic and political trends, as well as complex global power shifts, suggest that Washington will face lasting constraints as it seeks to exercise influence in the twenty-first century. No country will be more powerful than the United States for the next several decades, yet it is likely to confront ongoing political volatility at home, and its power in Asia will probably continue to decline as China grows stronger. Meanwhile US allies will still be limited in their defense capacity. If the United States is to guarantee its own national security and assist its allies, it will need to repurpose its alliances for this tempestuous world.

How can Washington grapple with twenty-first-century deterrence and defense challenges despite domestic turbulence and global power shifts? America's alliances must be reformed to adapt to the changing nature of conflict. Chapter 7 argues that Cold War alliance logics now hinder security because adversaries know them too well and have figured out how to circumvent them. Over the course of seventy years, adversaries have learned where Washington's conflict thresholds lie. They have also developed methods of aggression that skirt the international law governing nuclear and conventional war—law on which US security guarantees are based. Thus, as Russia and China have reemerged as competitors, they have increasingly relied on nonmilitary conflict and coercion, avoiding America's alliance commitments and bypassing deterrence altogether.

A sound twenty-first-century alliance logic requires Washington and its partners to confront these novel forms of conflict and competition, which may jeopardize the political independence of the United States and its allies without a resort to full-blown war. Fortunately America's allies—now wealthy, consolidated democracies—are up to this challenge, even if their conventional militaries cannot readily stand up to China's or Russia's. Indeed, the new strategic landscape is one in which US allies are better able to contribute to their own security and that of their American partner than they once were. Now more than ever, security is not exclusively a function of military power; it requires intelligence, law enforcement, and technological capacity; international coordination; and homeland security efforts. On these terms US treaty partners are well positioned. They can spend more for collective defense in the nonmilitary domain, illuminating the path to more symmetric alliances. This would make US security guarantees more effective and increase support for alliances at home.

Shields of the Republic

In his 1943 book *U.S. Foreign Policy: Shield of the Republic,* Walter Lippmann argued that the goal of American foreign policy must be to shape international politics in ways that serve to protect liberty and prosperity at home. Foreign policy, Lippmann observed, "consists in bringing into balance, with a comfortable surplus of power in reserve, the nation's commitments and the nation's power."[14] A country's international objectives must align with its domestic capacity to support them, both financially and politically. According to Lippmann a crisis of "solvency" occurs when a country's international commitments are poorly matched with its vital domestic reserves.

America's postwar strategists shared this view. Their object was to protect the republic through an ambitious, pragmatic, and ultimately solvent defense and deterrence strategy: alliances. These alliances were never missions of benevolence, intended above all to protect others. Rather, they were means for accomplishing strategic ends. The security of the American homeland and economy required a forward defense strategy; alliances were the tool of choice.

I adopt Lippmann's subtitle, with a slight modification. "Shields" is pluralized because alliance purposes and logics can change over time and, indeed, have changed throughout American history. America's first alliance helped it survive and win the Revolutionary War. Its distinctive Cold War system supported a peacetime grand strategy reliant on defense, deterrence, and allied control to hold the balance of power. These logics are still relevant to contemporary strategy, but America's shields must once again be refit to the objectives at hand.

Although Lippmann's subtitle is apt, I embrace it with some hesitation. In *U.S. Foreign Policy* and his subsequent *War Aims*, Lippmann argues that foreign policy solvency can be achieved by dividing the world into spheres of influence—hierarchical domains in which political, economic, and military strength is wielded disproportionately by one major power. He envisions granting spheres of influence to the British and the Soviet Union, both US wartime allies. America's postwar planners may have shared Lippmann's view about the goals of foreign policy, but they did not share his strategic aims. Instead of granting spheres of influence, they opted for a grand strategy that sought to limit the Soviet sphere using alliances. Likewise, I argue that, in the twenty-first century, the United States should seek to avert closed spheres of influence in Asia and Europe. The titular allusion therefore should not be interpreted as a full-throated endorsement of Lippmann's postwar geostrategic agenda.

Still, Lippmann's warning of a foreign policy solvency crisis warrants attention. Today America's alliance system is approaching insolvency, not because it is too financially costly to maintain but because American citizens and leaders are disconnected from its origins and fundamental purposes. The system outlived the adversary it was designed to restrain, prevailing with a strong record and at tolerable expense, before it began to succumb to the strategic languor of the privileged unipolar period. Nearly thirty years after the USSR's demise, and amidst China's rise and a revanchist spasm in Russia, American policymakers have not fully reconceived the role that alliances should play in twenty-first-century national security strategy.

Nor have they offered to the American people a narrative that details precisely why its alliances were salvaged from the embers of the Cold War. It is small wonder that many citizens, lacking a clear explanation of the system's Cold War record and its current potential, have come to see alliances as evidence of hegemonic overextension—outdated luxuries of a hyperpowerful America at its apex, which the country can no longer afford.

Quite to the contrary, today's power rivals and domestic volatility make alliances necessary to US foreign policy solvency. If policymakers seek to preserve the country's position, they would be wise to take heed of America's singular alliance achievements. History shows that alliances are powerful, dynamic tools that can continue to support peace and prosperity. Yet, despite their extraordinary record—indeed, because of it—the republic's shields are now in peril.

1

AMERICA'S ALLIANCE LOGICS

For the first century and a half of its existence, the United States had precisely one alliance. The 1778 military arrangement with France was valuable but highly controversial, and Americans could hardly wait for it to end. What they hoped to be rid of, according to a homespun tale, were the "entangling alliances" that America's first president supposedly cautioned the country against in his Farewell Address. Largely out of deference to George Washington's warning, American leaders eschewed alliances until the Second World War. The change was a watershed. Between 1948 and 1955, US leaders extended defensive security guarantees to twenty-three countries in Europe and Asia. Seventy years later the number of allies had grown to thirty-seven. Why did a country once doggedly committed to an independent foreign policy suddenly emerge as the most ambitious peacetime alliance architect in history?

The United States did not simply discover an appetite for alliances during the early Cold War period. Between the Revolution and the postwar moment, it transformed the ends to which these pacts would be used. The infant state had formed its alliance with France for the sake of independence and survival, and Washington warned against any further pacts for similar reasons. The early republic was young and vulnerable, its sovereignty was far from guaranteed, and alliances could enmesh it in Europe's endless conflicts. By the dawn of the twentieth century, Washington's strategic premises were growing obsolete, yet America's leaders clung to them, even when the First

World War obviated their rationale. Only during the Second World War and its immediate aftermath did US policymakers come to understand that the country could no longer guarantee its own survival. It would need a new theory of how to achieve national security—a new grand strategy.[1] The result was a sprawling and innovative system of defense pacts in Europe and Asia. Each alliance had unique qualities, but an overarching strategic logic united the project. The pacts that had once posed a risk to the independence of the United States would now help it to secure the peacetime balance of power and would become essential to its survival.

A Farewell to Allies

The Franco-American pact was a traditional bilateral military alliance. In exchange for France's wartime aid against Britain, the rebellious colonists guaranteed French colonial possessions in North America. The French offered supplies and later troops, ships, and skilled commanders.

Washington's Continental Army could not have prevailed without France's intervention, but Americans quickly came to see the alliance as a liability. The Continental Congress had little bargaining power when it signed the treaty and became increasingly dependent on it as the war dragged on. Concerned by their reliance on Paris, the Americans opted to negotiate a separate peace with Britain. In 1793, when France and Britain again went to war, Washington proclaimed American neutrality, rendering the 1778 alliance effectively, though not formally, moot.[2]

Over the next few years, the risks of the alliance only multiplied. The 1795 Jay Treaty improved Anglo-American relations, leading the French to fear that the Federalists were directing a volte-face against them. The French began a series of interventions into US politics in hopes of securing the Francophile Thomas Jefferson as the country's second president. The effort failed—John Adams won the coveted office and would, in 1800, negotiate the end of the US-French pact—but many, including Washington, feared continuing French subversion. The meddling made Washington's last year in office deeply unpleasant, and his Farewell Address contains barely veiled references to French treachery.[3]

The warning against "entangling alliances"—the specific language actually appears in Jefferson's 1801 inaugural, not Washington's text—was a contextual response to the alliance woes of the early United States. The first president believed that the infant United States needed political separation from Europe's seemingly endless troubles if it was to develop self-government and power of its own. "Our detached and distant situation invites and enables us to pursue a different course," he said in the Farewell. "Why, by interweaving our destiny with that of any part of Europe, entangle our peace and prosperity in the toils of European ambition, rivalship, interest, humor, or caprice?"[4]

Yet Washington was not implacably opposed to alliances, as the decision to partner with France demonstrated. He understood that there was a place for alliances in foreign policy, if they were used judiciously. And, despite his exhaustion with the French pact, he rejected the idea of breaking it. He also counseled that future "extraordinary emergencies" might call for "temporary alliances."[5]

Washington's early successors, including other US founders, had a similarly nuanced view. They were willing to entertain the prospect of tactical alliances when the need dictated—so long as those arrangements did not imperil the country's sovereignty and autonomy. Thus, while Jefferson took a firm line against any relationship that could jeopardize American independence, he weighed the prospect of a defensive pact with Britain that might allow him to drive the French out of Louisiana.[6] Had he been willing to risk warfare at Britain's side, he might have also managed to grab Texas in the gambit, but ultimately he demurred. And James Monroe, prior to his presidency, supported the idea of an alliance with Spain to protect free navigation on the Mississippi River.[7]

There is no evidence of another US president again considering a formal alliance in the nineteenth century. After all, for a hundred years America did not need one. With favorable geography, a small navy to patrol the coasts and army to guard the frontier, no overseas colonial holdings, and strong norms against foreign intervention, the young country was largely free of European interlopers.[8] This was particularly so after the War of 1812, when the British began to guarantee their former enemy's security through unofficial assurance. It was a case of convergent interests. Both the Americans and the British wanted European powers out of the Atlantic—the British to protect their trade routes and the Americans to claim the New World as their sphere of influence, as outlined in the Monroe Doctrine. But the United States could not enforce the Monroe Doctrine; instead that job fell to the Royal Navy. For the rest of the century, the United States was protected implicitly by British sea power, leaving the country to provide for its continental defense.[9]

In the second half of the nineteenth century, the American conception of national survival filled the continent and spilled beyond it, but the United States never relied on alliances with outside powers. Neither the Union nor the Confederacy had formal allies, and the frontier settlement, while terribly bloody, involved no military defense pacts. The century's close finally saw the United States risk its foreign policy independence through entry into the contest for overseas empire. In the four month–long colonial paroxysm of the Spanish-American War, the United States took Cuba, Samoa, Guam, Puerto Rico, and the Philippines and separately annexed Hawaii, giving it interests more than 3,000 miles from its shores, despite the fact that its military remained largely focused on continental defense.[10] Americans then spent more than a decade subduing the Philippines by force. Yet, throughout this process, the United States still managed to avoid alliances.

While the United States was taking territory in the Pacific and the Caribbean, Germany was rising in Europe. By century's turn it was apparent that Germany could eventually pose a direct threat to the United States—if it defeated the Royal Navy first. In 1914 the Germans set about doing just that, precipitating the transformative convulsion known as the Great War. Two years later the conflict was stalemated, and President Woodrow Wilson was preparing Congress and the American public to join. In a rousing speech delivered to some 2,000 onlookers on May 27, 1916, Wilson acknowledged that a barbarous conflict had upended President Washington's guidance: the security of the world would be determined on Europe's battlefields, and the United States would have to partner with other nations to defend it.[11] Indeed, the catalyst of US entry into the war was not Germany's threat to the United States itself but to Britain and France. What convinced Wilson and other Americans to fight was Germany's unrestricted submarine warfare in the Atlantic. The danger was not directly to US vessels and their passengers: the same subs could isolate France and blockade Britain, leaving the Western Hemisphere undefended.

Still, when the United States joined the war, it did so as an "associated power" rather than a formal ally—a uniquely Wilsonian legal distinction. In an effort to preempt criticism from congressional Republicans, who clung to Washington's Farewell as gospel, Wilson had publicly promised that he would never consent to an entangling alliance. He also initially refused to allow American troops to be amalgamated into Allied military units, to escape the impression that US soldiers were under the command of foreign nations. And associated-power status allowed the United States to avoid assuming the Allies' specific war aims, which had been codified long before Americans joined the fray.[12]

When the First World War ended, Wilson put forward a bold vision for postwar peace centered on the League of Nations. But he failed to captivate congressional Republicans, who were unconvinced that the League was not itself a formal alliance. In a speech decrying the League, Senator Henry Cabot Lodge admitted that the wartime associated-power status had averted the sins of a standing military alliance but argued the League would be a brazen violation of Washington's Farewell.[13] Lodge and his fellow Republicans objected to the League's vague, universal commitments and preferred instead a more traditional, joint Anglo-American security guarantee to France. But Wilson disapproved, and the United States wound up joining no formal agreements of any kind.[14]

Democrats and Republicans alike understood that the United States could no longer remain secure and aloof from European politics, but they disagreed on the proper response. Instead of adopting the League's collective security commitments or more limited, traditional pacts, the US leaders approached alliance and balked. The dangers of their folly would take two decades to mature.

Extraordinary Emergencies

American leaders deferred their reckoning with alliances but could not avoid it. As Europe and Asia were devoured by the Second World War, the United States would form with Britain its first formal post-independence defense treaty. The two held mutual suspicions: Americans blamed Britain for helping to start the last war that had engulfed them; the British lamented American abandonment of the League of Nations, and they knew that US power could soon eclipse their own.[15] But as the continent succumbed to Germany, the United States realized its security depended on Britain. Indeed, US survival had become inextricable from Britain's because Europe's fate would determine the global balance of power.

It took time for policymakers to reach this conclusion. Through the war's early years, President Franklin Delano Roosevelt insisted on cautious distance from Britain and thought often of Wilson's wartime and postwar failures. The public was even more hesitant. Americans were not ready to enter another European conflict, nor a formal alliance to preserve Britain, so Roosevelt offered everything short of one. Washington and London shared intelligence and held secret naval talks. Eventually Roosevelt agreed to supply the British with aircraft parts and munitions and to allow Americans to trade freely with belligerents through the 1939 cash-and-carry policy. After the fall of France in 1940, he signed the destroyers-for-bases deal, granting Britain fifty vessels in exchange for leasing rights to eight bases. As Germany ratcheted up the pressure on Britain, FDR announced the Lend Lease Act, authorizing him to transfer any war materiel necessary to the defense of the United States. When Hitler attacked the Soviet Union in his 1941 Barbarossa offensive, the almost-allies accelerated their joint planning to send war aid to Stalin. But there was still no formal security pact.

By August 1941 British Prime Minister Winston Churchill hoped for an American declaration of war. Instead he got the Atlantic Charter, a statement of principles that would govern the postwar world and demonstrated Washington's confidence that the United States would lead the peace. Roosevelt's calculation was transformed in December, when the Japanese attacked Pearl Harbor. Hitler had agreed to extend the Tripartite Pact with Japan and Italy beyond its original defensive provisions, which meant that the United States now found itself at war with both Japan and Germany.[16] Within weeks of entering the war, the United States announced its formal alliance with Britain.

With his war declaration and arguably well before it, Roosevelt recognized that George Washington's foreign policy premises had been subverted.[17] Technology had triumphed over happy distance: power could now be projected across oceans, diminishing the usefulness of those barriers. It was not only ships, such as the conflict-defining aircraft carrier, that could easily traverse the vast expanses that once insulated the United States. So too could Japanese and

German bombers, placing the US homeland at risk. Since geography no longer assured that the United States would be safe while the world was at war, the country would have to parry threats before they arrived. The destroyers-for-bases deal had acknowledged as much more than a year before Pearl Harbor. The United States had begun to build forward bases in the Atlantic and the Caribbean because homeland defense could not be accomplished solely from the continent.[18]

The threat to the United States was all the more daunting because it was bifurcated. American military planners had not anticipated a two-ocean conflict and did not have a two-ocean navy to work with. The ocean barriers suddenly appeared liabilities, and Britain's tenuous position compounded the problem. The Atlantic was not, in fact, an impregnable natural barrier; it was a defensive bastion only to the extent that the British dominated it. If Britain was secure, then the United States could keep its navy in the Pacific, where it had been almost exclusively for many decades. If Britain lost control of the sea, the United States was vulnerable to German naval and air power. Germany had begun to use commerce and its navy for coercive purposes in Latin America; if Hitler was able to neutralize both the British and French fleets, he might use Latin America as a launching point for an aerial invasion of the United States. These strategic conditions gave the United States a direct interest in Britain's survival. If the Royal Navy fell, America could only survive as a garrison state. As the balance of power in Europe dissolved, civilians and military planners alike agreed that if the United States did not wish to live in isolation, allied democracies would have to be its front lines.[19]

A military alliance was therefore imperative, and it worked remarkably well. The American and British high commands fused with extraordinary success and kept control of the world's oceans. The United States was able to supply the allies with a stunning two-thirds of all the military equipment used during the war.[20]

In the midst of conflict, it was already plain that this strategic shift was permanent. The basic requirements of US survival had changed, making reversion to the prewar posture impossible. Even with Japan and Germany defeated, the US homeland would remain vulnerable, for any adversary with wealth and technological savvy could develop a long-range navy and air force. Jet engines, ballistic missiles, and nuclear weapons rendered obsolete what remained of America's precious geographic buffers. In 1943 the Joint Chiefs of Staff began planning a network of overseas bases to create a defensive perimeter far from the continent.[21] But the problem was much bigger than force posture: the world was facing a power shift rarely seen in history. In defeat, Germany and Japan would be not just chastened but eviscerated and much of Europe and Asia razed. America would stand alongside just one power peer, and it would have to rehabilitate its adversaries while ensuring that their military potential was neutralized.

With the war concluded in October 1945, President Truman laid out the stakes in his address to Congress. "Our geographical security is now gone," he said. "Never again can we count on the luxury of time with which to arm ourselves."[22] The atomic bomb had cowed Japan, but US leaders knew their monopoly on the technology would not last, which meant that extraordinary emergencies could now unfold swiftly, unannounced. The strategic conditions that would compel the formation of the postwar alliance system had solidified: the United States was victorious, ascendant, and exposed.

A Postwar Superpower Strategy

The United States' role as a young superpower was undeniable by 1945, but neither its precise strategy nor its need for alliances was clear. American leaders were suspicious of the Soviet Union's intentions but did not yet see the two countries as in direct competition and were unfazed by its military strength. And while the econom-ically revved United States would have to assume Britain's role as global financial hegemon, it had little immediate interest in taking political leadership by forming new defensive commitments.

The broad strategic contours of this new world came into focus early: the United States would try to guarantee its safety by preserving its military dominance in both the Atlantic and Pacific. To do so it would have to practice defense beyond the continent. By establishing overseas bases, including in rehabilitated Japan and Germany, the United States could interdict incoming attacks, project power in peacetime, and punish aggressors in wartime, all with less risk to the homeland.[23] But bases were not alliances.

Within two years, postwar superpower cooperation had frosted into rivalry. The Soviet Union refused to accept free elections in Eastern Europe and rebuffed US plans for Germany. The United States responded with the Truman Doctrine and the Marshall Plan, manifesting its intent to resist communism and encourage capitalist democracy. By 1948 the Soviets had blockaded West Berlin, compel-ling the United States and its closest partners to mount 200,000 aerial-supply missions in one year to keep the city from caving to the pressure.[24]

As the Cold War standoff crystalized, the Joint Chiefs warned of potential Soviet domination of Eurasia. US leaders agreed that the Soviet Union's expansion could menace vital US interests; Soviet he-gemony in Europe or Asia would cripple the US economy and im-peril national security. George Kennan, the US chargé d'affaires in Moscow, powerfully summarized many of these concerns in his ac-claimed "long telegram" to the State Department, which argued that the United States could not allow the industrialized core of Europe or Asia to fall to communism. Later he would identify five critical military-industrial power centers in the United States, United Kingdom, Germany, Japan, and the Soviet Union. The West con-trolled four of them, but if even one changed hands, the balance of power would shift in the Soviets' favor. By 1948 Washington's objective was becoming clear: the US could not prevent Moscow from consolidating its position in the East, but it could and would defend the Eurasian periphery and prevent vital areas from slipping into Soviet control.[25]

With the specter of conflict returning to the continent, France, Britain, Holland, Belgium, and Luxembourg signed the Brussels Treaty in 1948, agreeing to aid one another in the event of an attack. All five had been devastated by the war, and their capabilities were sapped, so they asked the United States to join the pact. Washington considered the request but ultimately declined. It did, however, endorse the agreement. In a demonstration of bipartisan approval for the cause, the Republican chair of the Senate Foreign Relations Committee, Arthur Vandenberg, also secured a resolution to support the treaty.[26] The simple act of contemplating a Western European defense arrangement alongside its own emerging strategic objectives transformed the Truman team's calculations. Top aides had already concluded that the United States could not survive in the postwar world if Europe fell. Now they began to consider a transatlantic defense pact—for the first time, a peacetime alliance might keep America safe.[27]

Brussels to Washington

The novelty of the strategic moment meant that the potential transatlantic alliance was a tabula rasa, and few of its constituent details were obvious. Devising them would be a politically sensitive process.

Congressional Republicans remained committed to the idea of foreign policy independence and would not easily consent to Europe's postwar defense demands. Vandenberg, whose support was critical, was running for president and did not want to inspire other

Republicans to challenge him by backing an unpopular treaty. Truman, who was up for reelection, was similarly uneasy about publicly endorsing such a controversial project. He also worried that ratification might be impossible to secure from a Republican-controlled Senate.[28] It therefore made sense to delay pursuit of a treaty until after the election, in hopes that the voters would return a Democratic Senate that would back ratification. At the very least, the delay might reduce the chance that the treaty would be politicized during the campaign.

The administration therefore began its treaty project slowly and deliberately. One of its early steps was to research the legal and political issues that would govern the United States' security guarantee to Europe. Truman officials argued that, for reasons of legitimacy and political expediency, a defense treaty for Europe should be consistent with the commitments of the infant United Nations, rather than a route around it. To this end, the administration examined as a possible model the Inter-American Treaty of Reciprocal Assistance, which was designed to be consistent with Article 53 of the UN Charter, sanctioning regional organizations.[29]

The treaty, also known as the Rio Pact, was signed in 1947 by the United States and many Latin American and Caribbean states. It was the first US postwar multilateral treaty. FDR had used a wartime security assurance to prevent Hitler from gaining Western Hemispheric base access, the pledge had been formalized in a 1945 treaty, and the Rio agreement was a peacetime extension of that pact.[30] The Rio Pact was a negative security assurance from the United States, meaning that Washington pledged to prevent adversaries from intervening in the region. But under its terms it was almost impossible to authorize US military intervention, as two-thirds of members in the treaty organization—the Organization of American States—had to approve.[31]

Truman officials were confident that they could convince the Senate and the public of the merits of a Rio-like agreement for

Europe, but they also understood that such a pact would not fulfill the fragile continent's needs. European partners sought a promise of automatic US intervention in case of an attack; conflict would directly trigger US action, with no membership vote needed. By contrast the Rio Pact was less a true security guarantee than a formalization of the Monroe Doctrine. It codified a sphere of influence and created an organization for dispute resolution, but it did not ensure that the United States would intervene in case of attack. A transatlantic agreement also could not be governed by Article 53, which subordinated the activities of regional organizations to the UN Security Council. This gave the Soviet Union a potential veto over the activities of any regional body, which was clearly untenable for a defense promise that sought to protect Western Europe from possible Soviet aggression.

US officials looked next to Article 51 of the charter, which guaranteed every state the right to engage in individual and collective self-defense without permission from the Security Council. This became the basis of the eventual North Atlantic Treaty's Article V—the pledge that members would treat aggression against one as an attack on all. The administration's effort to comply with the UN Charter evoked protest in Congress. Detractors argued that committing to institutionalized collective self-defense would force the United States to abandon its independent foreign policy traditions in favor of an alliance of the very sort President Washington had warned against. Nonetheless, by staying within the bounds of the charter, Truman's team shrewdly reconciled the alliance with international law.

Senators also wrestled with the relationship between the North Atlantic Treaty and the Constitution. The Senate Foreign Relations Committee was especially concerned about Article V, the all-important mutual defense clause. The draft language promised "forthwith military or other action" following an attack. Democrats and Republicans alike were appalled that the administration would make a pledge that sounded automatic.[32] In doing so the administration was effectively proposing to shift significant war-making authorities from Congress to the executive branch. The language had to be reworked: the treaty would not foreordain a military response but would instead leave ambiguous the form of aid the United States was obligated to provide. Many committee members were mollified, but some holdouts still saw this formulation as a delegation of Congress's cherished power to make war. The committee also insisted that the treaty include a reference to decision-making "by constitutional processes," in an effort to prevent congressional war powers from being usurped.[33]

When the treaty was made public, Secretary of State Dean Acheson delivered a speech insisting that Congress would not lose its war powers. He averred that the North Atlantic Treaty did "not mean that the United States would be automatically at war" if an ally were attacked. At hearings before the Senate Foreign Relations Committee a month later, Acheson reiterated the limited scope of the commitment. "Article V . . . does not enlarge, nor does it decrease, nor does it change in any way, the relative constitutional position of the President and the Congress," he asserted.[34] A "guarantee" that left the United States flexible to determine its own response to attacks on allies, subject to intervention by Congress, was inherently Janus-faced. But no other arrangement would satisfy Capitol Hill.

A final issue for America's new alliance was its durability. The North Atlantic Treaty would be valid for a twenty-year term, renewable indefinitely; it was clearly not a temporary alliance in response to an extraordinary emergency. The Farewell Address was once again eulogized on the Senate floor, this time by the treaty's remaining detractors. The final vote, however, was decisive. On July 21, 1949, the Senate voted 82-13 in support of the pact. Senators from both parties agreed that America's peacetime national security could not be obtained without a secure and independent Western Europe. Almost a hundred and fifty years after terminating its first alliance with

France, the United States ratified the North Atlantic Treaty. But even its architects did not fully comprehend what it would become.

The Korea Conversion

The United States had accepted that it could not decouple its survival from the security of its international partners and intended to prevent another war in Europe through peacetime statecraft. But what would the young superpower do to realize this agenda?

Despite its strategic ambitions, Washington did not increase its overseas military commitments. In fact, the United States continued to draw down its deployed troops across the Atlantic and Pacific. Civilian policymakers like Kennan and military minds including General Douglas MacArthur believed the United States should adopt an offshore security posture, prioritizing the defense of the Aleutian Islands, Japan, Okinawa, the Philippines, and Guam. Accordingly the United States removed the last of its postwar troops from South Korea in 1949. In his now-infamous National Press Club speech in January 1950, Acheson pledged that the United States would defend a perimeter to include these offshore countries but failed to signal a stake in South Korea or Taiwan.[35] This choice of perimeter did not seem an obvious blunder—the United States was, after all, devising a novel forward defense strategy in real time. But the omissions of South Korea and Taiwan quickly became an elementary lesson in deterrence theory.

When 75,000 North Korean troops crossed the thirty-eighth parallel on June 25, 1950, they provoked a global crisis. The Korean Peninsula had been divided along the parallel, under US and Soviet trusteeship, since the end of the war. Two years prior the United States had called for a unified, independent Korea, but the Soviet Union refused its plans for elections and reunification. The Truman team then decided to support an independent South Korea.[36] But the backing was tepid, as demonstrated by the troop drawdown and Acheson's speech. After the North Korean onslaught, the United Nations called for aid to the South, and the United States obliged, sending troops and offering General MacArthur as UN Commander.

The defense of the South transformed the nascent alliance strategy in Europe. Europeans were reassured that the United States rushed to South Korea's aid, but they also gained a clearer sense of just how vulnerable they were. After all, Germany was divided much like Korea—partially administered by the Soviets, with Berlin itself submerged in the communist zone. Suddenly it seemed obvious that Germany could not survive as a political no-man's land, and its collapse would put the West in peril. German troops had to be integrated into defense plans for Western Europe; eventually, Bonn would need to become a full treaty partner.

The Korean War also demonstrated that the US defense guarantee needed to be far more robust, forcing the United States and its partners to assemble a durable military infrastructure. The result was NATO, the North Atlantic Treaty Organization. The Americans had pledged to support Europe using nuclear weapons and airpower, but these might not deter an opportunistic ground invasion akin to the North's on the Korean Peninsula. So the United States sent troops to Europe and in 1952 built a Paris headquarters where the NATO allies could plan for Europe's defense. The allies agreed to a joint military structure with a unified command, alliance-dedicated troops, and leadership by a supreme allied commander. General Dwight Eisenhower was the first to hold job, and the privilege was permanently reserved for an American. The United States also began to negotiate Germany's highly controlled rearmament and eventual admission into the alliance.[37]

These new NATO arrangements met with little resistance in the Senate, a striking turnaround from the earlier debates. Consensus was forged of the Korean example: deterrence and military cooperation now meant the difference between security and global peril. Before the war on the peninsula, this had only been a hypothetical concern. Now, remaining partisans were few and far less vocal than they had been when Truman and Acheson were pushing for ratification. It was beyond doubt that traditional US strategy was an artifact.

Eisenhower retained his commitment to NATO when he assumed the presidency in 1952. His defense team made a rigorous review of American national security and concluded that the country could not "meet its defense needs, even at exorbitant cost, without the support of its allies." To contain the Soviet threat, the United States needed to continue to increase its base presence, plan for overseas operations, and prevent major industrial states from falling to communism. In these efforts, alliances were deemed "essential."[38]

Allies to the East

The Korean War upended US plans for defending Asia against the Soviet Union. Before the invasion, the Truman team hoped to defend the Asian periphery with a modest American commitment only. Afterward, both Truman and Eisenhower sought to extend security guarantees to Asia.[39]

Once the war was underway, the need to secure the Asian periphery was acute, but the United States did not attempt it with a single treaty. As in Europe, US strategy for Asia aimed to hold the line against Soviet and Soviet-allied aggression and to permit the evolution of stable, independent, democratic governments that would eventually be able to contribute to regional defense. Policymakers sought to achieve this through a series of bilateral defense pacts that were tailored to US objectives and each country's defense needs. Like the North Atlantic Treaty, American treaties in Asia invoked Article 51 of the UN Charter in their defense pledges. But the United States found little initial appetite in Asia for a NATO-like multilateral defense pact. Many in the region were deeply fearful of a militarily rehabilitated Japan and could not yet make common cause with postwar Tokyo.[40] In several cases US officials also feared that reckless leaders in Asia's proto-democracies might entangle Washington in their own conflicts and chose to tailor their alliances to constrain those states.[41] Moreover, the United States extended pacts only to those countries with which it shared an adversary, but Asian countries often did not have common foes—there was no Soviet analogue against which to collectively defend. Some alliances, including those with South Korea and Japan, were backed up by tens of thousands of deployed American troops. But these numbers paled in comparison to outlays in Europe, and no NATO-like integrated organizational structure was sought.

The individual US defense pacts in Asia owed much to timing and historical contingency. For example, while the United States allied with Japan in an effort to protect itself in the bipolar, nuclear-armed world, the structure of the alliance also reflected narrower concerns. The circumstances facing Japan in the early Cold War left a strong imprint on this bilateral alliance and those that followed.

The Truman administration feared that war-weakened Japan would be co-opted by the Soviet Union. Officials did not foresee actual invasion, but they worried that Japan's fragile economy and feeble institutions would leave it vulnerable to subversion.[42] As a broken state with leadership adrift, Japan might become dependent on Soviet aid or amenable to communism. If it could be guided toward democracy, however, it was more likely to be a reliable partner to Washington. Japan's industrial potential made its democratization all the more tantalizing—rapid growth, political stability, and firm alignment could make it an ideal alliance partner and the cornerstone of American strategy in Asia. Truman's advisors planned to sign a peace treaty with Tokyo when it appeared to be politically stable and sufficiently aligned with the United States.

But American enthusiasm for Japan's potential was not shared throughout the region. Tokyo had invaded and subjugated much of

Asia, and its neighbors were not eager to see it restored and bristling. While many Asian countries might have preferred to see Japan totally disarmed, the intensifying Cold War standoff meant that it could not be stripped of its defenses entirely. A pacified Tokyo might bow to the Soviets. Instead, the United States would be responsible for Japan's controlled rehabilitation. By maintaining bases and troops in Japan, the United States could guarantee its political transformation and cautious rearmament as part of a broader peace settlement. Once the Korean War broke out, Japan became a genuine political and military crucible. It was evidence that the United States could be a reliable defense guarantor, using its military presence to build stability and protect the balance of power, rather than simply reacting to probes from the communist world.[43]

There was no perfect time to conclude a US-Japan treaty, which would necessarily spook other Asian partners. The occupation dragged on long enough to overlap with the region's next war. Eventually the Truman administration, wartime allies, and Japan set a date for peace: the Pacific War and postwar occupation would formally conclude in September 1951 with the signing of the San Francisco Treaty. Simultaneously, the United States would extend to Japan a defensive alliance to ensure its political independence. Upon learning that Japan would receive a security guarantee, Australia and New Zealand demanded their own in exchange for signing the pact. The Philippines learned of the exchange and lodged its own request.[44]

The United States obliged, and the San Francisco Treaty was signed on September 8, 1951. Japan was restored to sovereignty. It renounced claims to its former colonies and placed the Ryukyu Island Chain in US trusteeship, providing territory from which the United States could project power throughout most of Asia.[45] In a discreet ceremony the same day, Washington and Tokyo signed the US-Japan security treaty, guaranteeing that the United States would protect its ally from unprovoked attack. A week prior, the United States had concluded its first two Pacific security treaties: one with Australia and New Zealand, the second with the Philippines. In the span of just one week, the oblique but essential American security guarantee had found its way to the Pacific thrice over.

While Japan accepted peace, war in Korea raged. The United States fought alongside the South, although the two were not yet allies. Rather, Washington and twenty other nations rallied to the South's cause under the auspices of the UN Command. After more than two years of bloodshed, however, the Americans, who supplied the overwhelming majority of foreign military support, sought an end to the conflict. When the Eisenhower administration took office in 1953, its most immediate national security priority was ending the stalemated war.[46]

But American military officials were not looking simply to disengage. They feared another invasion if they did so, which meant US forces would have to remain on the peninsula. Policymakers began to consider a security agreement with Seoul. They also believed that the prospect of a defense treaty might hasten the war to its conclusion by overcoming one major obstacle to a drawdown: South Korea's president, Syngman Rhee. Rhee rankled his US partners by repeatedly insisting on nothing less than full defeat of the communists and complete reunification of the Korean Peninsula. He was, Eisenhower said, "recalcitrant." State Department officials went further, describing Rhee's "messianic sense of personal leadership." But a mutual defense treaty might convince Rhee to accept an armistice and ultimately a narrower settlement.[47] Such an alliance would not only serve US interests by helping to dissuade another communist advance, but it could also foster control over Rhee. The US and South Korean militaries had successfully established a single wartime command; a similar peacetime structure would give US military leaders opportunities to constrain Rhee and ensure he did not instigate a second conflict.[48]

The administration's gambit paid off. Rhee accepted alliance on the condition that the Americans provide military training to his troops and station 50,000 of their own on the peninsula.[49] Two months after the Korean War armistice was penned, the United States and South Korea concluded their mutual defense treaty. John Foster Dulles, the secretary of state, signed the treaty on behalf of the United States. Dulles was an influential supporter of the alliance strategy and was largely responsible for the proliferation of US security commitments in Asia. So dedicated was he to alliances that both contemporaries and later scholars have accused him of suffering from "pactomania," an affliction that caused him to look for an alliance solution to every geostrategic problem. While Dulles's treaty fixation was generally validated, his enthusiasm also led to overreach.

Nowhere was the pactomania malady more evident than in Dulles's creation of a multilateral alliance in Southeast Asia. The catalyst was France's failure to hold its colonial position in Vietnam: two days after the French were defeated at Dien Bien Phu, Dulles proposed an alliance with Thailand. This quickly evolved into an eclectic multilateral security guarantee that also included the United Kingdom, France, Australia, New Zealand, the Philippines, and Pakistan. The Manila Pact, signed on September 8, 1954, became the basis of the South East Asia Treaty Organization (SEATO), which Asian members hoped would be their regional NATO analogue. But the pact was primarily for the purposes of defense consultation, and although several members clamored for SEATO-dedicated military forces and a joint command structure, Washington resisted. SEATO quickly proved to be ineffective, primarily because the threat of American conventional or nuclear retaliation was poorly suited to deterring lower-level communist subversion such as guerilla war.[50]

Finally, the Eisenhower administration fixed its sights on Taiwan. The Republic of China had become the outpost of the nationalist Kuomintang party following the Chinese Civil War. Taiwan was not an early Cold War priority for the United States, but China's role supporting North Korea in the Korean War led the Eisenhower team to reassess the island's strategic value. But an alliance with Taiwan would not be a simple proposition. Like South Korea, Taiwan had an ambitious leader who sought reunification on his own terms. Chiang Kai-shek wanted a US security guarantee, but he also wanted to retake mainland China and drive out the communists. Americans knew they would have to restrain Chiang if they were going to ally with Taiwan.[51]

In late 1953 Chiang began to lobby for a mutual defense treaty with the United States, and the State Department agreed to open negotiations.[52] Chiang's goals proved an immediate sticking point. The nationalists wanted the treaty to extend to the offshore territories of Quemoy and Matsu, which the People's Republic of China also claimed.[53] The Americans knew that protecting Taiwan's claim could entangle them in conflict. But the French collapse at Dien Bien Phu had further convinced Eisenhower of the need for a Taiwan treaty to counter the Sino-Soviet axis, so his team forged ahead.[54] Then, in early fall 1954, the Chinese shelled Quemoy. They were resuming an earlier imbroglio, but they also hoped to convince Washington to abandon the treaty.[55] Instead the Eisenhower administration went forward with the security guarantee for Taiwan proper, excluding Quemoy and Matsu. To further restrain Chiang, the United States also demanded his agreement that he would not expect American aid if he used force offensively.[56] As with Korea, the United States managed to provide a defense commitment while taking special precautions to minimize risks.

America's Alliance Logics

Since America's founding, its alliance rationale has evolved alongside the country's developing understanding of its security needs. During the Revolution, the goal of the emerging United States was to win a particular war, and the alliance with France reflected this. In the post World War II years, America returned to alliances, but of an entirely novel sort. This new kind of alliance served a grand strategy

predicated not on victory in a single conflict but on maintenance of
the balance of power in Europe and Asia. The same tool of statecraft
has served distinct strategic purposes.

The decision to reject alliances, which held in the United States
for some 150 years, was also a function of grand strategic logics. For
the founders, America's first alliance was a sui generis case compelled
by a truly extraordinary and existential rationale. When that rationale no longer applied, the alliance was duly ended. George Washington's warning against entanglement persisted precisely because it
was consistent with the country's broader strategy. Nineteenth-
century American leaders were fully cognizant of geopolitics, and
their reading of the global situation counseled foreign policy independence rather than alliances. The priority was to achieve national
security and prosperity by settling the continent and establishing reliable self-government, tasks that could be hampered by alliances
with European governments. Britain had good enough reasons of its
own to protect the Western Hemisphere from incursions, which left
the United States free to avoid the liabilities of alliance while it pursued its own goals.

In the early twentieth century, the United States once again ex-
perimented with alliance-like partnerships. The aim this time was
not just to win a specific war—the First World War—but also to
shape the postwar balance of power and the peace in a manner that
benefited the United States. But the aversion to enduring entangle-
ments ran so deep that the country failed to formalize peacetime
partnerships and lost the opportunity to achieve longer-term strategic goals. The United States secured its desired war outcome but
was unable to establish a durable postwar balance of power.

When catastrophe struck anew just twenty years later, the United
States was coaxed once more off the sidelines. The strategic situation had changed yet again. Now the United States would fight not
only to preserve the global balance of power, but also for its own survival. With the British weakened and much of the rest of Europe

and Asia razed, the costs of failing to ally seemed a near-certain Axis triumph and a world in which America was alone and exposed. The knowledge that British hegemony would not survive the war, and the suspicion that America could take up that mantle, provided further motivation to ally closely. By prosecuting the war in tandem with Britain, the United States could not only influence the war effort but also position itself as Britain's successor. This was a wartime alliance with aims that reached beyond the conflict. The partnership was structured both to clinch victory and to assure that the United States would not retreat again—that it would remain to lead the peace.

The transition toward broader alliance goals that began with the Second World War solidified in the early Cold War years. The treaties brokered by the Truman and Eisenhower administrations were not constructed to win one conflict, or even to win a war and shape the peace. These alliances were intended to last for decades. The United States had identified a strategy in which it would maintain a significant military, economic, and political presence to hold the Eurasian periphery and prevent Soviet dominance. Over time the focus of this strategy expanded to include not just the Soviets but other communist powers, including China and North Korea.

The logic of the Cold War alliance system was especially unusual because there was no armed conflict with the principal adversary. The United States intended to use alliances to keep the peace from breaking in the first place. Of course, for millennia, powers had pledged themselves to military cooperation of various forms, sometimes with such specificity that they seemed to be planning a war on paper. Treaties could enumerate potential adversaries and specific military contingencies that would bring alliances into force. Occasionally treaties would detail responses so specific that they would include troop commitments.[57] America's peacetime treaties looked entirely different. They also differed from nineteenth-century European peacetime efforts. European powers had sought to maintain a continental balance through the mutual consent of other major

Year	Alliance	Participants	Primary threat	Purpose
1778–1783	Franco-American	Kingdom of France, American colonies	Great Britain	independence, survival
1917–1918	Entente Powers	France, Britain, Russia, United States (as associated power)	Central Powers	maintain balance of power in Europe through armed force
1942–1945	Allied Powers	United States, Britain, Soviet Union, China, United Nations	Axis Powers	maintain balance of power in Europe through armed force; survival
1949–1991	Atlantic alliance, hub-and-spokes system in Asia	NATO, Japan, Philippines, South Korea, ANZUS, Republic of China (until 1979), SEATO (until 1977)	Soviet Union, China, North Korea	maintain balance of power in Europe and Asia through defense, deterrence, and allied control; survival

Fig. 1.1   America's alliance logics, Revolution through Cold War

powers, as in the Congress of Vienna. Later, German Chancellor Otto Von Bismarck also turned to military alliances. But these partnerships were intended to counter specific military threats. There was no precedent for the Atlantic alliance—a standing guarantee that looked beyond any single war to deter faraway conflict using entirely new means.

One innovation was Washington's explicit invocation of the UN Charter to authorize the alliance, something it was under no obligation to do. Customary international law had long recognized the right of self-defense and even collective self-defense. But the United States chose to justify the Atlantic alliance on the basis of the charter in part for political reasons—it could not be accused domestically of overriding the nascent UN before it had been fully tested—and to demonstrate that the alliance, like the UN, was a force for peace. The Atlantic Treaty became a template; subsequent treaties also invoked Article 51. Doing so justified the relationship between US alliances and other international institutions. The decision was also important for the UN Charter, whose ink was barely dry. By enshrining Article 51 in a series of global alliances, the system served to legitimate a fragile body of international law.

The logic of the alliance system was not dictated purely by global security concerns. Domestic political issues also colored the new alliance structure. The White House could not create the peacetime system if it wrested war powers from Congress. The alliance project was therefore guided by a fundamental constitutional question: How could the United States make an advanced security commitment in peacetime without upending the separation of powers? The answer, ultimately, was vagueness—language committal enough to satisfy the allies without promising anything so firmly that Congress would balk. A similar balance was struck in all subsequent American defense treaties.

But while certain details held from one alliance to the next, the system was not standardized. Its architects understood that national security demanded different sorts of alliance, depending on the benefits offered—and liabilities incurred—by each potential partner. Individual pacts were therefore tailored to the circumstances of the participants, even if the various treaties amassed to form a coherent whole.

A single cogent logic nonetheless prevailed throughout the system. The United States sought to maintain the peacetime balance of power in Europe and Asia through defense, deterrence, and allied control. This was true even though, as a novice security guarantor, Washington had to learn the requirements of alliance management on the job. The Korean War had demonstrated in stunning fashion that America's immediate postwar plan had been flawed; there was no model for a modern peacetime security guarantee, much less a vast system spanning Eurasia. Many elements of the structure would have to evolve.

With the North Atlantic Treaty, the United States had hoped to provide a strong political guarantee and the promise of airpower, but it ended up developing a vast multilateral military structure and making significant material commitments to continental Europe. Similarly, events led the United States to commit tens of thousands of troops to South Korea and Japan but none to Australia and New Zealand. And, of course, the entire system rested on the implicit threat that the United States could use nuclear weapons on behalf of an ally—a form of far-flung deterrence that had never been possible before.

After abjuring alliances for 150 years and entering them only during extraordinary emergencies, the new superpower crafted a novel and ambitious alliance logic. A tool that the United States had used exclusively for finite, urgent commitments became the bedrock of a durable global strategy.

Alliance Alternatives?

How should we understand the significance of the unprecedented American decision to form a peacetime network of security guarantees? One way to comprehend this strategic shift is to consider how the twentieth century might have been different had the alliance system formed sooner. What if the United States had not disavowed alliances in the wake of the First World War, but instead embraced them? How would the two decades that followed have been different?

Any reasonable answer to this question depends on what precise shape that alliance embrace would have taken. The United States could, for instance, have joined the League of Nations in 1919. But even if the United States had joined the League, the body was unlikely to have forestalled the next war. One of the League's principle goals was to ensure that member states, such as Germany, did not go to war with each other. But its provisions on this score were too weak to prevent conflict. The covenant entered members into compulsory dispute resolution and held out the possibility of sanctions if they did not abide by the judgment of the arbitration. But members were nonetheless allowed to make war with each other so long as they had observed proper procedure. The League created a formal process to govern conflict but did not claim to eliminate it.

The League's few encounters with war demonstrate that it was not up to the task of preventing major conflicts. The League Covenant "failed its first great test" in 1931, when Japan, a member state, invaded Manchuria. The League's Lytton Commission responded by censuring Japan for attacking China, another member. But instead of submitting to the commission's verdict, Tokyo promptly withdrew. Later, in 1935, the covenant's collective security provisions were applied on behalf of member-state Ethiopia, which had been attacked by Italy, another member. But the League was unable to constrain Italy.[58] Washington's membership would not necessarily have reversed these outcomes, much less prevented Germany's aggression in the 1930s.

Moreover, even an American-backed League would have faced the frailties of a collective security system. Collective security agreements, like the League or United Nations, are broad efforts to keep the peace among the community of nations. Collective security does not target a specific adversary, and it has limited enforcement mechanisms. Members of collective security systems therefore cannot presume that the system will be able to deter all violators or defend victims once they have been attacked.[59] By contrast, collective defense involves specific, advanced commitments based on legally enforceable treaties, which seek to deter conflicts or prosecute them if necessary. The roles of the actors and potential repercussions are far more clearly delineated.

Let us instead suppose that the United States had taken another plausible path toward alliance—one not necessarily involving the League of Nations—by joining with Britain to guarantee French security after the First World War. In 1919, during negotiations at Versailles, France sought a more traditional alliance with Britain and the United States to protect against future German aggression. Senate Republicans preferred the French proposal because, unlike the League, it came with a specific and finite set of obligations. President Wilson, however, saw this as an ancien régime solution to a problem that his League could fix in a more enlightened manner. The treaty was never put before the Senate. The Brits forged ahead, but the guarantee collapsed as a function of poor design.[60] Had the United States joined with Britain, the pact may have been considerably stronger and the course of human history starkly different.

True, an Anglo-American guarantee would not have stopped Adolf Hitler's rise to power. And ample scholarship suggests that Hitler was committed to European conquest and would not have been easily deterred.[61] We must therefore suppose that the Anglo-American guarantee was insufficient to dissuade his earliest conquests and even his ambitions in France. In this world, Hitler would still have invaded Poland, Denmark, Norway, Belgium, the Netherlands, and Luxembourg in 1939–1940, bringing the Nazis to France's doorstep. With the 1919 Anglo-American pact in force, Hitler would have been met there by a combined French, US, and British force. After considerable exertion and sacrifice, including higher death tolls for all four major belligerents during the summer of 1940, Hitler may have been stopped altogether in the Battle of France.

Between 1939 and summer 1940, at least half a million people still would have fallen in the European theater—a tragedy, to be sure, but a fraction of the forty million who would perish by 1945.[62] Moreover, with Hitler's European objectives checked, and the United States in the fray, the Japanese likely would not have attacked Pearl Harbor. The Sino-Japanese War would already have resulted in 1.5 million deaths and could well have continued, but it is hard to imagine that the Pacific War would not also have changed course dramatically, yielding a death toll far short of reality's gruesome 30 million. It is possible, then, that an alliance vision far less grand than Wilson's, credibly established and enforced, would have saved tens of millions of lives worldwide.

American policymakers had a similar counterfactual exercise in mind in the years after the Second World War. Through disengagement, the country had abetted the devastation of the 1930s and 1940s. With the world ablaze, the United States was forced to defend itself from a belligerent power whose rise it might have helped to thwart at a diminished price. When the conflagration was extinguished, alliance appeared a prudent strategy to head off the emerging threat from the Soviet Union. But US planners knew they could not rely on an old-style treaty, the sort their predecessors refused in 1919. As bombers and nuclear weapons vanquished geography, and as Soviet influence expanded, American strategists developed new uses for a familiar tool. They hoped the novel approach would turn far-flung sovereigns into the shields of a mighty but exposed republic. These defenses would hold more steadily than they could have imagined.

2

DEFENSE AND DETERRENCE
IN THE COLD WAR

As the Cold War set in, US policymakers recognized that competition with the Soviet Union was a geopolitical reality. Those same policymakers hoped to prevent conflict through international institutions and laws, but they knew that the United Nations alone could not protect all of the nation's vital interests. If the United States failed to defend essential military-industrial powers in Eurasia—including defeated ones that might rise again—it could find itself an isolated bunker-nation. Thus alliances were layered on top of the new postwar institutions. The United States ringed Europe and Asia with security guarantees to contain Soviet influence.

The decision to form a far-flung network of alliances with small, war-ravaged states was not altogether intuitive. If one seeks to protect oneself, why not partner with the strongest possible allies? But early Cold War planners realized there were good reasons to ally with the specific weak states they chose. Most important was geography. In exchange for its security guarantee, the United States would gain access to bases ideally located for the purposes of forward defense and deterrence and would gain political relationships that made its guarantee credible. And because weak allies were dependent on US protection, the United States garnered influence over their leaders—leverage that it could use to stabilize and preserve its alliances.

This system came at some cost. In particular the United States had to reassure allies it was truly committed, necessitating considerable outlays in US troops and money. Washington also had to supervise the recoveries of Germany and Japan, to prove to other allies that these once-aggressive powers could be trusted as members of the US-backed network.

As Lord Hastings Ismay, the first secretary general of NATO, summarized, the alliance system was designed to "keep the Americans in, the Russians out, and the Germans down."[1] The network had to give the United States the forward bases and political ties it needed to hold off Soviet aggression, while reassuring allies that the United States would keep them safe.

Insofar as it can be measured, America's alliance gamble appears to have paid off, largely delivering on planners' objectives. With the strategy of forward defense and deterrence in place, no alliance members were ever attacked. Washington kept its allies in check, so that they did not threaten the system. And by keeping the allies' worst impulses at bay, the United States managed to avoid entanglement in faraway wars.

Why Did America Ally?

States often form alliances to balance against an adversary, offsetting its economic and military power and counteracting its threats. By pooling resources, allies defend against a rival who might otherwise be able to defeat them individually.[2] Thus in the late nineteenth and early twentieth centuries, for example, European powers generally chose to align with other strong states, in hopes of matching the warfighting capabilities of their competitors through defense collaboration.

The United States applied a very different logic in the early Cold War. The allies it selected had largely been decimated in conflict just a few years earlier. They were vulnerable to Soviet pressure and did not add much to America's military strength. It is tempting, therefore, to believe that the United States was providing a service on behalf of those in need. Those who excoriate Washington for spending on defense commitments to countries that cannot reciprocate seem to believe precisely that. But US leaders did not choose this alliance structure for altruistic reasons. Unlike European leaders of the pre-World War I era, they saw alliance asymmetry as advantageous.

Declassified documents from the early Cold War period reveal why US strategists made the choices they did: because they wanted to site bases far from the homeland. These would allow rapid response in case conflict broke out and would put the frontlines in Europe and Asia, not California or New York. Distant bases also heightened the deterrent effect of American power by demonstrating that the United States had the capability to fight far from home and the will to do so. The United States did not need fully reciprocal guarantees. Instead it needed geographically advantageous states on its side, so that it could defend and deter while exerting control over them, thereby ensuring its own survival.

Forward for Defense

Defensive alliances allow partners to make war preparations together by pooling their resources.[3] But allies can be useful apart from their military and economic might. An ally also can be geographically beneficial, particularly if it is proximate to potential adversaries. A major power might acquire bases on the ally's soil, improving its own defensive footing and impeding an adversary from attacking closer to home. This is known as forward defense.

This was a leading logic of the Cold War system. After a devastating world war, America's partners did not have much firepower, but they formed a perimeter around the Soviet adversary where the United States could site troops, naval vessels, aircraft, and other equipment. In exchange for basing rights, which require host states to cede some of their sovereignty, the United States promised security.[4]

Forward defense mitigated the vulnerabilities major powers felt after the advent of long-range air power, missiles, and nuclear weapons. But those weapons were also vital to the operation of a forward-defense effort. The United States could use its own nuclear and long range–strike capabilities to guard faraway allies. This marked a turning point in the logic of defense. Historically defense had largely been a tactical and operational problem of protecting borders. Modern military technology accelerated the capacity to deliver enormous destruction, so that defense became a strategic problem. Now the question was how the United States could keep its homeland safe when nuclear warheads and, soon, long-range missiles could arrive with only minutes' notice. The protection of the homeland and of allies could no longer be responsive, ceding initiative to the adversary: it required advanced preparation and positioning. Forward presence was the solution to this strategic problem, allowing the defender to maintain abroad the capabilities it needed to deny the adversary a quick victory if war erupted.[5]

Forward presence has other benefits, too. By working on the ground with its allies' governments and armed forces, the major power can help its allies build up their own capabilities and plan for potential conflict scenarios. And overseas troops can provide planners at home better intelligence on foreign threats.[6]

Military planners began studying postwar basing options as early as 1943, but America's postwar defense strategy did not crystallize until the early Cold War, when the Soviet Union emerged as the primary foe. Only then did it become clear that many US bases belonged in Europe. By 1947 the Joint Chiefs of Staff considered the need for bases in Europe to be urgent, and they encouraged the Truman administration to secure long-term basing rights.[7] Absent an American military presence, senior US officials argued, Europe would collapse in the event of a Soviet attack.[8] By 1948 American officials agreed that the Soviet Union was willing to use force to further its objectives, necessitating a US-led alliance based in Europe to resist.[9]

For the architects of the Atlantic alliance, the potential of one or another partner depended in part on the degree to which it would aid in forward defense. George Kennan evaluated prospective NATO members on the basis of the military value they could provide. Other officials considered which Western European countries would be most likely to grant advantageous base access.[10] This planning did not immediately come to fruition—only after the Korean War demonstrated clearly the value of forward defense did NATO establish its integrated military structure and the United States drastically increase its troop commitment in Europe. The sudden and calamitous invasion on the Korean Peninsula was evidence that the defensive logic of the Atlantic alliance needed to be implemented more fully.

In Asia, too, US alliances were driven by a forward-defense logic, centered on the so-called First Island Chain. American strategists identified as geographically advantageous the line of islands and archipelagos descending from the Aleutians, through Japan, and to the Philippines. This stretch would, strategists believed, serve as a defensive perimeter.[11] Kennan argued that the United States should adopt a maritime strategy against the Soviet Union, emphasizing control of the island chain and sea lanes to secure the Pacific, and General Douglas MacArthur announced the strategy publicly in 1949.[12] In 1951 Dulles, then a Truman administration consultant, argued that the First Island Chain, extending as far south as Oceania, should be the country's primary defensive priority. Every friendly country in that chain was a potential ally in Dulles's view. His advocacy nudged the Truman team toward extending alliances to Australia and New Zealand and Eisenhower to ally with Korea and Taiwan.[13]

Each component in the chain had a role to play. As early as 1945, US officials recognized that the Philippines was appropriate for forward basing. The country faced few external threats, and its geographic position made it strategically propitious.[14] Japan also was deemed a geographic jewel, useful for defense against Soviet sea power. From bases in Japan, the US Navy could hem in the Soviet Navy in the Pacific, or so the thinking went.[15] As American leaders prepared to sign a peace treaty with Japan, trading occupation for alliance, civilian and military brass argued that continued control of Okinawa and the Ryukyu Island Chain was crucial for US naval power projection. Japan was only more valuable after the outbreak of the Korean War and the intensification of the Chinese Civil War, emerging as the hub for US operations in the Pacific.[16]

Over the course of the Korean War, the South, too, emerged as a strategic location. In the early years of the war, the Truman administration was no more eager to extend a formal defense treaty to the mercurial Syngman Rhee than it had been when it omitted South Korea from its defense perimeter in 1950. As the war dragged on, however, the administration focused on the benefits the South could provide in containing threats.[17] When Eisenhower took office, his team also looked to Korea as a possible land anchor of the First Island Chain that would help the United States hold the line against the Soviet Union and its proxies.[18] This dovetailed with President Rhee's demand that the United States promise the South protection in exchange for alliance. Eisenhower wanted the war over but was happy to comply: he agreed that 50,000 American troops belonged in South Korea for the long term. A US outpost in the South could prevent another communist fait accompli. If instead the United States decamped, as it had in 1949, communist forces might eventually gain a foothold in the South, making it impossible to defend South Korea and difficult to protect Japan.[19]

Taiwan too became an ally in part because of its value in forward defense. In the late 1940s, American strategists hoped that China would be unified under the control of Chiang Kai-Shek and would serve as a regional counterweight to the Soviet Union. Instead the Chinese Civil War left the mainland under communist control and aligned with Moscow. American planners flirted with the idea of intervening to seize Taiwan as an American base but decided the move was too risky.[20] The matter then lay dormant until the Korean War broke out, after which US strategists again began to advocate for forward deployment on the island. The Republic of China had the second-most capable noncommunist military in Asia, after South Korea's, and Taiwan's location just a hundred miles from the Chinese coast made it a useful foothold. Furthermore, strategists reasoned that if Taiwan were to fall into communist hands, it would become much more difficult to defend Japan, the Philippines, and even Australia. Taiwan was an indispensable link in the First Island Chain.[21]

In Europe and Asia, the United States intended to hold the balance of power by using alliances for forward defense. But the goal was not simply to have troops and equipment well positioned if fighting should break out. Forward basing also fulfilled a second goal of the alliance system: extended deterrence.

Allying to Deter

When a state practices deterrence, it aims to prevent another from taking an unwanted action by altering the way it evaluates that action's costs. At its most ambitious, deterrence seeks to prevent wars from breaking out when they might otherwise. This was the task that the United States arrogated to itself after the Second World War. As Bernard Brodie asserted in 1946, "Thus far the chief purpose of our military establishment has been to win wars. From now on its chief purpose must be to avert them. It can have almost no other useful purpose."[22]

Deterrence strategies come in two basic forms. A strategy of *deterrence by denial* aims to demonstrate to an adversary that it will not achieve its goals if it attacks. *Deterrence by punishment* seeks to

convince an adversary that if it attacks, it will suffer devastating retaliation. Put differently, denial demonstrates that the defender has
the capabilities it needs to prevail in a specific war, while punishment
communicates that the prospective war will be too costly for the at-
tacker to bear.[23]

When a state practices deterrence on its own behalf, it sends
signals that an adversary should not attack its homeland. But alliances can help a state to project deterrence, taking deterrence by
punishment and denial beyond its borders. When a state aims to
dissuade attacks on distant allies it is practicing *extended deterrence*.[24] By making targeted threats and demonstrating its capacity
to secure its allies, a state can deter wars that might otherwise
have involved them. If deterrence is successful, those wars will
never erupt.

Achieving extended deterrence is much more difficult than establishing deterrence on behalf of one's own country. If an adversary
threatened the West Coast of the United States, and American leaders
responded by promising devastating punishment in return, no one
would doubt their sincerity. Extended deterrence, however, requires
the defender to promise that it will treat an attack on a foreign
country as an attack on its own, obligating it to assume great cost
and risk on behalf of others' immediate security.[25] Such a promise is
inherently less credible than a promise to defend one's own territory
and sovereignty.

Extended-deterrence guarantees become all the more tenuous if
an adversary has the ability to retaliate against the defender. Say the
United States promises to protect France from the Soviet Union,
which lacks missiles that can reach the United States. In this case the
United States will not face direct retaliation if it enters a conflict on
behalf of the French ally, so the defensive promise is relatively easy
to keep and its deterrent power is accordingly high. If, however, the
Soviet Union can strike the US homeland, then by pledging to defend France, American leaders are accepting the possibility that their
country will be struck in return. Will they really come through on

their promise? Would Americans really risk New York for Paris? This dilemma necessarily leads allies to question whether security guarantees can be trusted.[26]

Because of these complexities, a defender practicing extended deterrence must project its intention to intervene on behalf of the guaranteed party in advance of conflict. Alliances can help it do so. By making formal and public commitments—rather than ad hoc and informal ones—the defender signals to the world its intentions to protect the ally.[27] Formal alliances place the defender in an advanced commitment, and if it fails to respond when an ally is attacked, it may suffer politically costly reputational damage. A defender might also demonstrate the trustworthiness of its guarantee by signaling early its military capability on allied territory. By forward deploying "trip wire" troops or moving major military platforms into an ally's territory, it shows that an adversary cannot attack the territory without involving the defender.[28]

Before the emergence of long-range power-projection technology, it was nearly impossible for even a major power to extend deterrence to multiple allies that lay oceans away. But with the invention of bombers, missiles, and nuclear weapons, a once-impossible task became feasible for the United States. The country also had stronger interest in assuming this ambitious mission, lest its most valuable military and economic partners face quick destruction, making it the potential next target of attacks.

American planners focused on these logics. Numerous sources show that, as planners crafted postwar strategy, they discussed how they could use deterrence to prevent the outbreak of another catastrophic war. Writing to Secretary of State George Marshall in 1948, Kennan argued that the Atlantic alliance should not only defend Western Europe but also deter attacks against it.[29] In 1948 the Joint Chiefs of Staff worried mightily about how the United States would be able to defend Europe, given the relative weakness of prospective allies there—but the Joint Chiefs acknowledged that the pact had great deterrent value.[30] The Americans also emphasized the value of deterrence in an effort to win over skittish European allies. Recall that Europeans insisted the United States automatically declare war in case of an attack, but American leaders refused lest they run into congressional opposition and potential constitutional roadblocks. To assuage the Europeans, they replied that the pact's purpose was deterrence: the US security guarantee would prevent Europe from being attacked at all.[31]

Deterrence also drove alliance commitments in Asia. Dulles argued that the United States could deter attacks throughout Asia from its position on the Japanese archipelago, particularly if Japan was strong.[32] During the Korean War, the US intelligence community believed a security treaty with South Korea would allow the United States to establish what is known as *intrawar deterrence*, whereby an adversary in an ongoing war is dissuaded from escalating. By establishing effective deterrence in the midst of conflict, the United States might deter future Soviet-backed attacks on the South. With a US alliance in place, any Soviet-backed onslaught against South Korea—which was already illegal under international law—would become too risky.[33]

Similarly Taiwan came to be seen as a deterrence asset. During the Chinese Civil War, senior officials dismissed Taiwan's deterrent value, arguing that the United States could not be an effective security guarantor in the circumstances. But after the communist victory, these strategists reconsidered. If America's security interests lay in limiting Chinese power and disrupting the Sino-Soviet alliance, then Taiwan had a role to play. By 1954 the chairman of the Joint Chiefs was arguing that only US troops could keep the Chinese from overrunning Taiwan completely. And because the United States had a military-assistance group on the island and patrolled the Taiwan Straits, others argued that Washington had already made a de facto commitment to Taiwan's security, so it should sign an alliance treaty to reap full deterrence benefits.[34] This was still not an easy choice, because, as the National Security Council acknowledged, a US alliance with Taiwan would help to ensure that there would be two separate Chinas. If the Republic of China had American backing, neither the communists nor the nationalists could be destroyed without a world war.[35] Deterrence, if successful, would freeze the cross-Straits conflict in a stalemate. Indeed, deterrence seemed to be so powerful that it could reshape Cold War geopolitics altogether.

Allying to Assure . . . and Control

A third set of alliance motivations emerges from the difficulties entailed in making extended deterrence promises believable, and the coercive options that become available to deterrence-extending states. In addition to defending against or deterring attacks, formal alliance gives a defender opportunities to assure its allies that their security is in fact being protected.[36]

Assurance is difficult but often necessary to establish the credibility of a security commitment. To be credible, a defender must have reason to act as it says it will, coming to the ally's defense even at risk to itself. But, as we have seen, it is understandable that both allies and potential adversaries would doubt a defender's promises. This is especially the case when there is severe asymmetry between the defender and its allies. The weaker state is expecting to be defended, while knowing that it cannot reciprocate. Why would the defender follow through at great cost to itself? Moreover, the weaker ally never really knows what the defender is planning. Only the defender's leaders possess full information about whether they will really uphold their alliance commitments in wartime, and even they may not be certain until crisis arises. This leaves allies short of information and with a nearly unquenchable thirst for assurance. To slake it, the defender can deploy signs of commitment, such as cooperative military training and planning, regular diplomatic dialogues, and information and intelligence sharing. These signs of commitment aim to persuade the ally that its security is entwined with that of its guarantor, assuaging worries.

But if the cost of assurance is taxing to deterrence-extending states, they also gain an important benefit. The fears of weaker allies reflect their dependency, and that gives defenders control.

The weaker ally knows it cannot easily secure a new defensive guarantee, so it is beholden to its guarantor. The superpower's extended deterrence is a more potent source of defense than the weaker state can accomplish on its own through conventional self-defense and less costly than pursuing its own nuclear arsenal.[37] So weak allies do what they can to retain the defender's favor. They grant base access and other defensive benefits to the defender and may also cede to the defender some leverage over their national security policy. Dependence makes the weaker ally more susceptible to sanctions and political pressure, which in turn keep it from pursuing destabilizing activities.[38]

Deterrence-extending states can use their leverage for all sorts of ends. A guarantor may seek to ensure that its ally does not develop military systems that undermine its own strategy—for instance, an independent nuclear arsenal that complicates lines of authority and makes deterrence more difficult to uphold. As Victor Cha has shown, a guarantor may also convince its ally to abandon dangerous interests that it does not share, such as retaking territory lost in a prior war. The defender may further insist that the ally make consequential security decisions in close coordination—a boon when allies have been weakened by war but can be rehabilitated as strong and prosperous regional players. In cases like these, the defender is capitalizing on asymmetry by implicitly threatening to remove the alliance guarantee if the ally fails to comply. The very same asymmetry that can saddle the defender with extra assurance responsibilities pays off when the defender gains opportunities to shape weaker allies' behavior.[39]

Control over allies may bestow a security guarantor with yet another benefit: leverage in negotiations with the adversary. The guarantor's influence over allies' behavior provides chips in those negotiations. For example, by promising to stop its ally from developing nuclear weapons or retaking disputed territory, the defender can gain a coercive edge over a potential foe.

With each new alliance, US policymakers sought to achieve some measure of assurance and control. The Atlantic alliance was, at heart, an assurance mechanism from the start. US officials' central worry was that an economically and militarily decimated Europe would succumb to Soviet pressure. Alliances would provide the assurance Europeans needed to recover even as the Soviet threat loomed—the origin of the term "security umbrella."[40] Perhaps the strongest example of reassurance at work was the US relationship with West Germany. The United States hoped West Germany would redevelop its industrial capacity and eventually integrate into NATO. But Washington did not give Bonn a free hand. By controlling West Germany's rearmament and wider revival, the United States could also reassure other European allies that their former adversary would be restored as a benign regional actor.

Assurance and control were also compelling logics in Asia. Like Germany, Japan could be revived industrially and rearmed defensively, without unduly spooking other partners. The United States could use its control over Japan to reassure Asian countries that Tokyo would not be allowed to become aggressive again. The United States could also reassure those countries using treaties. Australia, New Zealand, and the Philippines were all deeply concerned about America's alliance with Japan, and Washington assuaged them by giving them guarantees of their own, thereby facilitating Japan's return to the world stage as a useful ally.[41] America's first three Asian alliances all sought to carefully rehabilitate Japan without causing regional alarm.

And, as we have seen, in South Korea a security guarantee enabled the United States to assure and restrain President Rhee. The Korean case became a model for Taiwan. Dulles, invoking the new Korea alliance, argued that the United States could begin treaty negotiations with Taiwan if Chiang agreed to curb his offensive instincts. The treaty would be exclusively defensive in nature and would make clear that the United States would not support aggression by Taipei against the People's Republic of China. Chiang ultimately agreed to these terms.[42]

Evolving Alliance Logics

While forward defense, deterrence, and allied assurance and control held as central logics across America's alliances, they did not feature in each pact in the same combination. Where potential allies lay further afield from adversaries, as in the case of Australia and New Zealand, forward defense and deterrence were less significant. There, US planners did not invest in integrated military planning, preferring to save resources for the defense of Northeast Asia. Instead the pacts with Australia and New Zealand were primarily motivated by the desire to reassure allies. Indeed, much of the Pacific alliance system began as an effort to assure a jittery region that Japan would be rehabilitated as a benign actor, and commensurately to exert control over Tokyo. The United States did not ally with Australia primarily for reasons of direct defense. It did so in order to gain Australia's confidence in and support for Washington's regional security system, which, in turn, afforded the United States greater strategic opportunities.

The goals of defense, deterrence, and assurance manifested in US efforts in both Western Europe and Asia, despite the fact that Washington took different approaches to the two regions. NATO was conceived as a holistic multilateral alliance from the start because US deterrence and defense efforts focused on a single, if vast, front line. In Asia, defense and deterrence were no less important motivators, but the discontinuous maritime geography in the region—and the need to defend allies against distinct adversaries like the Soviet Union, China, and North Korea—meant that deterrence and defense could be better accomplished through more focused, bilateral pacts.

Both approaches—multilateral and bilateral—enabled assurance and control through varying mechanisms. America's alliance logics themselves prevented a one-size-fits-all approach.

The power of these logics was only augmented as the first few years of the Cold War played out. When Washington's alliance entrepreneurship began—in 1948–1949 in Europe and 1950–1951 in Asia—American leaders recognized the need for forward defense and deterrence but hoped that the nuclear capabilities would keep its forward basing requirements modest. The strategic surprise inflicted by the Korean War, however, demonstrated that Soviet-backed adventurism was no abstract specter. It would have to be met with conventional power, so American strategy shifted in both theaters. In Europe the United States bolstered forward defenses and formed NATO's integrated military command in 1952. In Asia the end of the Korean War and the collapse of the French position in Vietnam led American policymakers to extend additional pacts in South Korea, Taiwan, and Southeast Asia to strengthen deterrence not only against the Soviet Union but other communist challengers as well. The Atlantic alliance extended membership to Greece, Turkey, and West Germany around the same time.

When the Korean War revealed the limits of Washington's early Cold War alliance strategy, the United States did not abandon the underlying logics. It redoubled its commitment to them. To some extent, the US appetite for alliance grew with the eating. In 1948 the country's foreign policy minds were hesitant to sign a defense treaty with Europe; by 1954 they were all too eager in Southeast Asia.

These new alliances were definitively not altruistic, nor were they instruments for fighting and winning a given war. They were innovative peacetime tools for securing a novel conception of the national defense. One by one, weaker allies took their place in a strategy that aimed to hold the balance of power in Europe and Asia and thereby keep the United States safe and secure.

America's Cold War Alliance Record

America's postwar planners may have produced an innovation in statecraft, but did their alliance strategy work? International relations scholarship suggests that alliances do advance the goals American planners set out in the early Cold War. Forward-deployed troops are proven to enhance deterrence in alliances. Alliances have also been shown to significantly lower the risk of conflict involving the allied states. And scholars have found that alliances with nuclear-armed states are especially likely to improve deterrence and reduce the risk that smaller countries will be targeted by adversaries.[43] The Cold War historical record reflects these findings. With an alliance in force, no US ally was a victim of an unprovoked attack, and no ally invoked its treaty commitment with the United States.

The United States also gained from its leverage over partners, most notably West Germany and Japan. Under US protection, the countries not only became central to America's military position in Europe and Asia respectively, but they also became consolidated democracies with vibrant economies—leading regional powers in their own right. Along the way, they adopted domestic and foreign policies that were highly beneficial to their patron. Former adversaries became fulcrums of American strategy in Europe and Asia, and since the Cold War ended, Japan and Germany have continued to play this role.

Scholars have also found strong evidence that security guarantees stem the spread of the world's most dangerous weapons. States that receive security guarantees from nuclear-armed powers are significantly less likely to pursue or acquire their own nuclear weapons. Cold War history demonstrates this nonproliferation effect. Between the 1960s and 1980s, the United States convinced West Germany, South Korea, and Taiwan to abandon nuclear weapons programs through implicit or explicit threats to end alliances.[44]

Moreover, alliances provided Washington with a benefit that early Cold War strategists did not anticipate: alliances lowered the cost of military and political action worldwide. Since the early 1950s, American treaty allies have joined every war the country has fought, although they were not required to by the terms of the alliance. European allies contributed over 20,000 troops to the Korean War, and South Korea alone sent 300,000 soldiers to Vietnam. Such multilateralism also improves the perceived international legitimacy of military interventions, as in Korea and in the Balkans after the Cold War. Evidence also suggests that by maintaining close defense relationships, the United States gained from allied diplomatic cooperation that would otherwise have been harder to secure.[45]

America's alliance record was not unblemished, however. American allies were involved in some interstate violence, especially where treaty application was contested or unclear. And deterrence did not prevent the use of force at all levels of the conflict spectrum. Taiwan and South Korea were involved in crises short of war despite the US security guarantee. Within NATO's borders, Greece and Turkey have skirmished with one another, and the alliance may have exacerbated tensions between them.[46] And, late in the Cold War, the United Kingdom went to war with Argentina over the Falklands. The closest of US allies was at war with a member of the Rio Pact, although the United States itself did not become involved militarily.

The United States also failed to stop its French ally from acquiring nuclear weapons, and in 1966 France left the NATO military structure rather than submit its weapons to centralized control. The French departure was part of a broader assurance crisis that seized NATO as the Soviets acquired intercontinental ballistic missiles, precipitating a New York-for-Paris extended deterrence dilemma.[47] Elsewhere, Washington's attempt to establish SEATO never advanced, and the organization foundered—alliance setbacks to which I return in Chapter 3.

But, despite these stumbles, America's alliance record is actually more impressive than may be apparent. The United States granted security guarantees to states that faced high likelihood of attack. These states were especially likely to seek their own nuclear weapons and other independent defensive capabilities and to become embroiled in Cold War conflicts. Against all odds, they did not.

Still, could it be that the success of America's strategy owes to some cause other than alliances? How do we know it was alliance that maintained peace? Political scientists have established that states with alliances are less likely to become victims of attack, but it is harder to confirm exactly why this is so in any given case. Was an adversary deterred from attacking the ally because of the defender's strong signals of commitment, or did the adversary never wish to attack at all? Indeed, while the logic of deterrence is straightforward, international relations scholars cannot calculate exactly whether it is working.[48]

Furthermore we do not know if the power of alliances lay in the security guarantees themselves or in the process by which the United States formed them in the first place.[49] Washington did not extend security guarantees everywhere it might have, choosing instead to grant defense pacts to states with which it shared clear interests and adversaries. This perfectly sensible approach to strategy makes it hard to know whether formal alliances intrinsically have great deterrent power, or whether the preexisting confluence of interests between the United States and its closest partners was enough to send strong signals to Cold War adversaries.

It is also possible that other post-1945 forces help to explain the security the United States and its allies enjoyed. The post-World War II period has been called the "long peace" due to the lack of overt war between major powers, which, in turn, helped to preserve the stability of smaller states and international politics as a whole.[50] To be sure, there have been numerous international conflicts since 1945, but none saw the leading states square off against each other directly. Explanations for this period of relative calm include the structure of the Cold War international system, divided as it was between American and Soviet camps; the presence of nuclear weapons on both sides of the competition; increasing economic interdependence, which reduced the incentives to go to war; the spread of democracy and its ostensibly pacifying effects; and international law and strong norms against territorial conquest.[51]

These are not necessarily contrary explanations, however. Indeed, each can be linked to the power of US alliances. Alliances are thought to be more stable in bipolar systems; nuclear weapons implicitly support US security guarantees; alliances and beneficial trade flows are closely connected; nearly all American allies are now consolidated democracies, although they did not begin as such; and alliances explicitly invoke international law that prohibits aggressive conflict and outlaws territorial conquest.[52] Alliances are not only inextricable from some of these other potentially salutary forces but directly exploit and advance them. If alliances' precise pacifying effects are vexing to measure, it is in part because alliances are vectors for some of the other post-1945 forces that are thought to have contributed to peace.

In sum, when peace prevails and crises do not arise—that is, when *general deterrence* is effective—it seems likely that the power of alliances is at play, but it is difficult to confirm this with certainty. It is easier, however, to examine the role that alliances play in *immediate deterrence*—efforts to resolve brewing crises before they spiral into conflict. A case study of one of the highest-stakes standoffs of the Cold War helps to demonstrate how forward defense, deterrence, and allied control and assurance may have helped the United States and its allies defuse wars before they started.

The 1961 Berlin Crisis

The 1961 Berlin Crisis was the last of three major political flare-ups over the contested status of the German city. It is also a primary example of how an alliance allowed the United States to deter potential conflict, defend its national interest, and exert control over its ally to facilitate the settlement of a crisis.

At the end of the Second World War, Germany was partitioned between the victorious allies. The Soviet Union would administer eastern Germany, and the United States, Britain, and France would divide authority over the western part. The four powers would share occupation of Berlin, which was located a hundred miles inside the Soviet zone. At first American policymakers embraced the idea: four-power administration would keep Germany as a whole weak, and the United States could run things as it wished in its own areas. However, by the end of 1947, with the Cold War seizing Europe, the Western powers concluded that the Soviet Union would not cooperate in overseeing Germany. The country would have to be formally divided, and a less-than-sovereign West German state established to protect the Western Allies' zones.

In 1948 the Soviets responded by cutting off ground access between Berlin and West Germany, forcing the allies to stage a year-long airlift to supply their sectors. The blockade piqued Western fears that their position in Berlin was essentially indefensible. Western leaders worried that they might have to withdraw from the city altogether.[53] The Joint Chiefs wondered if "some justification might be found for withdrawal of occupying forces without undue loss of prestige."[54] Ultimately the blockade accelerated the process of building a West German state. It catalyzed the formation of the NATO alliance that same year. When the Soviets broke the US atomic monopoly in 1949 and North Korea overran the South in 1950, the United States only became further committed to the strategic defense of Western Europe. The Soviets, in turn, became more fearful of West German

Fig. 2.1   Divided Germany and Berlin

rearmament. Under these circumstances, West Berlin became a proving ground for the perilous postwar settlement.[55]

After 1949 Germany was officially divided into the Federal Republic in the west and the Democratic Republic, or GDR, in the east. Berlin remained suspended in the Democratic Republic, providing a porous border through which millions of Easterners crossed into the West during the 1950s. This mass migration drained the Democratic Republic, with grave economic consequences. Then, in

1955, the Federal Republic became a full-fledged NATO member, to Moscow's consternation. West Germany began rearming with Western imprimatur. The Soviets rightly suspected that West German leadership was seriously considering building an independent nuclear arsenal. The Soviets responded by forming and investing in the Warsaw Pact, which would defend against NATO and its members. East Germany was included in the alliance.[56]

The next major Berlin eruption came during the Eisenhower administration. In 1958, with fears about West German strength mounting, Soviet Premier Nikita Khrushchev issued an ultimatum to the Western powers. In six months, he said, he was going to sign a peace treaty with East Germany, ending the Soviet occupation and handing over all administrative functions to the East German government. That meant the Western powers would have the same amount of time to withdraw from Berlin. If they wanted to keep their access and military presence there, they would have to negotiate with the newly empowered East German government.[57]

The Western powers objected, insisting that the Soviet plan would undermine their rights to the city, as established in the postwar settlement. Khrushchev responded that the allies had already abrogated their rights by bringing West Germany into NATO. Khrushchev's deadline passed without consequence in May 1959, but he did not withdraw the ultimatum. The threat to sign the peace and eject the Western powers persisted for the rest of Eisenhower's presidency. With the status of Berlin a lingering question, the West German military continued to strengthen, and NATO integration proceeded apace.[58]

When John F. Kennedy was elected in 1960, he was well aware that he faced a deferred showdown on the status of Berlin. Thus one of the new administration's first major foreign policy moves was the introduction of a "flexible response" strategy anticipating tensions in Germany. Flexible response was intended to make more credible the large-scale US conventional defense guarantee in Western Europe, so that the United States would not have to immediately escalate to promises of nuclear war in the event that West Berlin was threatened.[59] Less than five months after Kennedy's inauguration, Khrushchev revived his threats over Berlin.

The tension was thick in June 1961, when Kennedy and Khrushchev met in Vienna for their first bilateral summit. The two leaders made an odd pair. Kennedy was a forty-four-year-old foreign policy novice. He had just experienced a stinging national security defeat in his flubbed Bay of Pigs invasion, for which his Soviet counterpart had excoriated him.[60] Khrushchev was an experienced statesman of seventy-five, known to be of erratic and irascible temperament. And he held at the ready the Berlin ultimatum, which he could easily renew. Feeling "unabating" pressure from GDR First Secretary Walter Ulbricht, the Soviet premier did exactly that.[61] Khrushchev restated his intent to sign the peace treaty with East Germany, terminating the occupation and, with it, Western access rights to Berlin. Under further pressure from Soviet hardliners who demanded swift action, he set a fall deadline for the treaty. Kennedy responded that the allies were not in Berlin by East German invitation but by virtue of their contractual postwar rights, which the Soviet Union could not abrogate. Kennedy also announced that Western Europe, West Germany, and West Berlin were vital American interests and would be treated accordingly.[62]

Khrushchev responded by threatening war if the status of Berlin was not resolved to his satisfaction. In doing so, he sought to call Kennedy's bluff. West Berlin was not militarily vital to the United States in any strict sense; the defense of West Germany was not contingent on it. Yet Kennedy worried that if he lost access to West Berlin, West Germany would slip out of the Western camp, either becoming neutral or realigning with the USSR.[63] Kennedy quickly began to coordinate with Britain and France as to the precise position the allies should take and the means they were willing to commit to preserve their position in Berlin.[64] British Prime Minister Harold

Macmillan and French President Charles de Gaulle quickly made public statements declaring their rights in Berlin could not be dissolved.

Upon his return to the United States, Kennedy established a task force on Berlin. The group concluded that Moscow's aims were three-fold: it likely sought the permanent partition of Germany; it hoped to end allied rights and access to Berlin; and it sought to gradually erode the rights of West Berliners, neutralizing Western power in the city. The Kennedy team began to coordinate contingency planning with its French and British allies. Planners anticipated the actions they would take under three conditions: 1) the Russians signed a peace treaty with East Germany; 2) the Russians signed the treaty and interrupted Western civilian access to Berlin; 3) the Russians signed the treaty and barred Western military access to Berlin.[65]

The superpowers also sought to demonstrate and intensify their military commitments to Berlin. In early July Khrushchev made a public speech restating his ultimatum. He also announced a one-third increase in the budget for the Soviet armed forces. And he sent separate notes to Kennedy, Macmillan, and de Gaulle threatening different American, British, and French national interests in hopes of dividing the alliance. Instead the allies coordinated their responses, replying as Kennedy had in Vienna: the Soviet Union had no legal basis for terminating Western rights in Berlin, and its threats to do so were the real danger to peace.[66]

In late July Kennedy made a speech of his own. He declared the United States' defensive intentions in Berlin but insisted he would protect Western rights in the city. He requested and received an additional $3.5 billion in military spending to fund Army personnel, airlift capacity, munitions, and other equipment. He also announced that he would triple the size of the draft, call up Army reserves, and field six new Army and two new Marine divisions.[67] Despite the urging of some of his advisors, however, Kennedy opted not to declare a state of emergency over Berlin, judging this to be excessively escalatory and preferring to save the option in case it became necessary later. He wanted military pressure to be credible, but he also wanted to leave room for Soviet retreat.[68]

Khrushchev was impressed by the US president's demonstrated commitment to Berlin and the seeming cohesion of the alliance in the midst of crisis. Soviet intelligence also detected Western preparations to reinforce Berlin in case of conflict with Moscow, which added credibility to Kennedy's words and his budgetary move.[69] Under duress, Khrushchev authorized a KGB disinformation campaign to exaggerate Soviet military strength around Berlin, revealing that he "took very seriously the military might of the United States and NATO."[70] Having previously told his son Sergei that "no one would undertake war over Berlin," he now admitted to Soviet allies that "war is possible . . . they can unleash it."[71]

Since the Vienna meeting, East Berlin had been hemorrhaging a thousand refugees a day. Khrushchev had to find a solution or face the wrath of hardliners at his Party Congress. What to do, now that the Allies had shown their resolve? He was faced with a dilemma: he could escalate, gambling for a peace treaty by risking nuclear war with NATO. Or he could settle for more modest objectives, cutting off the refugee escape route through West Berlin. He chose the second option.[72]

On August 7 Khrushchev declared that he would imminently "close the loophole" that was West Berlin, effectively warning the Western powers not to interfere. On August 12 Ulbricht signed an order to close the border, and by the next morning it was rendered impassable by miles of barbed wire and fencing. The East Germans had been stockpiling construction materials, and just a few days later the Berlin Wall bisected the city.[73]

Initially both sides sought to avoid further escalation. US intelligence received advance notice that the border would be closed, yet the Western powers did not interfere or even object for two full days after the closure. The Warsaw Pact alerted NATO that the barrier was a temporary measure that would not affect Western access routes. The GDR announced it was imposing travel restrictions on East Berliners but that no action had been taken against West Berliners. In spite of these assurances, Kennedy did call up 148,000 reservists, and he sent his vice president and a new battle group of 1,500 soldiers to Berlin. De Gaulle agreed to increase his troop contribution to NATO by 30 percent. And all three Western powers placed their garrisons on alert. But, in truth, they were relieved. Khrushchev appeared to be solving his own Berlin problem without jeopardizing the Western position. From the Soviet perspective, Hope Harrison writes, "the wall itself was the way . . . to bury the idea of a German peace treaty."[74] Allied leaders hoped the barrier had brought the standoff to an end.[75]

But the 1961 crisis did not end there. In late October a senior American diplomat was stopped at Checkpoint Charlie, a high-traffic crossing between East and West Berlin. He refused to be turned away. Within days ten US and ten Soviet tanks faced one another at the checkpoint. The tanks were loaded with live munitions, and both groups had orders to fire if fired upon. The US Strategic Air Command boosted alert levels; its West Berlin garrison and NATO echoed the alarm, raising again the possibility of a superpower nuclear exchange.

Kennedy and Khrushchev took to a backchannel to seek resolution. They agreed that the standoff had catastrophic potential and decided to withdraw. The Soviet tanks move backward by five meters; the Americans followed suit. Each group edged away in turn, until the impasse concluded without incident. It was the superpowers' only direct military standoff during the Cold War.

In late 1961 the Soviet Union abandoned its ultimatum. The United States had weathered the crisis without bending to Khrushchev's demands: the allies maintained their position in Berlin, including military and civilian access. By early 1962 Khrushchev declared that a peace treaty was no longer necessary. The four powers did not immediately conclude a formal agreement to resolve tensions, but by

1963 a modus vivendi of sorts had consolidated among them. With the wall in place, the political status quo could now be respected in Berlin and in both halves of Germany; the United States would permanently maintain a large military presence; the NATO alliance would continue to strengthen; and Washington would work to keep West Germany nonnuclear—which it did, by suggesting it might abandon the alliance unless Bonn gave up its nuclear ambitions. With the refugee crisis under control and West German power in check, the Soviet Union could accept the arrangement.[76] "It's not a very nice solution," Kennedy observed, "but a wall is a hell of a lot better than a war."[77]

Without Alliance: A Berlin 1961 Counterfactual

If NATO had not existed, or West Germany had not been a member of the alliance, the standoff over Berlin might well have been resolved in Moscow's favor. After all, the Soviets were in the stronger position because the location of the city put its Western defenders at an extraordinary disadvantage. The fact that West Berlin was not intrinsically all that valuable to the United States made it even harder to mount a credible defense.

Washington's alliances, however, allowed it to pre-commit to the defense of Berlin, bolster its commitment as the crisis intensified, and coordinate responses with Britain and France. West Germany's NATO membership also gave Washington leverage over rearmament in the country, which mollified the Soviets and gave them room to back down. The Soviets were dissuaded from pursuing maximalist objectives.

The United States would have had a far more difficult time defending its position in West Berlin if not for its alliance commitments. Without NATO, there would not have been 12,000 allied troops stationed in West Germany in 1961. The United States probably would not have had access to bases to host additional Army and Marine divisions or the high-end military equipment needed to thwart a blockade. The allies would not have had garrisons they could alert and stand down to signal their intentions. Nor would they have had tanks in the area, to send to Checkpoint Charlie when American access rights to Berlin were denied. Even with these in place, Khrushchev may have doubted whether the United States would really fight a nuclear war over Berlin, but he could not deny that Kennedy was at least treating the city as though it were a vital American interest.

Alliance also enabled timely, credible augmentation of the Western commitment to West Berlin during the crisis, deterring the Soviet Union without escalating the standoff unduly. During July and August, the Americans, the British, and the French all demonstrated a willingness to dedicate more troops to defend Berlin militarily. Without the alliance, the three powers would not have had contingency planning mechanisms to allow them to coordinate Berlin policy swiftly and to ensure that the Soviet Union did not find many cracks in their position. Their unified front helped to convince Khrushchev that they might really be willing to fight and that the wall was a preferable option. Their incremental use of pressure—another product of coordination—left him room to back down, and he took it.

Counterintuitively, the heavy US military presence in Germany, and West German NATO membership, also helped to convince Khrushchev that he could settle for something less than his ultimatum. Kennedy was sincere in his efforts to keep West Germany from developing its own nuclear weapons and even argued to British and French allies that they should abandon their nuclear weapons to encourage Bonn to stop.[78] Khrushchev would have preferred a weak West Germany with no NATO membership or Western military presence, but he could accept both if they restrained West Germany's pursuit of nuclear weapons. Coupled with credible defensive and deterrent options, the US promise to exert control over West Germany helped to end the standoff.

Against all odds, the United States and its allies would go on to retain their political position in West Berlin for the entire Cold War, keeping it out of Soviet hands. A political partition that seemed preposterously unsustainable in the 1950s managed to endure for four decades with the help of a defense pact.

A critic might contend that the United States would never have been in Berlin without the NATO alliance—that the commitment itself created the need for forward defense, deterrence, and alliance restraint. The United States would not have had to use an alliance to salvage its position in Berlin if it had not made an untenable political commitment in the first place. But this argument is flimsy because the division of Germany preceded the US peacetime alliances. The United States and its allies were committed to Germany before Washington decided to form the Atlantic alliance, supervise German rearmament, and bring West Germany into the fold. The political commitment to Berlin may have been dubious, but the political and military commitment to West Germany—the alliance—helped to salvage it.

One might also argue that the 1961 crisis is an unrepresentative example of a clear alliance victory—perhaps an extreme case in which the Soviet Union had atypically revisionist intentions that the United States managed to thwart. To be sure, the Soviet Union did not seek to take territory or subvert the sovereignty of US allies everywhere. Similar dynamics, however, can be observed in other Cold War crises over divided, frontline territories. During several dangerous crises after the Korean War, forward defense, deterrence, and alliance restraint supported the US objective of preventing another war between Seoul and a Soviet proxy. Analogous forces prevailed in the Taiwan Straits Crises of 1954 and 1958.[79] Indeed, throughout the Cold War, the United States and its allies had a strong record of bolstering immediate deterrence once a challenge had begun, preventing serious escalation and avoiding war. In several cases divided states that might have easily been overrun by Soviet proxies instead remained peaceful parts of the Western bloc.

Alliance commitments motivated Washington to intervene early and demonstrably in crises along Cold War fault lines, lest it become embroiled in larger and more costly conflicts later. When trouble emerged the United States reinforced its alliance commitments with strong public statements and demonstrations of military force, improving the local balance of power near the standoff at low cost to the United States.[80] The global balance of power cast a long shadow, too: in any one crisis, the United States and its allies might be outnumbered, but in aggregate terms, their strength dwarfed that of the Soviets.[81] The republic's shields provided defensive advantages that helped to keep conflicts stable and the Cold War from escalating into an open and catastrophic clash.

3

AT WHAT COST, ALLIANCE?

America's Cold War alliances accomplished their central goals. They enabled forward defense, to better protect the homeland. They facilitated deterrence, dissuading adversaries from attacking. And Washington could exert control over security partners while keeping them in the political fold. These partners also made contributions beyond their mandates, committing blood and treasure to assist the United States in out-of-area conflicts, such as the Vietnam War. And they provided diplomatic backing on all manner of political issues. In short, allies were essential to the United States' grand strategic objective of defending Eurasia to secure its own economic and military survival. But were these political and strategic advantages worth the price?

Empirically, this question is vexing to answer for two reasons. First, there are no controlled experiments in international relations, and we cannot rerun the Cold War to examine what costs the United States would have accrued to maintain its security without allies. (In much the same way, we cannot cleanly measure the causes of America's impressive alliance record, although we can feel confident that the results were as intended.) Second, while alliance costs can be measured in a number of ways, all of them are flawed.

The vast academic literature on alliances discusses many kinds of costs. They may be tabulated in defense spending that would not be necessary absent the alliance. They may manifest as lives lost and wars fought when a state is entrapped in conflict by an ally. They may reflect loss of political flexibility owing to constraints imposed by allies. Allies may also abandon commitments, forcing their partners to draw up new plans and pay for their implementation.

All of these metrics are ambiguous; all are open to multiple critiques. But to the extent that we can rely on them for evaluation, they suggest that US alliance strategy was not nearly so costly an endeavor as we might expect. The United States bore a larger financial load than its weaker partners, but most of this spending was not devoted to the material needs of defending allies. Rather, Washington's spending maximized US security while defending and controlling allies. In the process the United States faced few instances of true allied entrapment or abandonment. What little entrapment occurred during the Cold War was mild, resulting in inconvenience but no serious challenges to US security or freedom of action.

If the United States had not extended its Cold War alliances, or if it had ended them in an effort to reduce political and material costs, it may not have saved much. In exchange, it could have lost a great deal more. Without alliances the United States would have faced different, perhaps costlier, foreign policy burdens and would have missed out on the financial benefits of alliances. Washington's Cold War alliance strategy was almost certainly more affordable than an alliance-free strategy in a similar world.

Footing the Bill

In his 1961 inaugural address, President Kennedy warned America's partners not to free ride "on the back of the tiger" lest they "end up inside."[1] For longer than it has had alliances, the United States has worried about burden-sharing: Would allies pay fairly toward the common defense, and could they do more to contribute? Though these questions have long occupied American analysts and policymakers, it is not clear how they should measure burden-sharing or what constitutes a reasonable contribution.

Contrary to an increasingly common misconception, US allies do not pay dues in exchange for their security guarantees. Rather, each government independently determines what it will spend on national defense, including as it relates to the alliance. These outlays make it easier for the United States to fulfill its security promises, and they aid the US missions of forward defense and deterrence. One way to measure burden-sharing, then, is to compare allies' defense spending to their respective gross domestic products (GDPs) and see how each ranks against the others. As Fig. 3.1 shows, Washington outspent most of its allies for most of the Cold War. The gap was especially pronounced in the 1960s and 1970s.

It is tempting to look at this chart and conclude that US allies took advantage of their defender. But Cold War burden-sharing was lopsided because Washington wanted it this way. The United States extended its security guarantees with the expectation that it would gain in ways that are hard to express in dollar terms: basing access, deterrence capacity, and allied control. US leaders did not expect defense-spending equality or anything close to it in the early Cold War period. To the contrary, they sought asymmetric alliances in part because these would allow the United States to shape allied defense policies. If allies had been equal defense spenders, they might have reduced US spending on forward deployment, but they also might have developed their own nuclear weapons or other capabilities and strategies at odds with US interests.

It also does not make sense to expect equal spending, since the United States and its allies had different national security objectives. The United States was spending on a global force posture to prevent Europe and Asia falling under Soviet control, a condition that strategists believed would pose an existential threat to the homeland. The allies had more modest goals. They sought to defend themselves and contribute to the alliance within their regions. Without these

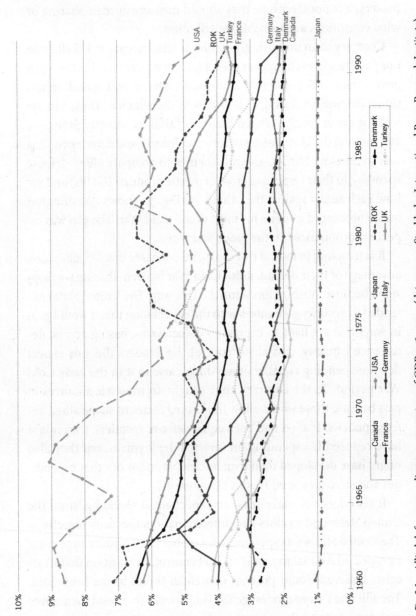

Fig. 3.1 Allied defense spending as a percentage of GDP, 1960–1991 (data source: Stockholm International Peace Research Institute)

partners, Washington might still have been able to prevent hostile powers from dominating Eurasia, but the United States would have borne the full cost.[2] One could reasonably argue that the United States obtained its foreign policy goals more cheaply thanks to its allies.

To further complicate matters, US spending on forward presence in a given country does not cleanly map to the cost of the alliance with that country. That is because the United States uses its bases to defend entire regions, not just the allies hosting them. Throughout the Cold War, the United States maintained its heaviest European defense presence in Germany and its largest Asian presence in Japan, yet each of those positions allowed the United States to defend many other allies. Moreover, each base was established because US planners believed those regional defense hubs to be necessary—not because the ally demanded it construct those bases or deploy a specific number of troops. The United States also maintained some Cold War alliances that included close political relationships but no base access at all, such as with Australia. We cannot, then, examine US defense expenditures on a particular country to evaluate accurately alliance burden-sharing. American spending on forward defense supports a broad and ambitious grand strategy selected for reasons of self-defense, not in response to the defense needs of particular base-hosting allies.

It is also important to keep in mind that allies' defense budgets can be spent in a variety of ways, some of which are helpful to the defender and some of which are less so. This further complicates the calculation of costs borne by the defender. If allies spend on research and development, major military platforms, or troop preparedness, their spending will be especially useful to collective defense and therefore will reduce the burden on the defender. If instead allies' defense budgets are taken up by inflated personnel costs, this will not bring nearly as much value to the alliance, and the defender will find fewer of its costs offset by its allies.[3]

Allies also can contribute to the common defense in ways that are not reflected in their military spending. During the Cold War, many allies defrayed US overseas basing costs without adding line items to their defense budgets. Some used nondefense funds to pay for construction and transportation. Others subsidized forward defense by granting free base leases or forgoing payments the United States would otherwise have had to make. Some combined these methods. Each partner fashioned their contributions in the manner most feasible given domestic political circumstances and constraints.[4]

More broadly, any comparison of American spending on overseas force posture to allies' defense contributions constitutes an inherently flawed burden-sharing metric. Such comparison is based on the faulty presumption that the purpose of US alliances is to do a service for the allies. But the United States has never spent on allies' defense as such. It assumed alliance commitments in order to preserve its own national security. Washington incurred costs associated with forward presence, deterrence, and alliance control because they promoted the national defense. Allies' contributions toward these costs was an additional benefit.

Despite the many quantitative and conceptual challenges that come with calculating burden-sharing, in the late Cold War period, Congress requested that the Defense Department do just that. In its annual "Allied Contributions to the Common Defense," the Pentagon evaluated several metrics assessing allies' contributions as a function of their ability to pay. Fig. 3.2 tracks allied spending according to one of these, the "fair share" metric. The metric divides the ally's share of the alliance's total defense spending by its share of the alliance's total GDP. If an ally accounts for 2 percent of the alliance's total GDP, and contributes 2 percent of total alliance defense spending, it has a ratio of one. A ratio of one implies that the ally is paying its fair share. A ratio greater than one implies largesse; less than one stinginess.

By the Pentagon's accounting, the United States spent quite a bit more than its fair share on defense throughout the 1980s. Among

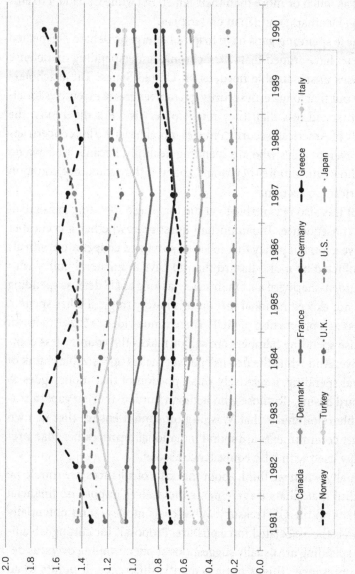

Fig. 3.2   Allied defense spending as function of ability to pay, 1981–1990. A ratio of one indicates spending equal to the ally's ability to pay, according to the Pentagon's "fair share" metric. A ratio below one indicates that the ally is paying less than its fair share; greater than one indicates that it is paying more than its fair share. (data source: US Department of Defense)

NATO allies, Turkey, Greece, the United Kingdom, and France also spent as much or more than their fair share, while Canada, Luxembourg, Denmark, and Japan underspent.[5]

These spending gaps have inspired energetic debate. Respected scholars have argued that allies' chronic underspending on defense imposes unsustainable burdens on United States. These scholars point out that long-term security guarantees create incentives for allies to spend less than they might otherwise. Put differently, the supply of American security induces moral hazard. This concern applies even to allies who are spending healthily, because we have no idea how much more they would spend if they could not count on American protection.[6]

But it is also reasonable to argue that these spending gaps are of little consequence. The important question is whether it is cheaper to have a foreign policy that relies on sustained cooperation with allies afflicted by moral hazard than to have a unilateral policy with no burden-sharing at all. On this view, as long as US defense spending does not exceed national means, it is hardly tragic if allies spend a bit less as a proportion of GDP. There is no evidence that American defense spending hampers growth or makes the country less competitive. And while the defense budget makes up a sizable chunk of federal spending, a relatively small portion of that money goes to forward basing. To those who bemoan burden-sharing gaps, a reasonable rejoinder is that Washington should ensure that its own budget commitments are sound in national terms, rather than preoccupy itself with false equivalence abroad.[7]

Finally, when we think about the costs of alliances, we should be mindful that alliance agreements themselves impose no financial burdens on the US Treasury. What costs money—and potentially lives—is the associated force posture. Proposals for cutting US alliance spending are usually suggestions about curtailing overseas defense presence. This is not a semantic difference. It points to an important reality that many miss when they refer to alliances as extravagant: in order to generate substantial savings in its own defense budget—that is, to close the gap between its "allied contribution" ratio and those of its thriftier partners—the United States would have to close overseas bases and return the personnel and materiel to the continental United States. Simply consolidating bases and relying more on rotational deployments would not generate substantial cost savings.[8] Leading scholars have argued for just this kind of move— ending alliances and shuttering related bases to curb commitments and spending. Such dramatic changes would require not just a transformed alliance policy but a completely different grand strategy—one that does not seek to secure the balance of power in Eurasia through forward defense, deterrence, and allied assurance and control.

The Political Costs of Alliance: Entrapment, Abandonment, and American Strategy

Cold War Entrapment

Strategists may attempt to tabulate the political costs of alliances by considering the dilemmas of alliance entrapment and abandonment. Entrapment occurs when a state is dragged into a conflict in pursuit of an ally's interests. Lesser forms of entrapment can occur when one partner behaves recklessly or takes an especially firm position toward an adversary due to its confidence in alliance support. Abandonment occurs when an ally fails to fulfill the terms of its security pledge by, for instance, refusing to assist in wartime or, less urgently, shirking commitments in peacetime.[9]

The likelihood of entrapment and abandonment is thought to vary depending on how power is distributed internationally. Allied entrapment and abandonment were probably less likely during the Cold War than other eras, such as the period preceding the First World War. With multiple centers of political power, alliances were less stable, and countries aligned and de-aligned with relative frequency. The structure of Cold War competition, by contrast, was conducive to durable alliances. Because the bipolar world was organized around two military-industrial power centers, the United States and the Soviet Union, smaller allies could not easily tip the balance of power. The loss of any one smaller partner was not catastrophic, whereas it is more likely to upset stability in a multipolar world.[10] Moreover, the independent interests of Cold War allies—in both the US and Soviet columns—were too minor to compel the superpowers to act against their own wishes.[11] Nonetheless, prominent scholars point to what they perceive as the serious risk of American entrapment by "reckless drivers."[12]

If America's Cold War alliances involved serious entrapment costs, the historical record would include cases in which the United States had been dragged into conflicts and crises despite having no direct stake in them. There are few such cases. American allies have proven no more likely to become engaged in conflicts with adversaries than are other states, suggesting that US security guarantees have not provoked adventurism.[13]

True, during the Cold War, the United States faced serious national security challenges in allied territory, including the Berlin Crisis and the Taiwan Straits Crises. But as we saw in Chapter 2, the strong US stand over Berlin was not a product of beneficent obligation to West Germany; US policymakers saw US national interests at stake. Alliance with Bonn helped to make the US commitment to West Germany more credible, but it did not entangle the country in an uninvited fracas. Likewise during the 1958 Taiwan Straits Crisis, Washington had an independent interest in averting a conflict between Taipei and Beijing; it was not simply ensnared in an ally's woes.

The United States also entered two major wars during the Cold War, in Korea and Vietnam. But in neither case was its participation a result of alliance commitments. The United States could not have been entangled by alliance with South Korea because the two did not have an alliance during the war. The dynamic arguably was just the opposite: Washington was dragged into war because it failed to commit to Seoul in early 1950. The United States later dangled the prospect of an alliance in order to win the South's support for an armistice. Vietnam, the most flagrant American military blunder of the Cold War, also was not provoked by alliance obligations. SEATO, the US defense pact in Southeast Asia, did not include Vietnam as a partner. Indeed, most of America's allies opposed the US war in Vietnam, and some worried that *they* would be entrapped.[14] South Korea and Australia did enter the fray, sending large numbers of troops to assist the United States, even though their own publics opposed the war. The United States fought in Vietnam because of its own perceived national interests and arguably paid lower, if still considerable, costs in blood and treasure than it would have if not for allies.[15]

In the first few years after the Cold War, the United States participated in two more major conflicts, in the Middle East and the Balkans. The Gulf War was precipitated by Saddam Hussein's invasion of Kuwait, with which the United States did not have an alliance. The George H. W. Bush administration committed troops to repel a violation of the UN Charter—not because it was obligated by treaty to protect Kuwait. Alliances played a greater role in the decision to take part in conflicts in Bosnia and Kosovo, as the United States sought to keep the North Atlantic Treaty relevant after the Cold War. But the Clinton administration also identified humanitarian interests and aimed to establish the United States' newfound global primacy through leadership in the Balkan conflicts. Neither Bosnia nor Kosovo were NATO members.[16]

Given the scholarly conventional wisdom that alliances cause entrapment, why is it so hard to find cases of American entanglement? There are several reasons. First, the United States has designed its alliances with terms that reduce its exposure to risky commitments.[17] Second, when it does commit to an ally, the United States tends to construct its treaty obligations vaguely, giving itself ample room to support its allies without entering conflicts.[18] And third, Washington has been selective with its alliance partners, rejecting requests for security pacts when it judges the associated commitments too dangerous.

A clear example of Washington's care in crafting treaty language is the 1954 agreement with Taiwan. Policymakers worried that Chiang Kai-Shek would exploit a US security guarantee, shrouding himself in American protection while launching attacks on mainland China. To guard against this, the United States gave itself an escape hatch in case Taiwan used force offensively. According to language attached to the treaty, Taipei needed to get Washington's agreement before any such use of force. That meant Chiang could not take just any aggressive action he wished and expect American support.[19] The alliance treaty also deliberately excluded several islands whose status Chinese communists and nationalists disputed. The United States opted to back Chiang through tensions over Quemoy and Matsu in 1954 and 1958, but Washington was not legally obligated to act as it did. During the first crisis, the alliance was still in draft form. During the second, Washington engaged because policymakers thought it wise to deter Mao's China. The United States was not legally compelled to take any specific action.

To the contrary, American treaty promises are designed to leave Washington with room to maneuver. Most US alliances are triggered by an "unprovoked attack" on the ally, but no language spells out what constitutes unprovoked attack. Treaties, moreover, do not indicate what the American response will be in case of attack. Recall that in 1948 NATO allies sought a treaty provision that would require the United States to automatically enter a war if Western Europe was attacked, and Washington declined. The North Atlantic Treaty and all subsequent treaties promise American consultation if allies are victims of attack, but the nature of defensive aid is not specified.

Ambiguous commitments give Washington flexibility in times of crisis. When Taiwan and China became locked in an escalating standoff in 1958, the United States made public statements on Taiwan's behalf, moved forces into the region, and provided naval convoys for Taiwanese ships. This was a nimble response short of war, enabled by Washington's freedom to design its action as it saw fit. In 1956 the United States used its leeway to stay out of a crisis altogether. Late that year two of the closest US allies, Britain and France, joined Israel in an invasion of Egypt. They hoped to regain the Suez Canal after Egypt's president, Gamal Abdel Nasser, nationalized it. But President Eisenhower opposed the intervention. Washington felt no obligation to participate, placing the United States in fleeting alignment with the Soviet Union and against its allies for the sake of preventing escalation.[20]

When the risks of entrapment run high, American leaders may never ally at all. US policymakers have made careful decisions about which international partners they should support, rejecting even close friends that pose excessive danger. Israel may be the most prominent example. Though a longstanding confederate on defense and intelligence issues, Israel is not a treaty ally. This is no accident. During the Kennedy administration, Israel requested a formal security guarantee from Washington. From 1961 to 1963, US policymakers seriously considered the idea. The prospect of alliance was attractive in no small part because US officials thought they could persuade Israel to abandon its nuclear program in exchange. But while Kennedy's team wanted very much to stop Israel from going nuclear, it felt it could not offer a guarantee without risking entrapment. A particular concern was the tension between Israel and Egypt, a country the United States did not count as an adversary. Ultimately the United States chose not to pursue the alliance. Today it is America's Middle Eastern partners—Israel and several Arab states—that are most often accused of "reckless driving," but none of them are treaty allies.[21] Formal US allies have records of highly responsible behavior.

Just as it is difficult to locate cases of US entrapment in allies' security crises, so too is it difficult to identify instances in which alliances have ensnared the United States politically. The United States has never been caught in an alliance treaty it wanted to escape. The early republic renounced the treaty with France when it became cumbersome, began to support France's rivals, and engaged in a naval war with Paris. There were no major political repercussions for the volte-face.[22] Similarly, a century and a half later, the United States was able to extricate itself from SEATO without issue. The alliance had never provided much benefit in defending against communist subversion, in part because SEATO members disagreed on where and how the treaty should apply. They also held sharply diverging views about the war in Vietnam and their obligations to support it. Britain and France quickly began to distance themselves from the pact. SEATO lasted until the 1970s only because Washington wanted to maintain a defensive relationship with Thailand, which it did by essentially bilateralizing the pact through quiet diplomatic notes. Well before his election, Richard Nixon had called the alliance an "anachronistic relic," and he encountered little resistance when he began to dismantle it once in office.[23]

If US hands were tied unduly by alliances, the country might never have achieved the important goal of opening formal relations with China. Doing so required a dramatic alliance policy reversal: before Nixon could go to China, the United States had to agree to Mao and Chou Enlai's demand to end the alliance with Taiwan and withdraw all troops from the island.[24] In 1971 National Security Advisor Henry Kissinger assented, paving the way for the historic presidential visit the following year.[25]

Ultimately it took longer to disassemble the alliance, as the move was politically unpalatable back home. Nixon postponed until after his reelection, and again until after the 1974 midterms. After Nixon resigned amid the Watergate scandal, Gerald Ford continued to demur. Jimmy Carter finally finished the job in 1978. In response to the abrogation, an outraged Congress passed the Taiwan Relations Act, which allowed Washington to maintain a looser security pledge to Taipei. The bipartisan congressional Taiwan lobby even brought a lawsuit against President Carter, but they could not stop him from ending the alliance and recognizing China.[26] Against determined bipartisan opposition, successive American presidents nullified a pact when they felt it no longer served the national interest.

If international relations scholars overstate the dangers of alliance entrapment, this may be because they focus on only one form of the problem: being dragged into war. In the case of the United States, this has not occurred, but Washington has arguably been ensnared in more modest ways. As US policymakers have discovered, when allies' goals differ, their influence on each other may result in commitments they would otherwise have preferred to avoid.[27] A security guarantee also may encourage the defender to get involved in an ally's crisis early, rather than to stand aside and wait for it to escalate. An alliance-extending state is therefore likely to participate in crises short of war in order to prevent the outbreak of serious confrontation.

The 1961 Berlin Crisis is one example. Had the United States not been allied with West Germany and other Western European states, it might have stayed out of the Soviet-induced imbroglio: no treaty required action in Berlin. But, thanks in part to these alliances elsewhere in Europe, President Kennedy felt a need to coordinate with partners and increase his military commitment to the city in an effort to bolster immediate deterrence. However, this probably helped to resolve the crisis on terms more favorable to the United States. Similarly the United States did not have a specific obligation to defend Quemoy and Matsu in 1958, but the existence of an alliance likely increased Eisenhower's perception that he should do *something* to support Chiang.

This effect is more nuanced than the entrapment or entanglement that scholars generally describe. It might be better thought of as alliance *dilation*—a subtle expansion of commitments beyond those indicated by the original alliance. Because of preexisting mutual interests, however, it is nearly impossible to identify what precise causal role alliances play in dilation. Expanded commitments necessarily arise when the United States has a genuine security interest in a relationship. That said, it would be wrong to contend that alliances never lead guarantors to devote resources they would not, absent the security guarantee. This subtle dilation does not entail costs as significant as we have been led to believe, but what costs accrue are nonetheless tangible.

Abandonment in American Alliances

The United States was never so close to its allies as to become obviously entangled in their wars or crises, nor did it become shackled to alliances its leaders preferred to discard. But what of the opposite alliance quandary? Was the United States ever jilted?

Abandonment occurs when an ally reneges on its commitment. An ally might officially sever ties, becoming neutral or realigning with another security guarantor. Or it might simply fail to hold up its end of the bargain by neglecting to give aid in a time of war.[28]

In the strictest sense, this has not happened to the United States. The country has itself ended alliances—with France, SEATO, and Taiwan—but never have allies backed away from their obligation with the United States. Because neither America nor its allies were directly attacked during the Cold War, allies never had the opportunity to slip a wartime commitment.

As with entrapment and entanglement, however, abandonment can take subtler forms. One is free-riding, which occurs when an ally benefits from an alliance without contributing to it sufficiently. As we have seen, it may not be appropriate to label allies free-riders just because they have smaller defense budgets than they might be able to afford. But there have been rare instances in which a treaty ally, seeking to exploit security guarantees, imposed meaningful political and material costs on the United States and other allies. The most damaging was the French effort under Charles de Gaulle to reap the benefits of NATO while shirking many of the costs.[29] De Gaulle's policy culminated in France's withdrawal from the NATO military structure in 1966, a move that, as Helga Haftendorn puts it, left "the survival and the future course of the alliance . . . in jeopardy."[30]

De Gaulle was on a mission to restore France to great power status. To this end he sought to build up the French armed forces and rein-vigorate the country as a diplomatic player that would secure its in-terests on the world stage even when these departed from NATO's. In particular he envisioned France serving as a mediator and pro-moter of détente, which in the 1960s seemed possible as the risk of war in Europe appeared to subside. Between 1960 and 1963, de Gaulle made known his opposition to Anglo-American NATO leadership and introduced several plans to raise France's profile within the alliance.[31]

A true believer in sovereign independence, de Gaulle worried that France would be overly constrained by NATO and the United States. At the same time, he feared that the United States would exercise its own independence, abandoning its commitments when convenient. The Soviets had a nuclear arsenal on par with the Americans' and were beginning to develop intercontinental ballistic missiles that would allow them to strike the US mainland: Why would the United States risk a strike on Washington to save Paris? De Gaulle's pre-decessor had initiated France's nuclear program, and the general embraced it as a way to guarantee France's survival if US security guarantees attenuated. Caught between a desire for autonomy and the need for protection, de Gaulle also opposed President Kenne-dy's doctrine of flexible response, which both asserted centralized American control and struck him as potential US disengagement from Europe.[32]

During the Kennedy and early Johnson administrations, US officials took pains to coax de Gaulle back into NATO's embrace. They toyed with multiple proposals to provide the alliance a multilateral nuclear stockpile, hoping to obviate de Gaulle's pursuit of his own. By 1963, however, de Gaulle was obviously trying to extricate France from NATO military planning and was refusing to participate in a new forward-defense strategy to protect Germany. Two years later American officials were reasonably sure that de Gaulle would abandon the alliance and began to order high-level government studies to examine their options in response. They also held wargames to analyze the defense implications of French defection. Johnson's cabinet considered threatening de Gaulle with the complete withdrawal of American protection to convince him to remain in NATO. But they decided the threat would not be credible—if the Soviets ever attacked Western Europe, it would be geographically and politically impossible for the United States not to aid France.[33]

By 1966 the French economy was at full strength, de Gaulle had just been reelected, and the United States was escalating in Vietnam, a war the general opposed. De Gaulle sensed an opening for mediation with the Soviet Union and an opportunity to execute his long-laid plan to leave NATO. He did so shrewdly, announcing his intention to withdraw France from NATO's integrated command without abrogating the Atlantic alliance. This was a move American officials had not anticipated. De Gaulle was renouncing France's peacetime military responsibilities to the alliance but was not defecting altogether. In essence, France was refusing to contribute to the alliance, even as it continued to claim to the alliance's protection. It struck the Johnson administration and many NATO allies as the ultimate evasion. The allies were outraged and immediately sought to limit the damage.[34]

The political and material costs of de Gaulle's defection were significant, not least because France was home to so much NATO infrastructure—President Johnson declared the alliance would have to "rebuild NATO outside of France."[35] The House Armed Services

Committee insisted that de Gaulle's decision had "done more to endanger the security of Western Europe than all activities undertaken by Communist governments since the beginning of the NATO alliance." All foreign forces and equipment, including 71,000 US personnel, would be expelled from France on April 1, 1967—April Fools' Day, as Senator Ernest Gruening noted dyspeptically—or else be forced to submit to French military command. A significant percentage of the US personnel were sent to Germany, with the remainder repatriated to the United States. Logistics and supply depots were also moved to Germany, along with $1 billion of materiel. US Air Force equipment and personnel were dispersed to other European bases. Far more cumbersome was the relocation of the allied headquarters and the NATO Defense College to Belgium. NATO also lost supply lines and petroleum pipelines that ran through France.[36]

In a further insult, the alliance had to negotiate with Paris over whether it could count on the use of French territory and airspace in the event of a war. If the answer was no, there would be a gaping hole in NATO defense plans. Even with that permission, the French defection would reduce the territory available in which to execute NATO's defense strategy because no alliance troops would be on the ground there. In all, the United States estimated its material losses at between $300 million and $1 billion worth of infrastructure and other defense investments in France.[37] This was not wartime abandonment, but it was about as costly as peacetime defection could get.

Yet France's departure proved a blessing in disguise for NATO, galvanizing the remaining members. It had not just been de Gaulle who was anxious about the advent of nuclear parity with the Soviet Union and the possible attenuation of US security guarantees. Most NATO members feared the alliance would collapse just as the USSR was becoming more capable. President Johnson used the shock of de Gaulle's withdrawal as an opportunity to revitalize the alliance. He quickly pushed through NATO approval of the flexible-response approach and agreed to give allies more of a voice in strategy through a new Defense Planning Committee and Nuclear Planning Group.[38] Other leaders in the alliance also seized the moment. Catalyzed by the French withdrawal, Belgian Foreign Minister Pierre Harmel initiated a year-long study to examine the future of the alliance, which ultimately devised a plan for strengthening deterrence and charting a course toward stability with the Soviets. The plan guided the alliance's strategy for the rest of the Cold War. De Gaulle's nationalist stance against NATO integration wound up inspiring a wave of defense institutionalization that would bring the allies closer together and carry them through the decades.[39]

There were other instances of alliance defection during the Cold War, such as New Zealand's. An energetic antinuclear movement developed in New Zealand in the 1980s, resulting in the country's decision to become a nuclear-free zone. This was akin to dropping a commitment to the United States, because American nuclear-powered ships were no longer allowed to make port calls. New Zealand was suspended from ANZUS and its status downgraded to "friend." But the United States and New Zealand continued to cooperate on important defense and intelligence matters, and the inability to port had little impact on US strategy.

In both of these cases, France and New Zealand continued to benefit from American security guarantees, despite contributing less to the alliance than they previously had—clear instances of free-riding. But while the costs of de Gaulle's gambit were considerable, they were hardly beyond America's means: even the highest estimated losses to the United States totaled no more than 1 percent of the costs of the concurrent Vietnam War.[40] Indeed, neither France's nor New Zealand's defection imposed costs outweighing the benefits of alliance. No Cold War–era or contemporary strategist or policymaker could credibly argue that the long-term advantages of NATO were offset by de Gaulle's escapade, and New Zealand's choice in the waning days of superpower competition was a minor irritant.

Does Cutting Ties Cut Costs?

We cannot measure precisely the financial burdens of alliance or the costs of alliance dilation and modest free-riding. Nor is there clear evidence of flagrant entrapment and outright abandonment to be weighed. It is therefore difficult to settle conclusively the cost-benefit accounting of America's alliance system.

Again, counterfactual analysis can help us divine some clarity from murky history. Faced with the contention that the United States overspent on alliances during or after the Cold War because allies failed to pay their fair share, the appropriate question is whether fewer alliances and slimmer force posture would have resulted in less cost. And what if the United States had maintained no major alliances at all during the Cold War? Would it have paid fewer political and material costs?

If the United States wished to spend significantly less on costs that have been associated with alliances it could attempt this through a significant reduction in its overseas force posture. This could be accomplished by ending several major American alliances, allowing the United States to close bases and withdraw troops. Such a strategy would end or amend the North Atlantic Treaty, the US-Japan security treaty, and the US–Republic of Korea mutual defense treaty, transferring to all allies the primary responsibility for their defense. These drastic moves would considerably reduce the size of the US military by cutting back on personnel, aircraft, naval vessels, and other major platforms. As a result, defense spending might drop from about 3.5 percent of GDP to 2.5 percent in contemporary terms.[41] Washington would free itself from many of its overseas commitments by adopting a wait-and-see approach, addressing international threats when and if they arose, much as it did before the Second World War.

The financial benefits of this homeland-defense strategy, as opposed to a forward-defense strategy, may seem obvious. With a smaller defense budget, the United States could invest in any number of needed domestic programs. There are some clear political benefits, too. By pulling back, the United States would guarantee itself against entrapment. There would be no advanced obligations with the potential to constrain foreign policy decisions.

If this were the end of the calculation, the cost savings of reducing alliances and reorienting American strategy might be compelling. But we must also calculate what the United States might lose along with its pacts. In particular, pre-commitment, for all its potential downsides, is what produces deterrence. The promise that a powerful defender will enter a conflict helps to ensure that the conflict never starts. If the United States detached from commitments, reducing its deterrence posture to only its homeland, it would no longer be able to prevent outbreaks of hostilities. This would, in turn, increase the chances of the United States finding itself involved in full-blown wars. Ultimately, saving money by cutting deterrence may actually raise the cost of defense in blood and treasure.

Furthermore, under this scenario, when Washington did decide to enter conflicts, it would do so without the advanced planning and coordination that forward defense enables. This would cause delays as troops and platforms move from the continental United States; surging forces in Europe or Asia would require weeks as opposed to days. The costs of deploying a large expeditionary force with no existing basing arrangements would be enormous. And once the United States committed to a conflict, deployment delays would put its forces at a disadvantage. As in the Korean War, the US military would likely have to spend months reversing losses before it made gains.

In this wait-and-see world, would-be US allies would have to provide for their own defense, potentially making cooperation with the United States more difficult. They would develop incompatible weapons systems and defensive doctrines that assumed no allied cooperation. There would be few opportunities to train together.

Military cooperation would drift.[42] Even if one-off alignments were formed for the purpose of fighting a given war, each participant would enter the conflict as an independent operator rather than as a member of a coordinated coalition. If this war were instead fought by longtime allies enjoying strategic and operational coordination, it would cost much less.

Consider what a leaner, alliance-free Cold War posture would have looked like. In the absence of deterrence and forward defense, the United States might easily have found itself joining additional wars on the Korean Peninsula or facing bolder Soviet attempts to take West Berlin or West Germany. Recall that the United States tended to extend Cold War alliances to states it was likely to defend anyway, preferring to pay tolerable upfront force-posture costs instead of much higher ones in blood and treasure later on. A wait-and-see approach would not have ended the Cold War or obviated America's interest in upholding the balance of power. Rather, the standoff may well have been hotter, forcing the United States to join active conflicts along Cold War fault lines from a militarily disadvantageous position.

Korea provides a cautionary tale. Because the United States disengaged, removing troops in 1949 and signaling diplomatic pullback in 1950, it soon found itself fighting over the very same territory. At the price of $341 billion (more than $3 trillion in current dollars) and 36,574 American lives, it was surely costlier for the United States to join this war once it had started than it would have been to form an alliance, maintain a troop presence, and deter North Korea from invading.[43] Similar conflicts may have arisen in West Berlin and Taiwan if not for forward defense and deterrence. The United States would not have been compelled to join those wars, but if it had participated, the challenges would have been considerable—far greater than those of deterrence.

Pruning alliances would also lead to economic sacrifice. Moving forces home can actually be more expensive than keeping them overseas. Some allies, such as Japan and South Korea, subsidize US forces so heavily that it is cheaper to station them abroad.[44] Moreover, ending American alliances could harm US prosperity generally. Economists have found that American security commitments bring sizable trade benefits. After Washington grants security alliances or deploys troops overseas, bilateral trade flows improve sharply. The data suggest that American security commitments increase regional stability, which in turn reduces the costs of trade. It follows that if American security treaties and military personnel are reduced, trade will also suffer. In economic models, a 50 percent reduction in defense treaties and troop levels reduces overall US bilateral trade by 18 percent. Cutting treaty relationships by half could reduce trade in goods by $426 billion. Cutting both treaty ties and military personnel by the same amount would lead to an annual loss of $577 billion in trade. This would be associated with a net reduction in US GDP of $490 billion per year, in 2015 dollars.[45] This trade is equivalent to nearly 80 percent of the modern US defense budget. Ending alliances and downsizing force posture may therefore reduce US defense spending somewhat, but it could not possibly compensate for the trade losses that would accompany disengagement.

A Price Worth Paying

American concerns about the financial and political burdens of alliance are as old as the republic itself, but they are not borne out in the record.

It is true that many US allies underspent on defense throughout the Cold War, according to the Pentagon's fair-share metric. But allies' relatively low defense outlays, as compared to US spending, do not tell us as much as many politicians, international relations theorists, and everyday citizens seem to believe. America's spending reflects the country's far-flung global strategy, not its alliance commitments per se. Moreover, spending-gap data do not support the conclusion that the United States would have incurred fewer political and material costs if it had pursued an alliance-free Cold War strategy. Without allies and a forward presence, Washington would have faced different kinds of entrapment and abandonment threats, which, if realized, would very likely have been costlier than those rare instances that occurred during the Cold War. The United States also would have forgone substantial economic benefits.

Contrary to conventional wisdom, Washington has rarely been entangled in conflict on behalf of its allies, and when it has joined them in crises, it has done so because it saw US interests at stake. US leaders never found themselves stuck in a treaty arrangement they wished to discard. The milder issue of alliance dilation has arisen; US leaders' view of the national interest sometimes expanded with its pacts. But while one might object to their reading of the national interest, it was at least in part that reading—not simply entanglement—that resulted in additional commitments. Finally, while the United States paid political and material costs for France's abandonment of NATO, these were negligible compared to the benefits the alliance provided over the decades.

Given the manifest benefits delivered by the Cold War shields, and the potentially enormous costs the United States would have otherwise assumed on its own, one can reasonably conclude that investing in alliances was a wise decision. The tremendous political advantages alliances provided at low cost likely help to explain their longevity. Indeed, Washington was so certain of the return on its alliances that it refused to discard them even when their Soviet raison d'etre suddenly disappeared.

4

ALLIANCES AFTER
THE COLD WAR

Between 1989 and 1991, America's principal adversary evaporated. Without war or revolution, and in a tectonic geopolitical shift, the Soviet Union willfully dismantled. The newly minted Russian Federation seemed to pose little threat. It was isolated internationally, its economy in tatters, and in fits and starts it appeared to be making peace with the US-dominated global order. Asia, too, looked favorable. Washington's relations with Beijing had been reasonably stable for twenty years, and China was too weak militarily to register as a national security concern.

With commanding global power, the United States no longer needed to hold the balance in Europe and Asia to keep itself safe and prosperous. America's alliances had outlasted the threats they were designed to address, and policymakers would have to decide their fate. Was it time to discard them? Or should alliances be maintained, and perhaps repurposed for this newly auspicious world?

For some international relations experts, the idea of salvaging America's security guarantees in the absence of a major adversary was nonsensical.[1] But many policymakers saw matters differently. Alliances, they argued, could serve purposes other than deterrence and defense. By anchoring itself to overseas commitments, Washington could make a case for its leadership in a world that no longer seemed to need traditional collective defense. Security guarantees could help the United States consolidate its Cold War gains and, in Europe, could help to spread liberal democracy. Both outcomes would further a new grand strategy based not on deterrence and defense but on prevention: ensuring that serious competition to American power never arose in the first place.

The Clinton administration embraced this new mission, preserving and transforming US alliances in the process. By 1999 NATO was intervening in Kosovo, a conflict that pit the alliance against entirely new adversaries and unmoored it from traditional notions of self-defense. But this detachment from historic alliance objectives gave way to backlash. The windfall of the 1990s created vulnerabilities that twenty-first-century competitors would come to exploit.

NATO after the Adversary

During the first two years of his presidency, Bill Clinton and his closest advisors made the decision to enlarge NATO.[2] The choice was not entirely obvious: with its adversary gone, the United States might have disbanded the alliance or transformed it to some other end. Maintaining and expanding it, however, would help to democratize and stabilize Eastern Europe. Clinton also saw NATO enlargement as a proxy for America's role in the world: advancing in the aftermath of the Cold War, rather than demobilizing.[3] Many senior officials also backed NATO enlargement as a humanitarian response to intensifying conflict in the Balkans.

Enlargement proponents, whatever their goals, agreed that Russia had to be involved in any effort to expand NATO. Moscow could not be treated like a vanquished foe; if the Russians felt threatened by enlargement they might abandon democratic reform.[4] NATO expansion was therefore carried out in consultation with Moscow and was decidedly not premised on a perceived need to counter a Russian threat. To the contrary, expansion went forward on the assumption that Russia was becoming a partner.

If NATO expansion was not a foregone conclusion, alliance transformation was. As Vice President Al Gore noted, "Everyone realizes that a military alliance, when faced with a fundamental change in the threat for which it was founded, either must define a convincing new rationale or become decrepit."[5] In the early 1990s, nearly every senior US official concurred that NATO would have to adopt a new military mission if it was to survive. There was, however, disagreement over just what this mission should be. Some strategists toyed with the idea of refashioning the alliance into a collective security organization—a more inclusive body that would not be directed against any adversary and could even include Moscow. But this would have had some of the same weaknesses of the League of Nations and would not have provided a sturdy security guarantee.[6] Others argued the alliance needed new military missions: "NATO must go out of area or it will go out of business."[7]

That NATO should welcome new members was an idea born not in Washington but rather Central and Eastern Europe in response to events of the early 1990s. In 1991 Soviet military officers opposed to the reforms that were dissolving the USSR staged a coup and briefly took control of the country. The following year, war seized Bosnia. Observing the dramas around them, the leaders of Poland, Hungary, and Czechoslovakia began to fear that the new Russia would reject democracy, and nationalism would overtake their region. They sought NATO's protection.

Clinton did not see Russia as a direct threat, but he was sympathetic to the entreaties from Eastern Europe, which offered a coherent rationale for continuing partnership: the United States needed to grow NATO in order to spread democracy and bolster fragile democracies against nationalist resurgence.[8] As far as Clinton and his advisors were concerned, this goal was not at odds with Secretary of State James Baker's ambiguous 1990 pledge, delivered to Mikhail

Gorbachev, that the alliance would not expand its borders eastward beyond East Germany. It was never entirely clear what Baker had promised, and any pledge offered was never repeated or codified.[9]

The Eastern European NATO aspirants probably expected that Clinton would be favorably disposed to their request. On the campaign trail, he had championed democracy promotion alongside aid to a reforming Russia. Once in office, he connected this agenda to NATO expansion, warning that democratic reform in Central and Eastern Europe was not guaranteed, but that the alliance could help to secure it.[10] Many of his closest advisors shared this view. Top officials were influenced by a *Foreign Affairs* article in which several leading analysts argued that NATO should become an alliance "committed to projecting democracy, stability, and crisis management in the broader strategic sense" while managing the relationship with Russia.[11]

Madeleine Albright, Clinton's secretary of state from 1997 through the end of his presidency, articulated a similar rationale: adding allies to NATO would foster democracy and further the integration of Eastern Bloc states into the West, thereby helping to avoid another war in Europe.[12] As National Security Advisor Tony Lake eloquently summarized, "We have arrived at neither the end of history nor a clash of civilizations, but a moment of immense democratic and entrepreneurial opportunity. . . . The successor to a doctrine of containment must be a strategy of enlargement."[13] At the core of this argument was a fundamental belief among political scientists and policymakers that democracies did not go to war with one another. It therefore held that the United States would be more secure if the circle of democracies expanded.[14]

When the administration looked to Yugoslavia, it saw a pressing need for NATO enlargement. As Bosnia was consumed by fratricidal conflict, the White House was increasingly convinced that conflict on Europe's periphery could endanger democratic consolidation. The case for alliance endurance was also tied to humanitarian concerns: on both sides of the Atlantic, leaders wondered what future NATO could have if it could not stop ethnic cleansing in Europe. Several months after deciding to enlarge the alliance, the Clinton administration also intervened militarily in Bosnia. NATO airstrikes helped to end the conflict, intensifying Central and Eastern European states' drive for membership.[15]

Finally, alliance enlargement occurred because there were few barriers to it. The United States was sufficiently powerful economically and militarily that no foreign power could thwart its NATO-expansion goals. Domestic political opposition might have changed Clinton's calculation, but the post-Cold War sense of strategic triumph was bipartisan. Thus the George H. W. Bush administration declared it was "improbable that a global conventional challenge to US and Western security will reemerge from the Eurasian heartland for many years to come."[16] And within the Clinton administration, most top officials could find a NATO-enlargement logic that appealed (those who did not tended to be defense officials, who worried that an expanded alliance would not be militarily sound). As for existing American partners, they were not prepared to doubt Washington. Western Europe was horrified by its failures to stop the conflict in Bosnia and deferred to the United States. Even Moscow, which hardly welcomed the growing pact, was so preoccupied with its own political and economic dissolution that it had no recourse. Foreign Minister Yevgeny Primakov likened his government's acquiescence to "sleeping with a porcupine."[17]

Consultation, Not Containment

The Clinton administration took care to minimize the likelihood that Russia would see NATO's growth as a threat, and NATO expansionists made choices that demonstrate they were not trying to counter Moscow. NATO enlargement was necessarily an outgrowth of American preponderance, but Clinton made genuine efforts to build a partnership with Russian leadership. The administration hoped it could bolster the Atlantic alliance and support Russian reform simultaneously.

Clinton and his top advisors did not share the opinion of those congressional Republicans who supported NATO enlargement as a form of containment. Russia seemingly was attempting to liberalize its economy and move toward democracy, and while Clinton recognized that backsliding was possible, his instinct was that Moscow was more a partner than a serious military threat. The administration therefore took a "dual track" approach that sought to expand NATO while also beginning a "strategic alliance with Russian reform."[18] Such an approach would have made little sense if its author, Deputy Secretary of State Strobe Talbott, and the administration as a whole wanted NATO to be a bulwark against Russia.

Russian leadership appeared to understand these relatively benign intentions, even if it did not fully embrace them. In 1993 President Boris Yeltsin not only accepted Poland's desire to join NATO but even entertained the notion that Russia someday might. On a number of occasions, senior officials on both sides of the Atlantic dangled the prospect of Moscow's membership. It seemed unlikely, and potentially destructive to the alliance, yet no American policymakers saw a reason to rule it out. Talbott urged Clinton not to use any names or dates when discussing the prospect of NATO enlargement with President Yeltsin—better to move him toward acquiescence rather than reveal a definite commitment at which he would bristle.[19]

The administration also sought to give Central and Eastern European states ways to associate with NATO without offering them membership prematurely or alienating Russia. This began with the North Atlantic Cooperation Council, a vehicle for collaboration with former Warsaw Pact adversaries. In 1994 the council was supplemented by the Partnership for Peace, which was designed to build trust between NATO and European nonmembers while allowing the alliance to defer the question of whether it should formally enlarge. Yeltsin himself was fond of the partnership, which he believed had postponed NATO enlargement indefinitely, relieving considerable domestic pressure on him. Clinton officials knew otherwise, but they did not disabuse him of this notion as they quietly studied the options for alliance expansion throughout 1994.[20]

That the specter of a renewed Russian threat was not the catalyst for NATO enlargement was also clear from the initiative's detractors. Secretaries of Defense Les Aspin and William Perry urged the administration to expand the alliance only if Russia's domestic reforms failed, and Assistant Secretary of Defense Ashton Carter believed the United States should continue to focus on military cooperation with Moscow, not on expansion. Chairman of the Joint Chiefs of Staff John Shalikashvili had operational military concerns: Central and Eastern Europe were largely unprepared to assume the requirements of membership. In the eyes of the general and many of his colleagues, enlargement would saddle NATO with thorny new defense commitments without bestowing it with the capability to uphold them.[21]

The White House pressed ahead despite the concerns of defense brass. By spring 1994 the National Security Council had begun to draft a NATO-expansion plan, and by summer most of the president's close advisors favored the policy. In the fall the administration officially decided to support enlargement. At year's end NATO launched a formal study to explore expansion. Yeltsin, dissatisfied but resigned to the outcome, declared that a "cold peace had replaced the Cold War." Anticipating that Yeltsin's successor could be more hardline, Clinton decided to push through enlargement before his counterpart left office. At the same time, Clinton reaffirmed President Bush's declaration that Russia was no longer a foe and pointed to ongoing meetings between NATO and Russian foreign and defense ministers as evidence. In 1995 he assured Yeltsin that the alliance had transformed since the end of the Cold War, no longer sought to contain Russia, and was focused on newer regional threats.[22]

The 1997 NATO-Russia Founding Act, which set up a council for ongoing cooperation between Russia and NATO, was intended as further confirmation that the revived alliance did not target Moscow. Through the act, the uneasy Russians sought a pledge that the United

States would not forward deploy nuclear weapons or permanent troops to new NATO countries. The Clinton team gave Moscow this assurance, although not in treaty form. Alliance planners had no qualms about the Russian request; they were not blind to the possibility of Russian revanchism, but they also were not preoccupied with it. They assessed that NATO possessed conventional military superiority and ample strategic warning, which allowed them to issue new security guarantees to Central and Eastern European states with no forward deployments.[23]

Outside of the administration, enlargement critics abounded. Most were foreign policy realists, focused on power balancing between the former Cold War rivals rather than on democracy promotion and concerned about the possible security implications of Russian blowback. A group of senior former diplomats who had served in Europe and Russia wrote to Secretary of State Warren Christopher arguing that enlargement imperiled the future of the alliance. Venerated scholar-practitioners including Kennan, Kissinger, Paul Nitze, and Brent Scowcroft were scathingly critical. Kissinger was particularly upset—the United States was bargaining with its defeated adversary and, he said, giving Moscow the chance to undermine the future of NATO. Kennan, who had opposed the formation of NATO in 1949, called enlargement "the most fateful error of American foreign policy in the entire post-Cold War era." Many other scholars shared this view.[24]

For policymakers, these complaints were unpersuasive. In 1997, with both Clinton and Yeltsin reelected, NATO leaders announced that Poland, Hungary, and the Czech Republic would join the alliance. But first the Senate had to ratify expansion. The opposition came from Republicans wedded to the idea of NATO as a Russia-focused alliance. Defense hawks derided the administration's extensive consultation with the Russians. There was also some question about how much NATO enlargement would cost. The administration's estimates varied widely, from $30 billion to $70 billion over ten to fifteen years. In a relatively benign security environment, defense requirements seemed indeterminate; there was no consensus on what enlargement would entail militarily.[25] An enlarged NATO apparently could spend as much or as little as it liked.

Whatever qualms some Senate Republicans had, they could not move the body as a whole. In 1998 the Senate voted overwhelmingly to enlarge NATO, and the three new members joined in 1999. The enlargement decision was in many ways "the culmination of everything we had been working for, everything for which we had risked nuclear war," said James Steinberg, Clinton's deputy national security advisor and later deputy secretary of state in the Obama administration. Throughout the Cold War, American foreign policy had been premised on the rationale that many Eastern Bloc countries "would eventually be restored to the Transatlantic community," he explained.[26] In 2004 seven more countries joined the alliance, followed by two in 2009, and one more in 2017.

By far the most controversial step was the decision to admit the Baltic states of Latvia, Lithuania, and Estonia, which had, under duress, been Soviet republics until 1991. Well before they were admitted, experts understood that the Baltics were essentially indefensible in military terms because they lie on the Russian border, and the alliance had forsworn new forward deployments.[27] This was further evidence that NATO enlargement did not seek primarily to deter and defend against Russia—and that the alliance had moved considerably beyond its founding strategic logics.

Alliances Adrift in Asia

The demise of the Soviet Union also left America's Asian allies without major-power adversaries. While strategists throughout the administration understood that China was on the ascent, it was simply too early for most US officials or their alliance counterparts to recognize the challenge Beijing would become. In the long term, the White House understood, alliances might be useful as a hedge against Chinese power. But for the time being China policy would be aimed at engagement. President Clinton was not primarily concerned about deterring China or defending against it; rather, he sought to promote democratic and free-market principles there.[28] And on matters of alliance, the Clinton administration was largely focused on NATO expansion and conflict in the Balkans.

Northeast Asian allies sensed that their region was not a priority, as evidenced by the decreasing stakes of their cooperation with the United States.[29] Over the course of the 1990s, diplomacy surrounding the US-Japan and US-Korea pacts concentrated on intra-alliance issues, especially trade policy and burden-sharing. With one clear exception—North Korea—national security objectives were secondary; the alliances were preserved largely as ends unto themselves, rather than as means of advancing strategic goals. Southeast Asian allies got even less attention. In the absence of defense and deterrence objectives, these alliances languished.

Intra-Alliance Angst

By the end of the Cold War, and in the years immediately after it, serious rifts formed between the United States and its allies Japan and South Korea. Both the Bush and Clinton administrations saw Japan as America's next major competitor. Policymakers were concerned with punishing Japan for its commercial and industrial policies; the future of the alliance was at best a secondary issue.[30] South Korea, too, looked more like an economic nuisance than a reliable friend. Defense planning documents from 1992 show American officials torn over the status of their Northeast Asian partners. Secretary of Defense Dick Cheney wanted them to contribute more to the common defense and wondered whether they should primarily be feared or trusted.[31]

Meanwhile the Japanese and Korean publics increasingly questioned the value of alliance. Politicians and activists asked whether, in the absence of a great power threat, close US ties still served their interests. Left-wing political factions rose to power in both countries, and with a relatively peaceful post-Cold War security environment, the governments in Seoul and Tokyo focused inward.[32]

In the immediate aftermath of the Cold War, then, the United States, Japan, and South Korea did not so much act as allies as squabble about the terms of their partnerships. They battled over economic policy and burden-sharing. American forward basing became a political flashpoint for Japanese and Korean leaders.

Even before the Soviet Union collapsed, more Americans feared the economic threat from Japan than worried about the military one from Moscow. Policymakers were fixated on gaining access to Japanese markets. Defense officials who emphasized the value of the alliance were accused of "shielding Japan" and subordinating pressing economic concerns to outdated military ones.[33] Trade friction ran high for the first Clinton term, and Japanese officials began to wonder if Washington would abandon them for some form of alignment with China.[34] By the end of the decade, however, Japan's flagging growth snuffed out American economic envy.

The trade relationship between Washington and Seoul was less piqued but still fractious. Washington sought greater access to Korean markets, particularly those for rice and automobiles. US officials also wanted more protections for American intellectual property. Members of Congress worried that South Korea was shifting its defense procurement away from the United States, and many complained that it was not putting enough of its growing economic capacity toward defense. In the early post-Cold War years, Seoul did agree to pay more toward US basing costs, but this did not assuage American worries.[35]

Alongside economic competition came rising political tensions as Japanese officials expressed doubts about military subordination to their US ally. Throughout the Cold War, Japan had been guided by the Yoshida Doctrine, which held that the country should concentrate on economic growth while the United States took responsibility for its security. This was a maximally congenial arrangement. Article 9 of the Japanese constitution prevented Tokyo from using military force except in cases of narrowly defined self-defense, but the United States would provide the defense and deterrence the recovering state needed. In exchange the Japanese generously supported American troop presence, granted unfettered base access, and made few demands on the United States. After the collapse of the Soviet Union, however, Tokyo presumed that Japan was on track to become Asia's regional hegemon. Japanese officials undertook a major strategic review that questioned whether the country should continue to rely on American protection. Some favored aligning more closely with China, others with international institutions. Either approach meant downgrading US influence in Japan. Tokyo ultimately affirmed the necessity of the US security guarantee, but there was hardly an enthusiastic consensus on the matter.[36]

When Japan had an opportunity to demonstrate its value to the alliance during the 1991 Gulf War, many American officials felt it made a poor showing. Japan's constitutional restrictions prevented it from sending troops, but it did not even comply with its ally's request to aid with nonmilitary logistics and transport. Instead Japan gave financial aid.[37] Tokyo was criticized for its risk-averse "checkbook diplomacy," and American officials questioned the security role that Japan could play if it could not contribute to post-Cold War missions.[38]

American officials had similar concerns about South Korea's alliance commitment. Seoul appeared to be charting a course for independence: the end of the Cold War, and massive economic growth, meant that the country did not need to rely so heavily on the United States. In particular, because South Korea's economy was driven by exports, it developed global interests of its own—interests that did not always align with America's. It began to explore relationships with China and Russia and with other formerly communist countries. South Korean domestic politics divided between two main camps: conservatives who supported the security alliance and took a hardline position toward North Korea, and progressives who sought greater reconciliation with the North and space from Washington.[39]

Another preoccupying intra-alliance issue was basing. The presence of US soldiers was already a major concern in Japan and South Korea when the Cold War ended, but matters only became more fraught in 1995, when three US servicemen abducted and raped a twelve-year-old girl in Okinawa. Amid outcry from the local population, the United States and Japan agreed to move American bases on Okinawa to less populous areas, lest the issue continue to inflate anti-American sentiment. The agreement has still not been fully implemented. The Okinawa negotiations were watched closely in South Korea, where several troubling incidents involving US soldiers and Korean civilians had led to a desire for a smaller American military footprint.[40]

North Korea

Much of the tension between the United States and its Northeast Asian partners reflected the listless character of the alliances. Allies can be at odds even when they are united around a shared goal, but when there is no mutual adversary, no clear strategic purpose, alliance strife may overwhelm achievement. Post–Cold War purpose returned to each alliance, if briefly, through an intensified threat from Pyongyang. But Japan and South Korea responded very differently, demonstrating that post-Cold War drift had already set in.

In 1993–1994 it became clear that North Korea was producing plutonium that could be used in nuclear weapons. A true crisis emerged when the North began to unload its reactor at Yongbyon. The United States considered responding with military force but instead made diplomatic overtures to Pyongyang. That culminated in the 1994 Agreed Framework, a deal that gave North Korea food and energy aid in exchange for compliance with the Non-Proliferation Treaty, to which it was a signatory. The initiative caused some consternation in Seoul, as officials feared they were being cut out of a bargain critical to their country's security. The United States and South Korea also had their differences over the implementation of the nuclear deal, with Seoul periodically worrying that Washington was giving North Korea too much in exchange for minimal changes in behavior. However, despite South Korea's interest in diplomatic autonomy, no administration in Seoul could any longer deny the need for an American security guarantee.[41] The North's nuclear ambitions provided a new alliance rationale.

The 1994 crisis had a very different effect on the US-Japan alliance. Washington consulted with Tokyo about using Japanese bases for the possible mission against North Korea but was rebuffed. A North Korean crisis would have put Japan in harm's way, yet Tokyo invoked its constitutional restrictions to justify its refusal to aid the United States in its own defense. Secretary of Defense William Perry later said that if a conflict had taken place and Japan had continued to refuse access, "it would have been the end of the alliance." Japan's estrangement evoked memories of its Gulf War paralysis just three years before, and US policymakers concluded that they urgently needed to coordinate more closely with both Seoul and Tokyo.[42] America and its allies had a clear regional adversary, and they were not equipped to cope with it.

The Nye Initiative and Its Aftermath

In 1994 Assistant Secretary of Defense Joseph Nye assumed his position with the intent of introducing new purpose to America's Asian alliances. In particular, he was concerned about China. At the National Intelligence Council, he and his team had analyzed possible futures for the region and concluded that in a number of plausible cases China would become a major regional power with significant military capabilities. The United States, he believed, would need its alliances to balance power in the Pacific. To that end, he sought to assure South Korea and Japan that the United States would maintain a significant post-Cold War regional defense commitment. The result was the February 1995 Department of Defense East Asia Strategy Report, often referred to as the Nye Initiative. According to the strategy, the United States would not reduce its troop presence in Asia; the number would remain fixed at 100,000, on par with US forces in Europe.[43]

Nye's strategy had plenty of detractors, including congressional Republicans who argued that the Pentagon's troop numbers were arbitrary—unmoored from any particular threat and lacking basis in warfighting or deterrence needs. These criticisms were understandable, but evidently Pentagon leaders felt that some threshold was needed to prevent Congress from pressing for further drawdowns. And the Nye Initiative did help to convince allies that they would not be surprised by a precipitous American withdrawal from the region, as when the Nixon and Carter administrations drew down from Taiwan and Carter attempted to pull troops from South Korea.[44] The exact defensive and deterrence value of the troops was indeed open to question, but in 1995 that was less important than their assurance potential.

Alliance Stagnation in Southeast Asia

While Washington tried to quell intra-alliance angst and keep its position in Northeast Asia, its standing in the south deteriorated with its full permission. After the Vietnam War, Washington deprioritized Southeast Asia, and Southeast Asia increasingly turned away from Washington. Thailand, a military partner but not a full-fledged holder of an American security guarantee, ejected US troops following the drawdown.[45] Anti-American sentiment accrued in the Philippines throughout the 1980s, and the looming expiry of a major basing agreement caused an alliance rift in 1991. The Bush administration was not willing to beg or overcompensate Manila to renew base leases, believing the strategic value of Southeast Asia to have dwindled in a post-Cold War world. The Philippine Senate voted to end American leases at Clark Air Base and the Subic Bay naval facility, bringing the US military presence in Southeast Asia to an end.[46]

There was no such post-Cold War schism in the US-Australia alliance, but there was a perceptible drift that suggested neither country was as valuable to the other as it had been. After the two sides managed a raft of 1980s policy disagreements ranging from the Strategic Defense Initiative to the Lockerbie bombing over Scotland, the end of the Cold War laid bare an emerging gap. Post-1991 Australian strategy emphasized integration with the rest of Asia and development of new, non-American partnerships. Australians perceived the United States to be indifferent to the future of the alliance and prickled at Washington's failure to consult with Canberra on several major national security issues. During his December 1991 visit to Canberra, President Bush was asked if ANZUS was "dead or dying." Similar queries were put to his Australian counterpart. By 1994 the US Department of Defense announced that it "would neither seek nor accept primary responsibility for maintaining peace and security in the region."[47] The US-Philippines and US-Australia pacts survived, but the partners no longer knew to what ends. Both alliances idled, yet there was no real reason to dismantle either.

By preserving its alliances in Northeast Asia while neglecting those in the Southeast, Washington inadvertently crafted two tiers of pacts. The ROK and Japan alliances had recouped some regional purpose in North Korea and received substantial attention to quell intra-alliance tensions. In the south, there was no strategy, leaving the area especially vulnerable when China reemerged.

China Strategy

Tellingly, the new East Asia strategy sought to shape the strategic environment to *prevent* the emergence of a peer competitor. By implication, China was no such competitor.[48] Americans encouraged

Beijing to join international institutions and liberalize its markets, on the theory that this would help it develop in a more benign fashion and never become a major security threat.

Defense Department officials understood that China could become a rival several decades on, but policymakers preferred an "engage and hedge" approach, which bore some similarity to its Russia initiative. That meant cooperating with Beijing on some security issues while preserving America's alliances in case China became more assertive.[49] The Pentagon was especially focused on developing confidence-building measures to reduce the chances of an escalatory US-China clash.[50] The United States did not, however, renovate its Asian alliances with the purpose of meeting an emerging China threat.

Two decades into the twenty-first century, it seems perplexing that the United States did not more vigorously counteract the long-term challenge posed by a rising China and revise its alliances to that end. But accurate prognostication would have been an extraordinary feat in the 1990s. Consider that, as late as the 1995–1996 crisis in the Taiwan Straits, Beijing looked nothing like a rival. The crisis erupted after the president of Taiwan accepted an invitation to visit the United States for a college reunion in the spring of 1995. After much wrangling, the United States allowed him to make the trip, which China opposed in an effort to isolate Taiwan. Over the summer, the People's Liberation Army (PLA) responded by conducting a massive military exercise and missile tests near Taiwan. It was the biggest mobilization of Chinese troops since the Sino-Vietnamese War of 1979 and the first modern demonstration of Beijing's military capabilities within the First Island Chain.[51]

But the United States was not impressed and mounted a muscular response. Two aircraft carrier battle groups were sent to the opening of the Taiwan Straits to show that the United States was prepared to defend Taiwan, with whom it had a quasi-alliance relationship under the Taiwan Relations Act.[52] The Chinese then stood down.

From the American perspective, the Chinese looked skittish. With a demonstration of American military prowess, Beijing had backed away from a cause it considered fundamental to its sovereignty. China had been far more bellicose toward a US partner than American officials had anticipated, but Washington cowed Beijing. In the throes of the standoff, Pentagon officials were stunned to learn that China had not detected the two carrier groups approaching the Strait; Chinese sensors were so unsophisticated that they had missed the massive military movement altogether. While China had asserted itself as a potential regional threat, it had a long way to go before its military capacity would put it in America's league.[53]

Chinese leaders came to a similar conclusion. They had seen un-bridled American might on display in the 1991 Gulf War. And now they were humiliated on what they considered their home turf. In 1996 China redoubled its spending on missiles and other technology that could keep the US military from operating close to its shores.[54]

These were early but formative steps toward the bristling and tech-nologically savvy contemporary Chinese military. Pentagon officials understood that this future was possible, and certainly Nye was concerned. But some of those same officials also recall mid-1990s classified intelligence assessments which held that the PLA was un-likely to become a modern fighting force to rival the United States. Even officials who studied Beijing's strategy closely underestimated dramatically the pace and scope of its military development.[55] At century's turn, scholars still agreed that the PLA was nowhere near peer status. Furthermore, China-watchers believed that Beijing would face hurdles at home before it could become a major power: it would have to reconcile Leninism and capitalism in a swiftly growing economy without unleashing social forces that might threaten the regime. This seemed a formidable task—possibly an insurmount-able one. There was simply no consensus that China would become a significant strategic competitor and therefore no foe against which to direct the strategic energies of Asian allies.[56]

NATO's First War: A Case Study
in Alliance Rehabilitation

On March 24, 1999, NATO went to war for the first time in its fifty-year history. The operation heralded the alliance's changing role. With no superpower enemy to deter and defend against, NATO assumed new political and humanitarian goals—in this case, protecting Albanians in the Serbian enclave of Kosovo from ethnic cleansing. And, just as in the early years of NATO enlargement, Russia was seen not as a foe but as a critical diplomatic partner.

Kosovo's status within Serbia had been contested for decades, and Serbian President Slobodan Milošević had a long history of oppressing Kosovars. He had not targeted Kosovo during the Bosnian war, but after the peace settlement he turned against the Kosovar Albanians. His forces drove 1.3 million people from their homes and pushed 800,000 out of Kosovo entirely. When Milošević attacked the Kosovo Liberation Army in spring 1998, NATO set its sights on creating a Kosovo protectorate within Serbia. After negotiations with Milošević failed to secure the province, the alliance began what it hoped would be a swift bombing campaign. Seventy-eight days and 27,000 munitions later, Milošević surrendered. A NATO-led force of 50,000 troops established the Kosovo protectorate.[57] By all accounts the NATO air campaign, without a single alliance casualty, accomplished its political ambitions.

NATO's first war exemplified the fundamental tensions of the alliance's post-Cold War rehabilitation. The Clinton administration argued that the mission would bring common purpose to an enlarged NATO, giving it legitimacy and credibility in its post-Cold War role. But that logic struck some as flawed. Should NATO have to go to war to justify its survival? At the very least, it was clear that NATO had deviated far from its Cold War purpose. It was using its military might to end a sovereign government's brutal ethnic cleansing campaign—a worthy goal, but one unrelated to the direct defense of its members.[58]

This made the Kosovo mission legally dubious. As a defensive military alliance based on Article 51 of the UN Charter, NATO was authorized to use force only if its members were attacked. Kosovo was not a NATO member and was internationally recognized as part of Serbia. NATO's use of force was therefore, legally speaking, an operation against a sovereign state—even if its goals were humanitarian. Several NATO members believed the alliance needed UN authorization to use force in Kosovo, as there was otherwise no legal justification for the mission. While negotiating with Milošević in 1998–1999, the United States and its partners managed to pass UN Security Council resolutions condemning human rights abuses in Kosovo and calling on Serbia to restrict its military activities, but none of these resolutions authorized the use of military force. Ultimately there would be no Security Council permission for NATO's intervention, and the United States did not seek it before the bombing campaign began. The failure of peace negotiations at Rambouillet, France, in early 1999 made clear that any request for a council vote would falter thanks to Russian opposition.[59]

NATO could hardly have denied that it was operating beyond its remit. Its objectives demonstrated as much. NATO sought to establish a protectorate in Kosovo, not its independence, and initially hoped to achieve this through demonstration exercises and humanitarian assistance.[60] As it neared a decision for war, NATO ruled out the use of ground troops and committed to what it thought would be only a few days of air strikes. It conducted the air war from 15,000 feet, in hopes of avoiding casualties that would split its coalition.[61] If the bloodshed in Kosovo had been a direct threat to members of the alliance, NATO would likely have been less reticent.

Thus an alliance whose mandate was for defense and deterrence on behalf of its members went to war with a very different rationale and a dubious legal basis. After the war a UN commission led by former South African President Nelson Mandela concluded that NATO's campaign was "illegal but legitimate." It halted the violence in Kosovo but did not conform with international law or NATO's core purpose.[62]

A final demonstration of NATO's transformation was Russia's role as a diplomatic partner in the conflict—a collaboration that would have been unthinkable during the Cold War. Russia and Serbia were historic allies, and Milošević sought to consolidate Moscow's support to counter NATO pressure. But American strategy sought the opposite. With its allies, Washington worked to ensure that Russia would not actively oppose NATO policy, even when it could not fully support it.[63]

In the lead-up to war, Russia was a vital interlocutor between NATO and Serbia, urging Milošević to accept the stationing of foreign troops in Kosovo to prevent diplomacy from collapsing. After Milošević's crackdown on the Kosovo Liberation Army, the allies secured Russian support for a UN resolution demanding human rights improvements in Kosovo, as well as a Russian abstention from a decision to impose sanctions on Belgrade. Moscow would not agree to any UN language that threatened the use of military force but privately expressed to Washington that it understood why NATO would make such threats.[64]

When NATO opted for war, however, Russia's leaders were irate. Foreign Minister Igor Ivanov called the air campaign the worst aggression in Europe since the Second World War. President Yeltsin warned that the war could lead to global conflagration. Moscow believed that, by proceeding without a Security Council resolution, NATO was neutering the United Nations. Russia demanded an end to the bombing, and in the final days of March sent several ships to the Mediterranean, prompting NATO fears that Moscow could be sharing alliance flight data with the Serbs. However, in the face of NATO unity at an April 1999 summit, Yeltsin reached out to President Clinton with an offer to help end the war through diplomatic means. Yeltsin appointed former Prime Minister Viktor Chernomyrdin to act as special envoy to Kosovo.[65]

Moscow's diplomatic intervention was crucial to convincing Milošević to surrender. Publicly Chernomyrdin expressed rage at NATO, insisting that the intervention had set back US-Russia relations "by several decades."[66] But the focus of Russian diplomacy was not Serbian grievances—it was ending the bombing, helping Serbia retain sovereignty over Kosovo, and ensuring that non-NATO countries were included in the postwar occupying force. Privately Chernomyrdin pushed Milošević to surrender almost entirely on NATO's terms. This meant that Moscow itself would have to sacrifice its interests, including agreeing to a NATO occupation under UN authority, as opposed to by UN forces. Moscow also negotiated with Washington over its own participation in the peacekeeping mission. Russia preferred to have a sector of Serbia under its auspices but agreed to distribute its 4,000 troops between the NATO sectors. Russian troops remained under Moscow's tactical command but allowed NATO to maintain operational control.[67]

Michael Jackson, NATO's commander in Kosovo, concluded that Russia's role "was the single event that appeared to me to have the greatest significance in ending the war."[68] The former adversary had helped NATO prove itself and establish a new purpose, one having little to do with self-defense and deterrence against a great power threat.

Beyond Defense and Deterrence

By the end of the decade, the United States and its allies had not only salvaged security guarantees but also taken genuine steps to update them for the post-Cold War world as they saw it. NATO admitted new members and carried out a successful air campaign in Kosovo.

It thwarted nationalist violence on the continent, demonstrated military prowess, and relied on a former adversary as a diplomatic partner. All this confirmed a novel alliance logic.

The United States and its allies in Asia settled into the new status quo. In 1996 Tokyo and Washington developed defense guidelines that laid out Japan's role and stabilized the alliance, and the Japanese government passed legislation that allowed it to help defend US forces. Japan and South Korea agreed to take on greater financial burdens for the stationing of US forces, such that by the late 1990s they were among the cheapest places on earth to post American troops. As North Korean nuclear and missile threats mounted, both allies sought closer defense coordination with the United States.[69] The thaw came against the background of reduced economic rivalry, as the 1998 financial crisis felled hard-charging Asian markets and years of recession took their toll in Japan.

After the attacks of September 11, 2001, US alliances held strong. Japan, South Korea, Australia, and NATO—invoking Article V for the first time—gave significant support to US wars in the Middle East. The British fought beside the United States in Afghanistan as early as fall 2001, and NATO led the UN-mandated International Security Assistance Force there from 2003 to 2014, with a mission that included 130,000 troops and twenty-eight reconstruction teams. As of this writing, NATO continues to train and advise Afghan security forces through its Resolute Support operation. NATO also led a mission to train and equip Iraqi armed forces and police from 2004 to 2011, despite considerable public and allied-leadership opposition to the US invasion. Japan provided fuel, supplies, and reconstruction support in Afghanistan and Iraq. South Korea sent troops and police to Afghanistan and Iraq, where Seoul had the third-largest presence, behind only the United States and the United Kingdom. Australia participated in the invasions of Iraq and Afghanistan, where it continues to train forces.[70] In the Philippines the United States supported counterterrorism training, providing a new rationale for alliance.[71]

Senior George W. Bush administration officials were heartened by allies' contributions and urged continued cooperation, specifically with respect to counterterrorism. The White House saw terrorism as the country's most pressing threat, and therefore the task to which American security guarantees should be turned. By operating jointly, the thinking went, Washington and its allies could demonstrate to terrorist adversaries the world over the efficacy of old pacts under modern threat conditions.[72]

But as the United States and its allies identified new reasons to work together, novel strategic circumstances developed around them. Wars in the Middle East were in many ways a diversion from the more fundamental challenges of Russian and Chinese power. Old rivals were beginning to reassert themselves, sometimes at the alliances' most vulnerable points. Improbably, America's security guarantees had outlasted their adversaries. But in their victory, they were not reequipped for the major security threats of the twenty-first century.

A Reckless Rehabilitation?

Leading foreign affairs thinkers argue that America's post-Cold War alliances were not only under-prepared for Russian and Chinese resurgences but also provoked them. According to this view, by preserving its alliances even as Cold War adversaries were on the wane, the United States incited a backlash that could have been avoided. Prominent scholars such as John Mearsheimer have argued that NATO enlargement was the "taproot" of Russia's 2014 annexation of Crimea and invasion of Ukraine, so undermining Moscow's security that it was compelled to lash out anew. Vladimir Putin has made a similar case to justify Russian revanchism.[73] For their part, China's leaders insist that the US alliance system in Asia is a "Cold War relic" that undermines regional stability.[74] But is there concrete evidence that America's decision to keep and repurpose its alliances provoked former adversaries?

If such evidence exists, it should be found in the case of NATO enlargement. But while there is no doubt that NATO's expansion contributed to Moscow's feelings of strategic diminution, it is another matter to claim enlargement caused Russia's revanchism. Russian backlash began before the decision to enlarge NATO was made. Russian nationalists opposed the Kremlin's economic and political reforms in the early 1990s, particularly following the "shock therapy" intended to induce rapid transition toward capitalism. And Russian anger was stoked further by demonstrations of NATO power and Russian impotence—namely, the Kosovo operation—than it was by NATO's post-Cold War continuation and growth. This antipathy intensified after the ruble collapsed in 1998. "There is no doubt that the economic prescriptions promoted by the United States and the IMF contributed to the Russian public's backlash against the West," Steinberg said. "Especially in the early years, US policy was driven more by economic orthodoxy than a sensitivity to political realities in post-Soviet Russia." As Talbott put it in 1993, the American approach needed "less shock and more therapy."[75]

The claim that Russia was provoked by NATO expansion also ignores the fact that, during the first few years of the expansion process, Russia did not see NATO as a menace. Quite the opposite—Russia's leaders accommodated themselves to the alliance's post-Cold War efforts and even joined them. Moscow enrolled in the Partnership for Peace, signed the NATO-Russia Founding Act, and for years maintained that it was considering membership. As late as 2002, Vladimir Putin publicly hinted at and privately sought Russian NATO accession.[76] Halting NATO's expansion did not become a Russian foreign policy objective until after the round completed in 2004.[77]

None of this is to say that Moscow was pleased by NATO's activities. In the late 1990s, prominent experts such as Scowcroft worried about Russian anxieties and argued that the United States should therefore slow the pace of NATO enlargement.[78] The Kosovo intervention, however, was probably more damaging than alliance enlargement. Moscow's reaction to the campaign was "strident condemnation"—the alliance was bombing a Russian partner in its former sphere of influence, seemingly confirming long-held fears that a reinvigorated NATO would upset peace and stability in Europe. As bombs were falling in Kosovo, Chernomyrdin declared, "The world has never in this decade been so close as now to the brink of nuclear war."[79] Russia became a diplomatic partner for lack of other options, and US-Russia relations may never have recovered from Kosovo's strain.[80]

The particulars of enlargement also suggest that it was not NATO's preservation and expansion that provoked Russia. During the first round of enlargement, Russia was largely quiescent. What it objected to most strenuously was extension of membership to the Baltic states of Latvia, Lithuania, and Estonia, three of the seven states added to NATO in 2004. The inclusion of these former Soviet republics exacerbated Moscow's declinist dismay. Even the most enthusiastic enlargement advocates acknowledged the political dangers of including the Baltics.[81] We might therefore conclude that a more limited expansion, or an expansion that included different states, could have been acceptable to Russia, or at least, rankled it less.

In short, the timeline of expansion does not support the strict causal claim that NATO enlargement provoked renewed Russian aggression. Anti-Western and nationalist sentiments in Russia were not born of alliance expansion, per se, but were primarily piqued by economic policies and exercises of NATO power that contributed to and reinforced Russia's sense of diminution. In the dissolution of the Soviet Union, Moscow had experienced the sort of geopolitical loss and economic shock normally reserved for catastrophic defeats in war. Russia was almost certain to begrudge NATO's resilience, but that does not establish that enlargement drove the revanchism that dismembered Crimea and Ukraine.

Nonetheless, there exists a more modest and plausible linkage between post-Cold War American alliance renovation and twenty-first-century geopolitics. These refurbishments—at first ad hoc, later directed toward counterterrorism—lacked clear focus on major-power defense and deterrence, inadvertently helping to create significant strategic vulnerabilities. Whether or not Russia's leadership saw NATO expansion as a true threat in the 1990s and early 2000s, it claims to do so now, after the enlargement process landed the alliance on Moscow's doorstep. NATO's newfound proximity to Russia makes the alliance much harder to defend and increases the chances for escalation and hot war. This is a liability NATO courted during a moment of triumph. Imbued with the elixir of unipolarity, NATO leaders were distracted from the strategic imperatives of defense and deterrence. Meanwhile in Asia, the two-tiered system of pacts was at best focused on North Korea, and at worst, diverted and listless.

Thirty years later, America's shields have endured the end of the Cold War but lost their luster. They outlasted their foes but were unprepared when rivals emerged anew. A long-postponed alliance reckoning has now arrived.

5

THE DAWN OF
MODERN COMPETITION

In late 2017 the United States made a foreign policy proclamation that many analysts on both sides of the domestic political divide considered overdue. For years national security efforts had focused on counterterrorism operations in the Middle East. The White House's 2017 National Security Strategy and the Pentagon's 2018 National Defense Strategy identified a different leading challenge: "revisionist" competitors—Russia and China, specifically—that posed threats to US interests around the world.

The White House and Defense Department were acknowledging that the post-Cold War period of uncontested dominance had ended and major-power rivalry was again a defining feature of international politics. Their proclamations raised more questions than they answered, however. What does American strategy seek to achieve as the country competes with Russia and China? How will the United States keep itself secure with its primacy on the wane? The world still awaits Washington's responses.

Leaders in Moscow and Beijing, however, are somewhat clearer in their objectives. In pursuing them, they have made America's alliances strategic targets. Since the early 2000s, under Vladimir Putin, Russia has viewed the United States as a menacing superpower. In the 2008–2012 period, Russia's foreign policy became expressly revanchist, with an aim of rending NATO and the European Union.

By 2014 Russia had begun to use systematic disinformation campaigns with the goal of destabilizing Western governments and alliances. In the United States and Europe, Russia has covertly supported political candidates and causes opposed to multilateralism and alliances. In its region it has been more bellicose, though it denies using force or else invents pretexts to justify doing so. Russia is a declining power, but it still poses a military threat to NATO's eastern flank and is a disruptive actor in the West.

In contrast to Russia, China is in a position of strength. It has fashioned a strategy predicated on its economic and military ascent. After decades biding its time, hiding its capabilities, and seeking integration with the West and its neighbors, it has become more assertive. Now China seeks to undermine America's Asian alliances, which stand in the way of its restoration as the leading power in Asia and its emergence as a global superpower.

Russian and Chinese national security interests are distinct, and their divergent power trajectories mean that their leaders will advance these interests in different ways. But both countries are taking aim at US alliances. China and Russia have each developed conventional military strategies that target US partners and sap the credibility of Washington's security guarantees. But as states facing a militarily stronger opponent—the United States—Russia and China also pursue their geopolitical aims using means designed to prevent American retaliation. Through maritime law enforcement, economic penalties, hacking, and disinformation campaigns, Russia and China effectively challenge American power without firing a shot. And Moscow in particular uses force in limited, obscure, and deniable ways to avoid triggering US defense commitments. These "subconventional" strategies also aim to exploit and widen existing gaps in American alliances.

Fundamentally, both Moscow and Beijing hope to make their immediate neighborhoods friendlier to their regimes and eventually achieve dominant spheres of influence, although only China really has that power. To reach this goal, they will have to expunge the considerable US influence already in these regions, which requires them to unravel American alliances.

Reform to Revanchism: Russian Strategy after the Cold War

The dissolution of the Soviet Union led many Western analysts to embrace an almost-teleological assumption about Russia's future: with communists out of power, the people of Russia would disavow empire and move toward a freer economic and political system.[1] But the post-Soviet trajectory was not so evident to Russians themselves. No sooner had the flag of the Russian Federation been raised than competing camps began to vie over the new country's future.

Three schools of foreign policy thought were most prominent. There was the pro-Western view, espoused by liberals who also supported market reforms and democratization. Others argued for a power-balancing approach. They tended to favor some reforms but less alignment with the West. Finally, hardline nationalist-imperialists sought to organize domestic and foreign policy around the restoration of Russia's greatness and traditional sphere of influence. The liberal-reformists, aligned with President Yeltsin, were initially ascendant. But their leading position was short lived. By 1993 the failure of US-backed economic shock therapy had convinced many policy elites that rapid liberalization was perilous and that Washington was to blame for the difficulties of Russia's transition.[2]

For the next decade, Russian foreign policy embraced the balancing approach, as "Slavophiles" gained the upper hand on "Westernizers." Restoration of Russia to the great power ranks became the central object of foreign policy, and progress toward that goal would be measured by comparing Russia's global standing to Washington's.[3]

As the NATO-enlargement debate demonstrated, Moscow had no compelling reason to fear a US invasion in the 1990s, but antiliberalism and remnants of Cold War competition stoked anxiety nonetheless. As early as 1991, Russian officials had begun to contemplate how the United States might strike the Russian homeland through states formerly in the Eastern Bloc. With these concerns in mind, Russian officials decided that the "near abroad" of former Soviet republics would have to serve as a geographic buffer to guarantee its sovereignty.[4] To ensure that NATO was held at bay, Russia would attempt to secure a sphere of influence, dominating its backyard as in Soviet times and ensuring deference from its neighbors.[5]

The term "near abroad" was never cleanly defined, but analysts understand it to include the former USSR minus the Baltic states and, of course, Russia itself. Belarus, Ukraine, Kazakhstan, Kyrgyzstan, Tajikistan, Turkmenistan, and Uzbekistan are considered the highest-priority states from a power-balancing perspective. They are followed by Moldova, Georgia, Armenia, and Azerbaijan in a second tier. Under this scheme, Russia prizes the unity of Central Asia and noninterference by other major powers therein. A third tier of priority includes all former Warsaw Pact countries, including the Baltic states.[6]

For the first decade of the post-Cold War era, Russian leaders saw no conflict between their desire for a strategic buffer and NATO's for expansion, to which Russia acquiesced. But while Russia accepted NATO's growth and even sought closer ties to the alliance, it was sidelined from European integration, isolating it politically and economically as it declined. The post-Soviet Russian economy contracted by 43 percent in GDP terms and did not reach 1990 levels again until 2007, when Russia finally paid off its debts.[7] By that point Moscow had ushered the country through a painful transition, but great power status was still receding, and its strategic buffer zone appeared elusive.

Russia's Strategic Turn: 2008–2012

Between 2008 and 2012, Russian foreign policy lurched toward nationalism and imperialism. Foreign and domestic policy became inextricable from Putinism, a conservative doctrine emphasizing the need for a strong state to protect Russia from enemies at home and abroad.[8] Russian leaders abandoned their 1990s quest for integration into the prevailing international political system and came to view the United States as uninterested in, or disrespectful of, Russian interests.

Several events motivated this shift. One was the Kosovo War, which helped to solidify in Russia the image of the United States as a rogue superpower.[9] Then there was the Baltic states' 2004 accession to NATO. The Russians also bristled at the US decision to invade Iraq in 2003 without UN imprimatur. Finally, after disputed 2003 elections in Georgia and 2005 elections in Ukraine provoked pro-democracy uprisings—the Rose and Orange Revolutions, respectively—Russian leaders became convinced that the United States was fomenting upheaval on their periphery. It seemed that Washington and its European allies were encroaching upon Moscow's security through the use of political warfare, drawing few casualties and maintaining plausible deniability. At its annual summit in Bucharest in 2008, NATO pledged that Ukraine and Georgia would eventually become members—a precarious commitment given these states' location in the heart of Moscow's near abroad.[10] In 2008 Russia invaded Georgia—its first use of force since its 1989 withdrawal from Afghanistan.

By this point Putin and other Russian leaders firmly believed that the United States had a sinister agenda to thwart Russia's restoration. In 2010 this view became official Russian military doctrine, as further NATO enlargement was labeled a direct national security threat. In 2015 Russia's National Security Strategy reiterated that view.[11]

It would be wrong to claim that deterioration was the only option for US-Russia relations after 2008. At times, the Obama administration's "reset" seemed like it might stabilize the bilateral slide.
Most notably, in 2010 the two countries signed the New START arms
control agreement. They also cooperated in attempting to restrain
Iran's nuclear ambitions and on North Korean nuclear sanctions, and
they worked together to accelerate Russia's accession to the World
Trade Organization (WTO).[12] President Obama canceled the deployment to Eastern Europe of a planned missile defense system,
which detractors viewed as a major concession to Moscow.

But even as the reset was proceeding in fits and starts, Russia's
economy was succumbing to the global financial crisis. The hard-
won gains of the post-Cold War period that had brought Russia out
of debt evaporated. After much whiplash, the leadership in Moscow
concluded that the Western liberal model was utterly bankrupt.[13]
With its economy on the line, Russia relied more heavily on its oil
exports and on kleptocracy. In the words of one scholar, it became
"trans-imperial"—part of the globalized world for the sake of its survival, while increasingly corrupt and authoritarian at home.[14]

Russia also claimed to be increasingly victimized by American political influence. When the Arab Spring seized the Middle East in
2010–2012, officials in Moscow assumed Washington was the puppet
master. When Ukraine experienced more upheaval in the 2014
Maidan protests, Russia again saw Americans at work. In Putin's
telling, all sparks of democracy were the product of Western subterfuge. The United Sates was engaged in ideological arson, which
might well be a prelude to military intervention.[15]

By 2012 nationalist-imperialism had recaptured Russian foreign
policy. NATO and the EU were targets of pointed ire, and halting
the alliance's further advance had become a central foreign policy
goal. Russia also positioned itself as a counterweight to the West by
promoting global institutions in which it was a significant or dominant figure. The Kremlin registered few objections to the UN, WTO,

and other organizations in which it saw itself as fairly represented. But it backed the Collective Security Treaty Organization as a NATO alternative and the Eurasian Economic Union as a substitute EU. Through these regional institutions, Moscow sought to shore up its near abroad and insulate the region from what it saw as US-led efforts at democracy promotion. Much of Russia's government is organized toward those same ends: ensuring that the country's interactions with the outside world do not expose it to liberalizing forces.[16]

Revanchist Russia has done much more than play defense. In 2014 it began cyber and information campaigns against pro-democracy protests in Ukraine, nonmilitary offensives designed to pave the way for its annexation of Crimea and to bolster pro-Russian forces over demonstrators on the Maidan. Its intervention in the 2016 US presidential elections was an effort to derail the heavily favored candidate, who was likely to support NATO enlargement, further European integration, and popular democratic movements. Moscow's interference in that year's Brexit vote was, similarly, a wrench hurled at European unity.

Putin continues to strive for a sphere of influence through direct actions against Western and liberal states and institutions. But Russia's objective is not to just to disrupt others; its interference is a means toward the ends of survival and restored great power status, however elusive. Putin calls for a more multipolar world—a "new world order" in which Russia is one of several major players.[17]

Russia Secure, NATO Broken

Russia's pursuit of great power objectives is starkly at odds with its stagnation and decline. The Soviet Union boasted demographic stability, despite its devastating war losses. But post-Soviet Russia imploded demographically and economically. Russia's population fell by 5 million in the first two decades after communism. The economy is expected to grow no more than 2 percent annually for the foreseeable future and will remain highly dependent on hydrocarbon exports.[18] On the whole, population and economic data suggest Russia is weak and growing weaker.

It is also a domestic political shambles. Russia could reasonably be called an electoral autocracy. It has a parliament, but this and other formal institutions hold little sway. Elections are uncompetitive, and the legal checks and balances on Putin's power are fictitious. If anyone has influence over the centers of power, it is the kleptocrats: the vast elite patronage network, unaccountable to Russian society, that exists to extract payments and convert its wealth into power and access to government.[19] This combination of structural decline and rent-seeking autocracy encourages an aggressive foreign policy. Lackluster economic and demographic trends make for a short time horizon: Putin and his associates must secure their gains right away, or they are liable to lose them as the state grows feebler. They are therefore likely to run risks that leaders of a more stable state would not.

One of these gambles is massive military investment, which diverts funds desperately needed in the faltering society. Putin's is a renovation project, as the Russian military languished for years after the Cold War ended. With the collapse of the Soviet Union, Moscow's 207-division army became just 85 brigades. Forces withdrew from ten countries, and bases were closed in Cuba and Vietnam. The total armed personnel under the Kremlin's command fell from 3 million to 1 million.[20] Military spending plummeted from 21 percent of GDP in the final days of the Soviet Union to 4 percent in the early days of the Russian Federation. By 2006 spending had bottomed out at 3 percent of GDP, and the military was in a state of abject disrepair.[21] By 2016, however, a decade of arms buildups had brought spending to 5 percent of GDP. And Moscow has not stopped there. In 2018 the Kremlin announced GPV 2027, a military modernization program focused on improved force mobility and deployability, logistics, and command-and-control systems.[22]

But while military modernization is a priority, there is no realistic possibility that Russia will spend its way to great power status.

Russia's losses from the financial crisis continue to sting, and oil prices remain low, leaving few resources to draw on. Moscow's spending on defense dwarfs that on health care and education, yet the United States still outspends it on defense nine times over.[23] This has led Russia to take compensatory steps, including relying more heavily on its aging nuclear arsenal and equipping its army for smaller wars.[24] Russia also is investing in significant subconventional warfare capabilities.

Reflecting the sense of urgency among Russia's leaders, the military has been active despite the country's faltering economic and demographic foundations. Its combat operations in Europe have been efforts to maintain a buffer zone, or at least to blunt Western influence in its near abroad. The 2008 invasion of Georgia silenced talk of NATO membership for that country and for Ukraine. Its 2014 invasion of Ukraine was intended to derail Kiev's economic integration with the EU. In each case Russia's leaders saw military action as a justified response to an international system unfairly imposed on them. Russian forces still occupy pieces of Georgia and Ukraine, including the annexed territory of Crimea.

Russia-watchers on both sides of the Atlantic worry that Moscow will next turn on the Baltics, NATO's eastern flank. The prospect is a grave one, as the NATO-Russia Founding Act forswears the permanent installation of NATO troops or nuclear weapons in Latvia, Lithuania, and Estonia. Only local forces are available to defend the borders they share with Russia, which is equal in length to the West German frontier patrolled by eight allied corps during the Cold War. RAND Corporation wargames find that Russian troops could reach Tallinn and Riga, the capitals of Estonia and Latvia respectively, in fewer than sixty hours, snatching a quick victory from the alliance. If NATO came to their aid, Russia might try to cut off air and sea routes around the Baltics. Moscow could also attempt to take just a sliver of Baltic land, perhaps where an ethnic Russian population is especially dense, creating a dilemma over how NATO should respond. NATO would face the unhappy choice between escalation and backing down. The former is potentially catastrophic, as the United States and Russia are the world's leading nuclear powers. The latter would shatter the alliance.[25]

In considering whether to escalate, the United States would be at a disadvantage vis-à-vis Moscow since it would be acting on behalf of allies rather than itself. Naturally, American leaders and the public at large would be hesitant. Indeed, by extending NATO to include allies whose security the United States cannot fully guarantee, Washington has bifurcated the alliance: it can credibly promise to support its longstanding allies in Western Europe but cannot be counted on to defend the Eastern European allies most in need of protection. The challenges have only grown now that Crimea is in Russian hands, giving Moscow a favorable location from which to strike.[26]

More likely than a Baltic invasion, however, is aggression against a country auditioning for NATO membership. Moldova is one possible target. Its constitution makes it officially neutral, but Moldovans have long debated reunification with Romania, a NATO member with which they share a language and deep history. If the states were to merge, Moldova would be absorbed by the alliance. Russia maintains troops in the Slavic Transnistria region of Moldova in an effort to keep the country from becoming a NATO member by default.[27] Beyond Moldova, Moscow could take further punitive action against Ukraine or Georgia if either is poised to renew a bid for NATO's protection.

Thus far Russia's military operations have had their intended effect of halting NATO's eastward expansion. Russia pointed to the alliance's openness to Georgian and Ukrainian accession to justify its invasions, and both states' candidacies have since been derailed. Talk of further enlargement is now muted.[28] The political toll has been costly for NATO. By backing down in the East, the alliance heightens fears in the Baltics, where concerns about Russia are acute. The eastern and western halves of the alliance are thus at odds. Western Europe is less concerned about Moscow's direct military threat, while the eastern allies worry aloud. Without using force against the alliance, Russia has eroded its unity and its capacity to assure members.

Two decades into the twenty-first century, Russia's geostrategic objectives have taken on an ever-more caustic edge, running headlong into America's biggest alliance. Moscow endeavors to protect its territory and regime, exert influence in its near abroad, prevent interference in its domestic affairs, and be treated as a great power. But it furthers these goals by fracturing and containing the EU and NATO.

Chinese Strategy after the Cold War

For China and the United States, the close of the Cold War did not mark a dramatic shift. The bilateral relationship had been largely stable since President Nixon's 1972 trip to Beijing and President Carter's decision to recognize the People's Republic diplomatically. And by the early 1990s, the Chinese economy was intimately linked to the West. Since Deng Xiaoping established the program of "reform and opening up" in 1978, China had increasingly relied on market forces to fuel its growth and had become enmeshed in US-led international institutions. China, moreover, had distanced itself from Moscow during the Sino-Soviet split of the 1950s and 1960s. The collapse of the Soviet Union was concerning to Beijing, but not perilous.

From the Chinese perspective, Deng's reforms were necessary to preserve the regime and keep the country safe. The reforms also came with a kind of strategic doctrine: China should "hide its capabilities and bide its time." Deng argued that China should improve its ties with advanced economies in order to boost its own growth. It should not present itself as a military rival to major powers, lest it find itself in a conflict that could derail its rise. In time, Deng and other reformers hoped, international politics would become friendlier to a nondemocracy.[29] The "hide and bide" strategy encountered a few hurdles, notably the Tiananmen Square massacre of 1989, in which government troops mowed down several hundred prodemocracy protesters, the state declared martial law, and the United States and others responded with sanctions and arms embargoes. In spite of Beijing's human rights violations, the perception generally held that China's growth was good for the world.

US leaders hoped that China could be guided into the international system as a "responsible stakeholder."[30] This approach had two interrelated objectives. First, by welcoming Beijing into existing institutions and treaties, the United States and its allies would persuade China that its interests lay in adapting to and preserving the international system rather than challenging it. Second, the United States hoped that China's growing economy would inspire some amount of political liberalization, on the theory that market forces would lead to rule-of-law institutions and a more open government. This pro-engagement approach never subsumed all of US strategy, and policymakers understood that China would only reform so much; Washington always sought to deter aggression in Asia. Nonetheless, enthusiasm for economic engagement sometimes took precedence over security concerns and the instinct to hedge against growing Chinese power.[31]

By the 1990s China was too strong to be seriously coerced from abroad, and it used its muscle to keep growing. Beijing joined the WTO and pledged market reforms on which it later reneged, as the government remained deeply involved in many aspects of the economy. It kept a tight grip on government-backed companies—so-called state-owned enterprises. Beijing engaged in systematic industrial espionage to purloin foreign technologies, including those with clear military applications. The government also forced the transfer of major innovations in aerospace, chemicals, and high-tech infrastructure from Western companies to Chinese ones.[32]

Even as China grew, most seasoned observers thought its labyrinthine bureaucracy and managed economy would keep it from the great power ranks. After all, state-led economies did not have impressive track records. Instead its form of Leninist capitalism has proved remarkably resilient, and the Chinese Communist Party has only increased its economic role.[33] When the party started plowing some of the country's newfound wealth into military development in the 1990s, the results came faster than virtually anyone anticipated; US intelligence agencies systematically underestimated the extent of the buildup.[34] With its economy revved and its politics stable, Beijing saw itself as uniquely positioned when the Western economic model appeared to stumble.

Seeking Not Hiding: 2008–2012

Chinese foreign policy underwent a decisive shift after 2008, leaving Deng's hide-and-bide strategy behind. The global financial crisis appeared to weaken the West and expose the frailties of democratic capitalism, and American forces were still mired in Iraq. It seemed to China's leaders that the United States was in decline, and the moment was opportune for Beijing to begin its push for a leading role on the global stage.[35]

China's leaders have long thought of its security environment in concentric rings. The Communist Party's first priority is the defense of China's territorial integrity, both from external enemies and from internal separatist movements and instability. This requires China to ensure stability along its borders, in its western province Xinjiang, and in Tibet and Hong Kong. It also demands that Taiwan be prevented from achieving independence.[36]

With its immediate sovereignty concerns relatively stable, China looked to the next ring of concern: its nearby seas. Beginning in 2009 Beijing adopted a much more forceful stance toward maritime and territorial claims in the East and South China Seas. China started intercepting US military vessels and aircraft operating near its coasts, despite international law guaranteeing freedom of navigation. It has also used its growing coast guard capabilities to intimidate Japanese and Philippine crews around the Senkaku Islands and in the South China Sea. In one of its more brazen acts, the Chinese coast guard escalated a standoff with Philippine fishermen and seized Scarborough Shoal after promising to withdraw from the area, despite the fact that the shoal had long been in Manila's possession.[37]

Since his 2012–2013 ascent, President Xi Jinping has consolidated this muscular foreign policy turn. He has made explicit China's aspirations to become the regional leader, and eventually, a global power. The central foreign policy push of Xi's first five-year term was construction and militarization in the South China Sea, which he described as a victory at the Nineteenth Party Congress in 2017.[38] In the space of just two years, state-owned enterprises transformed seven tiny reefs into artificial islands. Xi's government then proceeded to construct military outposts atop them. With naval ports, runways, sensors, and anti-air defenses, the artificial island bases can project power in surrounding waters. Although the territories remain disputed, China's construction is now a fait accompli and militarization continues at a deliberate pace.

Having tipped the balance in the South China Sea, Xi moved his sights westward to the next ring of China's security priorities: the rest of Asia. His new vision for Chinese power is the Belt and Road Initiative (BRI). Launched in 2013, the sprawling infrastructure program comprises more than $575 billion of projects in at least seventy countries. According to official Chinese sources, BRI's 3,100 discrete projects include roads, highways, ports, dams, and surveillance infrastructure. Development is clustered in South, Southeast, and Central Asia and China itself, and most of the contractors responsible are Chinese firms.[39]

Through the BRI, Beijing seeks to keep growing economically by exporting excess labor and capital and generating profits for state-backed firms. Presumably, the government also hopes to gain political leverage in the target countries. China may eventually transform ports and other sites for military use, and it likely seeks to build access routes along its western periphery so that it cannot be encircled by rivals.[40] The initiative is too amorphous and opaque to permit neat prognosis concerning likelihood of success, and it certainly exposes China itself to major political liabilities. Nevertheless, the Communist Party may hope to use BRI to reestablish China's dominance in Asia.

A final security target is the international system broadly. A central narrative in China holds that the country was wronged by European colonial powers in the nineteenth century and again in the post-World War II settlement. An ally during that conflict, China was included as a founding member of the UN Security Council. But after the Chinese Civil War, much of the world recognized the legitimacy of only the Republic of China, excluding Beijing from many aspects of international affairs until the 1970s. Chinese strategists remain skeptical of postwar rules and institutions in which they feel disadvantaged. China's leaders also increasingly claim their right to act unilaterally, arguing that hegemons have the privilege of hypocrisy. To support their position, they point to numerous US violations of, and opt-outs from, international law: the invasion of Iraq, non-ratification of UN Convention on the Law of the Sea, and so on.

China is now a member of nearly all international institutions and regimes for which it is eligible, but it does not accept many liberal norms.[41] China has increased its funding to the UN and is now a global leader on climate change, albeit due to its own self-interest and the US abdication of responsibility for the issue.[42] It has insisted on reforms to the International Monetary Fund and G20 but has worked within existing frameworks in the service of these goals. At the same time Beijing has all but broken the WTO by maintaining its non-market structure. And China engages in systematic efforts to undermine the international human rights regime, which exemplifies the liberal democratic global governance that it sees as fundamentally threatening. For instance, China has pressed the UN Human Rights Council to prioritize state sovereignty over individual freedoms.[43]

On the regional level, China is less willing to follow existing structures of security cooperation as it seeks to reestablish itself as a regional great power. From its heterodox interpretation of the Law of the Sea and its South China Sea island-building campaign to its long-standing economic support for North Korea, Beijing has often secured its regional interests by undermining rules without replacing them. In most of these cases, China has not expressly sought scofflaw status. Instead, it uses existing rules to hinder prevailing institutions where they contravene its security interests. In the words of one scholar, China's international behavior is moderately revisionist without being revolutionary.

Given Beijing's objective of achieving great power status, it is likely that China will aim to avoid conventional conflict for at least the next ten to fifteen years. (An exception could be a war over Taiwan.) It will continue to take an à la carte approach to international laws as its interests dictate, increasingly flexing its muscles within Asia without courting war. It will accept the basic form of many existing institutions, without necessarily abiding by their liberal norms.[44]

In all likelihood China's hand will only strengthen. In 2018 the Chinese Communist Party eliminated presidential term limits, which means that Xi will likely remain in power into the 2030s. Facing no visible domestic opposition, he will be in a position to reestablish China as a regional military leader. Indeed, China has already demonstrated that it can threaten the United States and is willing to do so, in part by undermining American allies.

Anti-Access and American Allies

China's military budget grew from $21 billion in 1990 to $239 billion in 2017—a ten-fold increase. Beijing has used this bounty to conduct a dramatic defense overhaul. As of this writing, China has three aircraft carriers under development. By the early 2020s, China will have more naval vessels in the Pacific than the United States does.

And along with its growing naval presence, China is engaging in more frequent military exercises with a broader range of partners.[45]

But China is not just doing more. It is also building better. Following the stunning display of US military prowess in the first Gulf War and the American intervention in the Taiwan Straits crisis, China understood that it lacked the capability to fight and win against modern opponents. To correct that, it began investing in a high-tech fighting force, with a focus on precision weapons. In the early post-Cold War years, the United States was the world's leader in precision weapons, which it demonstrated in strikes against Iraq. Other countries have since adopted these weapons, and China's defense strategy now relies on them.[46]

The PLA seeks to neutralize the US military advantage in the Pacific through deterrence and by denying opportunities to intervene decisively, as Washington did in the Taiwan Straits. China's investments in ballistic missiles, anti-ship missiles, land-attack cruise missiles, air defenses, cyber warfare capabilities, and communications and sensor technology all appear to further a central strategic goal. China's weapons threaten US bases in the Pacific, aircraft carriers at sea, and combat-support assets. These advanced military resources would, for example, make it much harder for US forces to join a conflict to defend Taiwan, a nontreaty ally that nonetheless has substantial political support in the United States. Since the island is just a hundred miles from the mainland, Beijing may be able to establish air superiority before US forces stationed in Japan, Guam, and Hawaii reached the area.[47]

These *anti-access/area denial* (A2/AD) capabilities offer a relatively low-cost means of confounding US alliance strategy. Because they increase the risks of joining a conflict near China's shores and of maneuvering within the First Island Chain, these capabilities place US security guarantees and therefore allied assurance in doubt.[48] China is now powerful enough in conventional and nuclear terms that escalation could be incredibly costly. This puts Washington in a graver position than it finds in the Baltics. Would the United States really be willing to escalate on behalf of allies, knowing that the result could be war with such a well-armed adversary?

If allies' confidence in the United States erodes, they may increasingly hedge, preferring to retain more political autonomy. This would be a victory for Beijing, which would find it easier to lead a region in which American alliances have a diminished role. Particularly since the end of the Cold War, China's leaders have become vocal about their distaste for US alliances. Beijing consistently refers to American security guarantees as Cold War relics and makes no secret of its desire to see them gone. Like their twenty-first-century Russian counterparts, Chinese leaders have argued that post-Cold War US efforts to deepen alliance cooperation serve hegemonic purposes—in their case, that Washington is attempting to encircle and contain China.[49]

At a 2014 regional conference, President Xi called for an "Asia for Asians," which implied an end to America's alliances and the birth of a regional security system centered on Beijing. The idea has not taken off, but if China has not been able to cleave away US allies, it is at least making their choices more difficult. Its augmented military challenges the value of US security guarantees, while its growing economic clout makes it a hard partner to refuse. Before long US allies may come to believe they cannot afford to choose Washington over Beijing.[50]

The United States can live with a more powerful China—indeed, it will have little choice in the matter. Fortunately the two countries probably will not find themselves at war any time soon. Precisely because China desires to become the regional leader and climb to global power status, it will want to avoid major conflict with the United States or its allies. More likely Beijing will slowly but persistently seek to erode America's alliances. Like Russia, China will continue to employ a strategy that seeks to undercut US security guarantees without testing them directly.

Competitive Coercion: Below Article V

In the last several years, national security analysts have become enchanted with the study of "gray zone" or "hybrid" warfare—a type of conflict that is said to occur in the space between peace and traditional war. This includes low-intensity military campaigns, law enforcement and paramilitary efforts, cyberattacks, economic coercion, and social and political manipulation through espionage and disinformation. A key dimension of gray-zone warfare, as the name suggests, is ambiguity. Belligerents often attempt to shroud and deny their activities.

Much of the discourse over gray-zone competition is too imprecise to be very useful. And breathless public discussion tends to make the problem seem new, which it is not. In the early years of the Cold War, Kennan spoke of "the employment of all the means at a nation's command, short of war, to achieve its national objectives," which he termed "political warfare."[51] Subterfuge has been an element of war since time immemorial. But even if subconventional conflict, when carefully defined and considered in context, is an older challenge than some appear to believe, it is no less a genuine problem.

Gray-zone activities are campaigns used by states and nonstate actors to achieve political goals, mostly through the coordinated use of nonmilitary tools and through incremental advances toward an objective. For the purposes of this analysis, I describe these activities as *competitive coercion*. They are competitive in that they are deployed by power rivals to advance their political goals. And they are coercive because they compel a change in the political status quo, even if traditional military force is not involved.

Competitive coercion is a puzzling phenomenon. Chief among its vexing features is that it is a product of functioning deterrence.[52] Security commitments send a strong deterrent signal—"do not attack my ally or I will attack you"—but also a limited one. Because security guarantees are only invoked under narrow, publicly acknowledged conditions, they create openings for adversaries to exploit. If an adversary knows that an alliance commitment may be triggered by an unprovoked attack on the ally's homeland, it also knows that it may be able to avoid retaliation by taking actions that are less brazen or that are targeted where deterrence is not operative.

As such, competitive coercion is frequently surreptitious. Although it is premeditated, it is often deployed opportunistically, the better to find the cracks in existing deterrence schemes. And ideally competitive coercion will be hard to detect, at least at first. China's construction on South China Sea reefs is a good example. China's building activity was initially inexplicable; only later did it become clear that Beijing was upending the balance of power in the South China Sea with new military installations, and at that point no one could halt its progress.

Competitive coercion is attractive for two related reasons. First, nonmilitary coercion usually has lower upfront costs than military action. Second, because competitive coercion is conflict-avoidant, it comes with fewer risks than combat. In particular, competitive coercion minimizes the prospect of retaliation and escalation.[53] Where the challenge to the status quo is difficult to identify, its protectors have few options with which to respond.

Although competitive coercion has long been a tool of power rivals, its current prominence is in some ways a counterintuitive product of relatively recent innovations in global rules and institutions. For instance, the international system now enshrines a strong norm against territorial conquest, and states rarely opt to make formal declarations of war on their adversaries.[54] Under such circumstances, it makes sense that rivals would avoid blatant hostilities. But the problem is even more complex. A system based on rules is intrinsically ripe for competitive coercion because rules, through omission, delineate a space in which competitors are free to act. Consider the North Atlantic Treaty. Article V firmly establishes thresholds against conventional military activity but not other forms of conflict, so that rivals can comfortably move their aggression into other domains.

Moreover, as we have seen, the structure of deterrence makes competitive coercion especially appealing in the nuclear age. The presence of nuclear weapons on both sides of an escalatory dynamic induces caution in each party, but it may do so disproportionally for a security guarantor, such as the United States, whose threats to escalate are made on behalf of allies instead of its homeland. A guarantor is unlikely to escalate in cases where nuclear-capable rivals coerce allies, given the high stakes.

Finally, alongside the structure of the international order and the dynamics of escalation in the nuclear age, the qualities of individual states can move them to undertake competitive coercion. As discussed below, Russia and China have particular needs and endowments that lead them to favor competitive coercion and to enact it in distinct ways.[55]

Moscow's Playbook

Russia has increasingly resorted to competitive coercion because it seeks to accomplish grand aims using declining power resources. Its preferred tools have been low-to-medium-intensity conventional conflict and information warfare. Moscow does not attempt to deny that this is its strategy, although it often denies individual instances of coercion, stealth being itself part of the strategy. Russian leaders argue that their tactics are proportional because the United States exercises its own competitive coercion in the form of democracy promotion.[56]

Ukraine has been a frequent target of Moscow's competitive coercion. Russia made several military incursions into Ukraine before annexing Crimea in March 2014, but much of the fighting was carried out by proxies and unmarked forces. Moscow also backs separatists, whose demonstrations and demands provide pretexts for Russia's more overt actions. And while Russian troops now hold swaths of Ukrainian territory, including Donetsk and Luhansk in the country's east, Moscow vociferously denies any military presence in Ukraine and has suffered only mild diplomatic reproaches.[57] Moscow acknowledges controlling another Ukrainian territory, Crimea, but argues that it is legally entitled to do so.

No serious analyst doubts that Russia has deployed its military to dissect Ukrainian sovereignty, but not all observers are so careful. Convincing global publics of what should be undeniable is a goal of information warfare, at which Russia has long excelled. President Putin, who had a lengthy career in the KGB and has staffed his government with former intelligence officers, has revamped Russia's disinformation machine for contemporary pursuits. Russian information warfare exploits domestic and foreign media and recruits ethnic Russians abroad to amplify its messages and obfuscate reality. A primary tactic is to magnify the hypocrisies of Russia's adversaries in order to undercut the political fortunes of foreign leaders who might take a hard line against Moscow. The proliferation of open-access and otherwise-exploitable media platforms has extended the reach of Russian disinformation at low cost. Several Russian intelligence agencies are now charged with hacking, conducting sabotage, spreading disinformation, and perpetrating systematic blackmail abroad.[58]

Moscow may attack using informational tools exclusively, as it did during the 2016 US presidential campaign. Its election-related operations against Germany, France, and Britain all sought to aid candidates who would sow European disunity. But Russia also may, as in Georgia and Ukraine, pair such influence operations with low-intensity conflict. Propaganda can be a useful tool for engaging separatists who will aid Russia's on-the-ground subversion. The combination of disinformation and kinetic operations can be especially hard to counter because its origins and objectives may be poorly understood.[59]

Beijing's Playbook

Like Russia, China has a long history of noncombat operations. Sun Tzu, the ancient Chinese strategist whose influence in and beyond the domain of war has extended across the globe, esteemed a military that could "win without fighting." Mao Zedong was known for his asymmetric military doctrine, penning the manual *On Guerilla Warfare* to help China prevail in the second Sino-Japanese War. Today Beijing continues this tradition with some novel techniques.

One might expect otherwise. President Xi firmly controls the armed forces, law enforcement agencies, state-owned enterprises, state media, and even the legion of paramilitary fishermen known as the "maritime militia." With his historic accumulation of power, he might be less reticent about using force. Moreover, as a quickly rising power, China has the economic and military resources to advance its aims using conventional arms; unlike Russia, it need not be restrained for lack of capacity. Yet China's grand strategy is risk averse because it hopes to keep rising.[60] As its foreign policy has grown bolder, it has primarily relied on maritime assertiveness, economic pressure, and cyber intrusions rather than direct armed conflict.

Since 2009 China has adopted a more confrontational approach to its maritime domain—activities that date back to the 1970s but that are now more coordinated and sustained.[61] Some attribute this muscle-flexing to Xi's rise; others to China's growing desire for great power prestige, which could be gained by taking long-claimed territory. Whatever the case may be, China's competitive coercion relies primarily on its coast guard, its maritime militia, and state-owned companies, while the navy has only a shadowy presence.[62] The consummate example is its base construction in the South China Sea.

The bases, built covertly on territory disputed by the Philippines, Vietnam, Taiwan, and Malaysia, bristle with military platforms that threaten foreign armed forces, support Chinese coercion in the region, extend power-projection capabilities, and secure China's sovereignty claims. The United States is hamstrung to respond on behalf of its allies when the aggression in question involves a disputed reef rather that the legally acknowledged territory of the ally itself. Without firing a single shot or even deploying many military vessels, Beijing has significantly advanced its goal of dominating regional waters.

China's nonmilitary coercion extends beyond the maritime domain. Against US allies including the Philippines, Japan, and South Korea, Beijing has turned to economic pressure, refusing to import or export key products and cutting off tourism. On some occasions it has employed Belt and Road projects coercively by creating unsustainable debt, forcing target states unable to pay to lease projects back to China, as it did with a major port in Sri Lanka. Beijing systematically steals trade secrets—for instance Huawei, a corporate giant with close ties to the state, is accused of pilfering robotics technology developed by T-Mobile. China relies on its foreign investments to advance state interests, seeking to gain ownership in companies making sensitive technologies such as semiconductors or occasionally to buy military-adjacent real estate from which it could spy. And while China has never directly interfered with foreign democratic processes, it does use information campaigns to influence public opinion abroad. The United Front Work Department, part of the state party, co-opts and neutralizes foreign opposition by strategically deploying funding and recruiting the overseas diaspora. The department has undermined protests critical of the Communist Party by organizing counterprotests. It has also funded efforts to persuade foreign politicians to take positions more favorable to China.[63]

An Alliance Blind Spot

Today Russia and China challenge American alliances with high-end military strategies that aim to exploit a long-dormant credibility problem: the United States can never value an ally as much as it does the homeland. They also seek to undermine US alliances by using coercive nonmilitary tactics designed to skirt the boundaries of Washington's security guarantees. The alliances themselves are now under threat, as adversaries seek to make them less credible in military terms and nullify them through the use of nonmilitary coercion.

Should America have seen this coming? Some critics look to the last two decades of foreign policy and wonder why Washington devoted so much effort to wars in the Middle East rather than the rising threats of Russia and China. But while there is good reason to question America's recent wars, there is little evidence to suggest that the United States could have preempted the precise challenges that Russia and China now present, even if it had been less distracted in the early 2000s.

First, recall that through the first decade of the twenty-first century, both Moscow and Beijing appeared inclined to cooperate with the United States, and both seemed to be moving in relatively benign directions. Russia had acquiesced to NATO expansion, only beginning to bristle once the 2004 round was complete. Even then it sought cooperation with the alliance. While antiliberal, anti-American elements had been visible in Moscow for years, so too were officials who supported genuine economic and political reform. For its part, China appeared to be prioritizing its economy and international integration, which seemed to bode well for its prospects as a responsible rising power. Russia's military was in disrepair, and China's was too far behind to challenge the United States or its allies directly. US officials recognized the potential of Chinese and Russian challenges but understandably sought to neutralize them through diplomacy and co-optation rather than threats and other bellicose actions.

Second, strategic thought in Russia and China shifted between 2008–2012. Not only had each come to view the United States as irresponsible in its foreign policy adventurism, but the financial crisis allowed both to make the domestic case that the Western economic model was failing and that their respective forms of authoritarian state capitalism would prove more durable.[64] While some early signs of this strategic shift were evident in each country's foreign policy, such as Russia's 2008 invasion of Georgia, each also displayed continued interest in some forms of cooperation, such as on nuclear issues in North Korea and Iran. Neither became consistently more pugnacious until 2012, when Putin retook the presidency and Xi ascended to it.

Third, to the extent that the United States recognized China's and Russia's increasing aggressiveness—as in Russia's 2008 invasion of Georgia, or China's growing maritime assertiveness—it was poorly positioned to check them. The 2008 crisis forced Washington to focus resources inward. And widespread opposition to the Iraq War made combative foreign policy unpalatable. The American public wished strongly to avoid overseas blunders and escalatory dynamics, and the Obama administration was not eager to confront directly other major powers. America's rivals stepped up their assertiveness just as Washington had its own reasons to commit to relative modesty.

Finally, US officials likely had a hard time recognizing the strategic as opposed to tactical nature of Russian and Chinese competitive coercion. Although Russia invaded Georgia in 2008, derailing its NATO membership, there was no clear indication that it would do the same thing in Ukraine six years later in an effort to split the country from the EU. In 2009 China began to harass American military vessels operating near its coasts, but this did not presage its bizarre and systematic island-building campaign five years on. The ambiguity of competitive coercion made it harder to see these offenses for what they were: not isolated incidents but expressions of emerging strategies.

But while American policymakers might be forgiven for their relatively hands-off approach prior to 2012, subsequent inaction is harder to justify. The Obama administration could have done more to craft comprehensive China and Russia strategies in its later years. And under the Trump administration, the risks Moscow and Beijing pose to the United States and its alliances have only become starker, while the US response has been meager. As of 2017 the United States has defined Russia and China as its twenty-first-century great power competitors, but it is yet to determine what precise behavior it intends to deter and defend against. Nor has the United States developed plans that take into account the differences between Chinese and Russian motivations, goals, and capabilities.

Although Russia and China would like to insulate their regions from American influence, only China has the potential to do so. Russia will retain considerable capacity to spoil US objectives, but it lacks the wherewithal to achieve real dominion near its borders. Russia could, however, align with China, a strategy that has some advantages for both in the short-to-medium term and that could make their anti-alliance tactics even harder to parry.[65] If Russia provides normative and political cover for China as it pursues regional hegemony, American security and prosperity will be much harder to guarantee.

American alliances are not merely the objects of Russian and Chinese competitive coercion. They are also the answers to aggression in the maritime, economic, cyber, and information domains. But US policy in these areas is poorly coordinated among allies, largely because Washington itself is in disarray. If the United States intends to use its alliances as a means of prevailing in competition, it must find ways to work with allies to deter and defend against nonmilitary incursions. First, however, it must confront the challenges to US alliances that come from within.

6

THE SHIELDS WEAR
FROM WITHIN

Russia's and China's challenges to American alliances have taken too long to acknowledge. But just as this return to major-power rivalry was finally recognized, the United States plunged itself into political turmoil, calling into question Washington's ability to lead alliances in this new era of geopolitics. The adversity US alliances face comes from within and from without.

Donald Trump took power over America's alliances at a moment when they were especially vulnerable: faced with new challengers after years of drift. Since 2017 America's shields have been routinely held at risk, and US alliance management has become increasingly coercive. But the president's pique, which typically centers on burden-sharing, is hardly novel, and he is by no means the only alliance antagonist in a position of influence in the United States. As we have seen, Americans have a long tradition of alliance distrust. The current paroxysm in American foreign policy amplifies concerns that have resided in the body politic for some time.[1] More broadly, the foreign policy positions Trump staked out as a candidate and has pursued as president arise from basic doubts about the US role in the world. Trump, his supporters, and even some of his detractors implicitly question why the United States should sustain its security guarantees in an international environment that differs so greatly from the one in which they were created.

These views are mistaken. The United States will only be able to meet the challenges it faces from Russia, China, and others if it relies on alliances, a resoundingly successful tool of statecraft. Indeed, these rivals' use of competitive coercion demonstrates just how consequential they understand American alliances to be. They have turned to nonmilitary and subconventional means because, insofar as we can measure them, alliances work. Most Americans—elites and everyday voters—appear to agree, in spite of recent spasms of anti-alliance sentiment. But the United States will not be able simply to return to its role as a global alliance leader. Instead, persistent domestic economic and political factors, as well as complex global power shifts, will impose constraints on US alliance leadership. Furthermore, restoring the status quo ante is not desirable, because the strategic calculus for the United States and its allies is markedly different today than it was during the Cold War.

America's alliances will not suddenly be safe once the Trump moment passes: he is catalyzing their perdition, but if the system collapses it will be because it no longer suits the world that Washington and its allies face. This outcome is avoidable, although the probability of its realization increases with leaders' continued neglect of and antagonism toward alliances. There is still time to update alliances in light of novel domestic and international political conditions, but the urgency of the problem rises with each outlandish burden-sharing demand, each broadside against traditional partners, and each partisan battle over the security benefits of allied defense, deterrence, assurance, and control.

America the Antagonist

Since the 2016 presidential election, it has become uncertain whether Washington has the will and ability to maintain many aspects of its postwar grand strategy, including its alliances. President Trump has pursued a unilateralist foreign policy, demonstrating the power of the American executive to damage and to withdraw from international agreements. While he has not attempted to abrogate any formal alliances, he has held them at risk in unprecedented ways.[2]

For decades, Trump has demonstrated a visceral antipathy toward treaty allies.[3] As president, his criticism has become policy. Trump has refused to reaffirm the United States' Article V guarantee to NATO. He has threatened to pull back on defense agreements, vowing that the United States will "go its own way" if NATO allies do not meet his constantly shifting spending targets. He has castigated Japan as taking "tremendous advantage" of the United States and threatened to remove troops from Japan and South Korea if they do not quadruple their alliance contributions.[4] Indeed, he has repeatedly floated the prospect of removing US forces from both countries, arguing that they have to "protect themselves or pay us" just as North Korea's latest nuclear weapons developments suggest that these alliances are more needed than ever.[5] Yet in a concession to North Korean leader Kim Jong Un, he has canceled or downgraded military exercises, further rattling South Korean allies.[6] He has sided with President Putin rather than America's European allies—and the US intelligence community—by denying Russia's involvement in election interference.

That Trump's views have won support should not surprise us. Americans, including occupants of the White House, have long worried about alliance burden-sharing. President Eisenhower lamented that allies were "making a sucker out of Uncle Sam" and hoped to withdraw US troops from Europe. American presidents have also followed word with deed. As President Nixon sought to draw down militarily from the Vietnam War, he declared the Guam Doctrine of allied self-reliance in Asia, inviting a major political fissure with Australia and attempted nuclear proliferation by South Korea and Taiwan. Presidents George W. Bush and Barack Obama repeatedly expressed frustration with allies underspending on defense. And, as we have seen, respected scholars of international relations frequently criticize the balance of responsibility within US alliances.[7]

Today's alliance enmity, however, is of an entirely different sort than we have seen before. Whereas past leaders have sought to revise alliances, the better to serve their political needs and support their strategies, President Trump appears to wish to dismantle America's alliances altogether.

There are at least three reasons Trump's alliance antipathy is different. First, unlike his predecessors, Trump relies on the direct and arbitrary coercion of allies. While previous American leaders worked behind the scenes to coax allies to contribute more to defense, Trump makes his threats public and explicit, suggesting that he seeks to shame and alienate allies, as opposed to securing a "better deal." His demands are also inconsistent, making it impossible for allies to satisfy him. While arguing that allies underperform, are pathetically dependent, entangle the United States, and further no meaningful American interest, he has simultaneously threatened wars that would depend on allies to fight and win. Even as he expects allies to do more to come to America's aid, he has explicitly undermined security guarantees by questioning whether the United States should defend an ally that does not spend sufficiently.[8] The defensive, deterrent, and assurance power of alliances lies in their consistency and reliability. Trump does not need to legally sever alliances; by treating them as protection rackets—for which the protected parties can never pay enough—he obviates them.

A second reason to believe that Trump wants an end to alliances—or at least is indifferent to their endurance—is that his strategic views are rooted in a conception of US national security at odds with America's alliance project. This was never the case among his predecessors. For the last seventy years, policymakers have, on a bipartisan basis, supported a strategy of deterrence and forward defense. Trump, by contrast, prioritizes homeland defense almost exclusively. He emphasizes the protection of the continental United States, which he sees as totally extricable from the fate of the rest of the world.[9] In this vision, unilateralism and isolationism replace forward defense and deterrence. The redefinition of American security in these limited terms *should* vitiate security guarantees in the eyes of allies and adversaries alike: an America that prizes only homeland defense cannot credibly extend deterrence, by definition.

Third, Trump's foreign policy priorities contradict the national security interests of US allies, which further suggests that he does not merely wish to see them spend more on defense. By absolving Putin of responsibility for election interference, or focusing narrowly on punitive trade policy with China while praising Xi, the president undermines his own administration's claims that Moscow and Beijing are leading national security competitors and that they challenge allies in Europe and Asia.[10] By embracing adversaries, Trump contests the very notion that the United States and its allies face the same threats.

Trump's volatile, arbitrary, and unmistakably hostile approach may do lasting damage to alliances by shaking the foundations of extended deterrence and collective defense. Trump has made clear that US alliance management powers are almost entirely in the president's hands, and allies will not soon forget this. Even in a post-Trump world, Washington's allies will recall their benefactor's ability to hold their national security hostage.[11] Alliances function on the basis of shared threats but also require cooperation among sovereign states. By not only antagonizing allies but also undermining the basic premises of American grand strategy, the US president has eroded an edifice that will be difficult to rebuild.

The Benefits and Costs of Alliance Coercion

Some international relations theorists argue that coercion is a useful tool for controlling allies. According to this view, if one wishes an ally to change its behavior, threatening to abandon it may be an effective tactic.[12] Unlike more subtle forms of allied control, coercion is a blunt instrument that prioritizes immediate gain over long-term cooperation. It may nonetheless permit the renegotiation of alliance terms in a manner favorable to the coercer.

It is difficult, however, to know if coercion works in practice. It is true that, following the urging of multiple US presidents, NATO allies have increased their military spending for several consecutive years. But this may be a response to increasing Russian aggression, not Obama administration pleas or Trump administration threats. Major allies in Asia have also spent modestly more, but, similarly, North Korean belligerence and Chinese assertiveness are likely the central decision factors.[13] NATO allies insist that they are in fact responding to American spending demands, but the president is notoriously persuaded by flattery. Allies may well be assuaging Trump with rhetoric that does not express their true motivations.[14]

The Trump administration's tactics are unlikely to get much more out of allies than the very modest spending increases they have already provided. Indeed, Trump himself is a central impediment to more equitable burden-sharing: his objectives shift constantly, so that allies lack incentive to even try to satisfy him because they know that he will augment any demand as soon as it is met. Trump has spent his first term repeatedly moving the goal posts NATO allies set for themselves in 2014: a commitment to spend 2 percent of GDP on defense by 2024. On one occasion, Trump asked them to hit their spending targets six years early. On another he demanded they double their commitment to 4 percent of GDP—more than the United States itself spends on defense. In a most extreme case, the president proposed that South Korea pay the full cost of housing US troops overseas, plus an additional 50 percent fee for the security US forces provide.[15] When coercive objectives are erratic, they do not compel effectively. Allies cannot be sure that their efforts will satisfy, and they will always be waiting for the next demand to supplant the last.

If the benefits of coercion—especially the capricious sort in which Trump specializes—are small, the costs may be sizable. As we have seen, postwar American leaders saw value in asymmetric alliances in part because, by taking on the burden of defending others, they gained control over allies whose territory replaced the homeland as America's front line. Washington spent more on defense than its allies, but got far more out of its alliances than any one of them did. If the United States continues to emphasize cost-sharing above all other strategic priorities, it will reduce its ability to assure and control allies, which may in turn weaken the defense and deterrence benefits those allies provide. America may pay less, but it will also get far less in return.

A loss of allied control may take the form of political distance, as allies look for other relationships to replace their faltering partner. German Chancellor Angela Merkel has already declared that Europe can no longer depend on the United States, and French President Emmanuel Macron has lamented that, amid US neglect and browbeating, NATO is "experiencing brain death." South Korean President Moon Jae-In has prioritized his ongoing negotiations with Kim Jong Un, distancing himself from the United States. Both South Korea and Japan have improved their relations with China.[16] Distance undermines policy coordination and can seriously diminish a guarantor's political influence. It may even foster conditions in which allies to tilt toward rivals.

Coercive management may undermine alliance capacity even when it does result in more equitable burden-sharing. Recall that allied spending is not all equal, and a dollar spent by an ally on defense does not necessarily promote alliance coordination and goals. If allies capitulate to US threats of abandonment, they almost certainly will spend in ways disadvantageous to the alliance. When they fear the loss of their patron, allies are likely to invest in capabilities to protect themselves alone, not in collective defense.[17] These capabilities may not be interoperable with the patron's, making it very difficult to cooperate in wartime. Worse still, allies may pursue capabilities, such as their own nuclear weapons, that damage alliance strategy. Allies will also take political steps to make abdication less costly. In the US case, this could mean that European allies pursue goals through the EU rather than NATO and Asian partners rely on ad hoc regional coalitions. In both cases, the United States would find itself without a voice at the table where important political, economic, and strategic decisions are made.

The United States has always had leverage over its allies because it provided security that they could not obtain otherwise. By forsaking a carefully calibrated approach to cost-sharing and control in favor of blunt coercion, the United States may squander that leverage and all that it buys. In the words of one scholar, this "American strategy may contain the seeds of its own obsolescence."[18]

Decline and Fall?

The United States' current political volatility is perilous not only to its alliances but also to the post-World War II international system more broadly.

In the eyes of many international players, the trouble started long before 2016. The ill-begotten decision to invade Iraq and protracted wars in the Middle East appeared to be cases of the age-old phenomenon of hegemonic overextension. The 2008 financial crisis suggested a similar trend in economic terms.

But where mismanagement was once, arguably, born of excessive privilege, today it has become more concerted: since 2016 the United States has made a foreign policy of defying international norms. The White House has begun trade wars, abrogated international accords, maligned the very notion of global institutions, and sought rapprochement with the world's most venal dictators. These moves reflect the view of the president and his advisors whereby international politics is a zero-sum game in which the United States can win only at someone else's expense. This perspective is directly at odds with the postwar goal of maintaining the balance of power through strategic cooperation.[19]

Whether the United States can recoup its former leadership role depends on the answer to a single question: Is the current political moment an aberration, or is it the product of underlying forces that will outlast the forty-fifth president? There is some evidence to support both optimistic and pessimistic answers.

America the Resilient

In the rosier of the two tellings, America will be restored to its perch atop the world because Trump and his supporters represent an isolated shock that is no match for the resilience of the international system the United States built. There are a few reasons to believe this is the case.

First, Trump was narrowly victorious in an election that involved intervention by a foreign adversary. One could argue that his election did not constitute a signal of majority support for his vision. Furthermore, while he wields his iconoclastic foreign policy views as a badge of honor, the election surely did not turn on foreign policy, so we cannot assume that these views are widely shared.

Second, many of the alliances and institutions the United States has built are "hard to overturn but easy to join," as the international relations scholar John Ikenberry puts it.[20] Alliances and international institutions can sustain some damage without collapsing. American allies have demonstrated the will to reinforce the very accords that the United States abjures. For instance, the Trans-Pacific Partnership has gone ahead without Washington, and several major players are attempting to hold together the Iran nuclear deal that Trump withdrew from. This suggests that the system America designed may be able to endure even the designer's defection.

Third, public opinion appears to be on the side of maintaining the United States' traditional role in the world. Since Trump's election, Americans' support for global engagement—including reliance on international institutions, alliances, and agreements—has grown. During Trump's first term, the public became more convinced than ever of the value of maintaining security alliances and saw them as more effective than military superiority when it came to protecting US interests. In one survey many Americans agreed that allies should spend more on defense, but they also favored using diplomatic channels to encourage spending hikes—not threats or withholding of security. The public also trusts countries in Europe and Asia to be constructive players in world affairs and favors preserving or increasing America's forward defense commitments. Majorities of Americans from both parties support the defense of frontline American allies, such as the Baltic states, if they are attacked. Polling also demonstrates little enthusiasm for an "America First" foreign policy; Trump's brand of punitive, transactional unilateralism finds genuine support only among his core voting base.[21] These data suggest that the American public would not be averse to restoring traditional foreign policy pursuits, including a familiar approach to alliances. And there is only so much Trump can do in four years. If he leaves office after one term, the United States may be able to repent and find its place in the world preserved.[22]

Colossus Bridled

In a more pessimistic interpretation, the United States is not experiencing a jolting aberration but rather a seismic shift whose consequences will endure. The upheaval in America's alliances and broader foreign policy is not the singular handiwork of Donald Trump, but the product of forces that predate and will outlast him. According to this view, multiple significant perturbations have coincided to undermine American strategy for the long term.[23]

American foreign policy has become ever-more captive to domestic political polarization. This makes it harder for the United States to sustain the political consensus on which the past seventy years of foreign policy has relied, and comity is unlikely to return any time soon. Politicians and voters have sorted themselves into distinct groups and rarely cross party lines. Ideological purity wins the day, thanks in part to media outlets dedicated to confirming voters' beliefs.[24] Economic inequality and job loss due to automation, immigration, outsourcing, and trade may amplify these effects.[25] These trends, developing for two decades or more now, do not foreordain any particular outcome for American foreign policy, but they reduce the prospect of achieving consensus over what that policy should be.

An important dimension of this polarization has been increasing distrust of "globalism" on the right and parts of the left. A notable target has been free trade.[26] While this is not an issue specific to alliances, it may have negative effects on US political partnerships. Most of America's closest trading partners are treaty allies, so trade-policy volatility could stress those relationships. In general, animosity toward multilateralism—increasingly portrayed as a threat to sovereignty—bodes poorly for US alliances. This view has deep roots in American politics, from Andrew Jackson to the opponents of Wilsonianism and beyond. It came before Trump and will still be here when he is out of office.

While US public opinion generally remains supportive of alliances, that support is increasingly partisan, with Democrats much more likely than Republicans to support alliances in general and NATO specifically.[27] These opinions may reflect partisanship as opposed to a meaningful shift in ideology that will transcend administrations. Either way, the findings suggest that although the American public generally supports alliances it can also be mobilized against them, despite a long tradition of bipartisan support for alliance-based strategies.

These domestic trends could transform the process of foreign policymaking in profound ways. In particular, a partisan foreign policy is more volatile. With both parties seeking to politicize foreign policy for short-term electoral gain, policy will swing dramatically when administrations change hands. It may become impossible to make reliable, long-term commitments to allies.[28]

Public opinion data from outside the United States suggest that America has already lost considerable trust on the world stage. In Europe and Asia, perception of the United States has tumbled, with the confidence slide especially pronounced among treaty allies. In South Korea, for example, trust in the American president plunged from 87 percent to 17 percent in 2017. In 2016 64 percent of the world trusted the US president to "do the right thing" in international affairs; in 2017 that number had withered to 22 percent. American withdrawal from international agreements is cited as the leading reason for disapproval. Global public opinion of the United States has rebounded in the past—during and after the George W. Bush presidency, for instance. But the swiftness and magnitude of the recent confidence loss raise doubts about whether Washington can simply recoup its role as alliance steward. Indeed, it is not clear that others want the United States to continue playing this role. Global audiences increasingly see China as the world's economic leader. Although they do not prefer Chinese to US preponderance, longtime friends may nevertheless accommodate themselves to Beijing's rapidly growing power.[29]

A World in Flux

How the United States attempts to recover leadership and on what terms will depend on domestic flux and global perceptions. It will also depend on major-power shifts that will take place in the next decade and beyond. America's future as an alliance leader is contingent on developments among its most significant competitors, China and Russia, and on the capacity of its allies.

In economic and demographic terms, the United States will probably be well placed to resume its role as a global leader and security guarantor. The president has wreaked havoc on America's global position, but the country's underlying power indicators remain strong. GDP is expected to grow at least 2 percent annually for the foreseeable future, an impressive performance for an economy that is already the world's largest (Fig. 6.1). GDP per capita also will remain high by international standards (Fig. 6.2). Unlike many industrialized nations in Europe and Asia, which suffer from quickly aging populations, the United States has good demographic prospects, largely owing to healthy immigration. The country is likely to remain the global technological leader and will continue to be the world's highest military spender, retaining its many defensive advantages.[30] For decades the United States will remain the most powerful country in the world, although it will operate with more constraint than it has been accustomed to in the post-Cold War period.

While America has been divesting itself of leadership, however, its challengers have been preparing to fill the breach. If and when Washington reinvests in allies and multilateralism, it will face powerful rivals—Beijing in particular. China is on track to supplant the United States as the largest economy in the world by 2030 and has already grasped the top spot by some metrics.[31] China is experiencing serious population aging and decline, and its demographics will put pressure on social spending and economic productivity. But its state-managed capitalism has proven resilient thus far, and its investments in the domestic technology sector—particularly artificial intelligence—will help keep its economy growing.[32]

China is now the world's second largest military spender and is likely to remain in this position.[33] As we have seen, Beijing has largely relied on a military strategy that aims to prevent the United States from intervening in conflicts close to its shores, and in this it has been alarmingly successful. The Chinese armed forces also have persistent weaknesses, and analysts do not expect China to rival the United States for global military hegemony. But it will likely remain a force to be reckoned with in East Asia. And as its economy

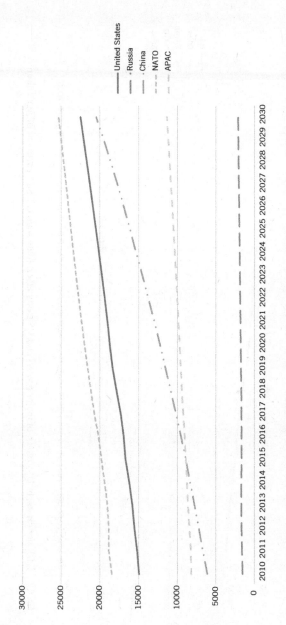

Fig. 6.1 GDP in billions of US dollars, historical and projected, of major powers and US treaty allies. APAC refers to Asia-Pacific allies. (data source: US Department of Agriculture)

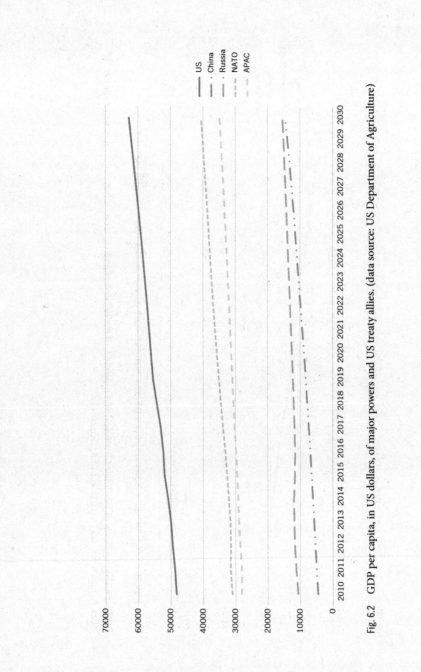

Fig. 6.2   GDP per capita, in US dollars, of major powers and US treaty allies. (data source: US Department of Agriculture)

continues to flourish, its ability to spread political influence through economic means will only increase.

Overall, China's continued rapid ascent portends challenges for the United States. Not only must Washington develop a strategy to defend its First Island Chain allies from Beijing's conventional military threats, but it also must work with them to oppose the most worrisome forms of competitive coercion.

Russia's outlook is different, marked by continuing slow decline, economically and demographically, with no real possibility of restoring superpower status. Russia will remain highly dependent on hydrocarbon exports, although it has unrealized potential in other industries. For instance, with a population highly educated in science and engineering, Russia could become a major tech power. But this sector has so far received little investment, and the state is not poised to make it a priority.[34] Despite these negative trends, however, Moscow will present security challenges in the years to come. Instead of spending on domestic development, the Kremlin prioritizes military modernization and is plowing money into hybrid, cyber, and nuclear assets. Russia will remain a conventional military threat in its immediate neighborhood and in lower-cost domains like cyberspace. A restored US alliance strategy would be wise to keep focus on Russia, even if Moscow's ambitions far outstrip its means.

China's sustained vigor and Russia's desperate defiance make for a potent cocktail of security challenges. To meet them, America's allies will have to contend first with their own deficits. Like Russia and China, many American allies in Europe and Asia are experiencing demographic stagnation. Japan has one of the world's oldest populations, with an old age–dependency ratio above 45 percent. And while South Korea and Australia are younger, both have rising dependency ratios themselves. Japan's and South Korea's populations are expected to shrink significantly. Most European states are also experiencing demographic contraction and will soon grapple with formidable old age–dependency ratios.[35] These trends may place pressure on social spending, diverting investments from defense and the productive economy. And in some cases, there could be less to invest in general terms. European countries can expect annual GDP growth of just 1.5 percent for the next ten years. Among Asian treaty allies, Japan will have the most sluggish growth at just 1 percent annually, but South Korea and Australia should perform much better, on par with the United States.[36]

Russia's recent military spending binge has helped it keep pace with America's European partners, even though they are economically in better shape. Western Europe's defense spending fell after the Cold War, reducing its military power in absolute terms and relative to Russia's. This trend has only just begun to reverse, and there are still substantial holes in European allies' conventional defense capabilities. For now, Asian allies are also raising defense spending modestly, and they are contemplating necessary strategic changes. But they are so outclassed by China that they will continue to experience relative decline and will need to work with the United States to pursue asymmetric defense strategies.[37]

American allies will nonetheless retain some significant advantages. While their GDP growth will be modest, they will have high GDPs overall. They fare better still when measured in terms of GDP per capita, a sign of productive and sophisticated economies. With developed technology sectors and highly educated populations, US allies are capable of considerable high-tech advances for commercial and defense purposes.[38] Most importantly, when American and allied capabilities are combined, they are formidable. Collectively the United States and its treaty partners dwarf Russia and China on defense spending (Fig. 6.3).

The geopolitical outlook, then, is one in which the United States is uniquely powerful, but no longer enjoys global primacy. Washington can continue to lead global affairs and respond to major-power challengers, but doing so unilaterally will outstrip its capacity. The United States is economically and militarily strong but it cannot

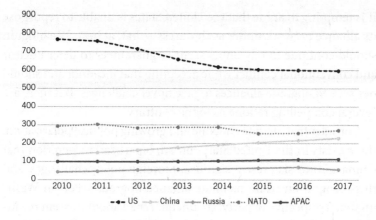

Fig. 6.3   US, allies', and rivals' military spending in billions of US dollars. (data source: Stockholm International Peace Research Institute)

afford to shoulder an even greater defense burden than it has in the past, which is what unilateralism would demand. Fortunately, Washington need not take this approach: allies' developed economies, technological prowess, and combined military spending can make them valuable partners in the years ahead. Yet a reasonable observer might wonder if seventy-year-old alliances really can be reshaped for a world that has changed so drastically since their inception.

The Case for Repurposing American Alliances

Quite apart from any one president's alliance hostility, the challenges of domestic political disarray, rising power competition, and international-system change call into question whether the US position as a security guarantor can be preserved. Indeed, most of the evidence suggests that Washington will not recoup the leadership position it has held in the past, no matter the foreign policy proclivities of whatever chief executive happens to occupy the Oval Office.

It is tempting to argue that the United States is unable to repurpose its alliance network under such duress—that, at best, Washington should continue to rely on its security guarantees to deter nuclear and conventional conflict while accepting that it cannot and should not seek to upgrade alliances to face novel challenges. But there are several compelling rationales to the contrary.

Consider that, despite endemic and growing political polarization, there exists in the United States broad, bipartisan recognition that China and Russia present significant foreign policy challenges, and this recognition could facilitate alliance upgrades. Few in Washington, irrespective of party, are unconcerned about Russian revanchism or Chinese assertiveness. It may be that even a riven US Congress could reach consensus on the need to deter and defend against Russia and China in order to protect American security and prosperity. Leaders in both parties have been at odds with President Trump over his esteem for Putin and have at times been willing to take legislative action to counter the White House's deference to Russia. Congress has imposed new sanctions against Moscow and opposed sanctions relief. It has passed with bipartisan backing military aid packages to Ukraine to support its fight against Russia. Similarly, despite domestic political chaos and Trump's affection for President Xi, Congress has united behind the pro-democracy movement in Hong Kong, opposed Beijing's oppression of its Uighur minority population in Xinjiang, and generally favored policies that will make the United States more competitive with China.

Relatedly, there is widespread elite and public support for alliances as a foundation of American strategy. Bipartisan congressional backing for alliance-preserving measures—such as the NATO Support Act, which prohibits the use of federal funds to withdraw the United States from NATO—suggests that alliances may be relatively safe.[39] Even if affirmative preservation were not an option, security guarantees would be hard to dismantle because they are based in treaties, which are approved by the Senate. Formally ending an alliance does not necessarily require the Senate's approval, but Congress's investment in these treaties gives it multiple options for protecting them when they are in danger.[40] Alliances may therefore be among the sturdier pillars of US strategy in an otherwise-tempestuous domestic environment.

The United States likely can retain its alliances, in spite of the political headwinds arrayed against them of late. But should it? Given the enormous costs of unilateralism in a world of increasing major-power competition, the answer should be an obvious "yes." But preservation is not enough. US alliances must be reformed with an eye toward parrying competitive coercion. Nuclear and conventional deterrence and defense should remain organizing principles of US alliances, but Washington and its partners will increasingly face subconventional and nonmilitary threats in the years ahead. If they do not rebuff these challenges, alliances will continue to erode.

Washington will also need to upgrade its strategy for the sake of allied assurance. Alliance renovation will, for example, have to account for partisanship—and sometimes in ways that may not directly advance security goals. For instance, although more equitable burden-sharing should not be America's primary alliance objective, policymakers should seek allies' aid on this front, to mitigate domestic political opposition. Policymakers and diplomats also need to find ways to compensate for the muddled foreign policy signals that a polarized America may produce. Moreover, they will need to assure allies that Washington is capable of remaining a credible alliance leader even as its global role has been transformed.

The reckoning ahead will not be easy on the United States or its allies. It will be financially costly and will strain political relationships domestically and abroad. It will require creativity, as high-tech but sputtering European and Asian partners devise new ways to contribute beyond defense budgets that can only rise so high. It will demand political courage from leaders who are inclined to cower to base voters. But if the reforms are thoughtfully crafted, the results will be worth the costs: the restoration of fundamental purpose to the republic's shields, precisely when it is most needed.

7

DEFENSE AND DETERRENCE
FOR A NEW ERA

Seventy years ago, the US alliance system was crafted in the service of a grand strategy that aimed to keep the country safe by preventing a hostile hegemon from dominating Eurasia. Today these alliances need new purpose, derived from contemporary strategic objectives and the realities of modern power competition.

At a high level of abstraction, the United States' alliance goal is similar to that of the postwar moment: to keep America safe by preventing a hostile hegemon from overwhelming Eurasia. However, both the rivals and their means have changed. Russia harasses Western democracies and institutions, although it cannot truly assert itself as a great power. China, however, may be able to accomplish what the Soviet Union did: establish a closed sphere of influence—a geographic zone in which it exercises dominant political, economic, and military power, albeit in twenty-first-century terms. That could place the security and prosperity of the United States at risk, jeopardizing its access to markets and vital political relationships.[1] The same is true of states that traditionally have been US allies. All share an interest in keeping Eurasia open and its states autonomous.

Restored rivals have brought with them new terms of conflict. In prior eras closed spheres of influence were usually the result of force and formal hierarchy. Whether by territorial conquest or economic and political suzerainty, hegemons blatantly subverted the independence of smaller states. In the twenty-first century, such dramatic action is unnecessary. China could sequester parts of Asia through economic or technological coercion. And while Russia has been more aggressive in its use of force, it is not fighting traditional wars. Instead it combines military violence with information and cyber warfare, all in a manner carefully calibrated to ensure that defense pacts are never invoked against it.

Responding to modern threat conditions will demand new alliance strategy. It will not do to simply maintain existing alliance structures and methods, because rivals have exposed their gaps and allies already have doubts about America's ability to lead. But nor can the

Year	Alliance	Participants	Primary threat	Purpose
1778–1783	Franco-American	Kingdom of France, American colonies	Great Britain	independence, survival
1917–1918	Entente Powers	France, Britain, Russia, United States (as associated power)	Central Powers	maintain balance of power in Europe through armed force
1942–1945	Allied Powers	United States, Britain, Soviet Union, China, United Nations	Axis Powers	maintain balance of power in Europe through armed force; survival
1949–1991	Atlantic alliance, hub-and-spokes system in Asia	NATO, Japan, Philippines, South Korea, ANZUS, Republic of China (until 1979), SEATO (until 1977)	Soviet Union, China, North Korea	maintain balance of power in Europe and Asia through defense, deterrence, and allied control; survival
1991–2012	Atlantic alliance, hub-and-spokes system in Asia	Enlarged NATO, Japan, ANZUS, Philippines, South Korea	regional conflicts, out-of-area terrorism (after 2001)	secure US unipolarity; intervene in regional and out-of-area conflicts; consolidate democracies
20??–Future	Atlantic alliance, hub-and-spokes system in Asia	NATO, Japan, ANZUS Philippines, South Korea	Russia, China, regional competitors	maintain global balance of power through military and nonmilitary defense and deterrence

Fig. 7.1   America's alliance logics, Revolution through twenty-first century

nation afford to turn away from collective defense, for the costs of unilateralism are simply too great. Alliances are still needed, but they must be reformed to deter and defend against actions below the military threshold. The United States and its allies cannot address every such action. But they should identify the types of coercion that will directly imperil their security and political independence and coordinate plans to respond. Doing so, moreover, will allow the United States and its allies to rebalance responsibilities within alliances. Nothing less than the future of American security and prosperity is at stake.

Reforming Alliances for the Twenty-First Century

If leaders of the US alliance system intend to prevent harmful spheres of influence, keep Asia open, and Europe independent of Russian coercion, they will have to change dramatically the way alliances operate. The alliance system needs new strategic logics that address competitive coercion, as practiced in different ways and for different reasons by China and Russia, as well as military defense and deterrence. Allies need to redistribute some of the burdens of security partnership, to better take advantage of US partners' competencies and to reflect today's global distribution of power. And allied leaders, especially Americans, need to tell the alliance story differently so that policymakers and the public understand the continuing promise of collective self-defense anchored by strong US commitments—and the peril that Washington courts if it loses this system.

Update Thresholds for Collective Defense

Implementing an alliance strategy that protects against coercion will require new collective-defense triggers. The United States and its allies will have to develop thresholds for responding to information warfare and cyberattacks that evade the current terms of defense pacts.

The nature of conflict has shifted beneath these pacts. Their success has bred innovative rejoinders designed to project power without activating their security guarantees. These guarantees are highly visible to challengers because they are based in Article 51 of the UN Charter, which enshrines a right to "individual or collective self-defense" in the event of "armed attack."[2] But just a few decades after this vision of self-defense was codified in international law, observers realized that belligerents had already found ways to create and exploit loopholes. In 1970 the prominent legal scholar Thomas Franck lamented the small-scale proxy wars between the United States and Soviet Union that had obviated the UN Charter framework:

> The great wars of the past . . . were generally initiated by organized incursions of large military formations of one state onto the territory of another, incursions usually preceded by mobilization and massing of troops and underscored by formal declarations of war. Because it was so familiar to them, it was to aggression of this kind that the drafters of Article 51 addressed themselves. Modern warfare, however has inconveniently bypassed these Queensberry-like practices.[3]

Rather than mourn the passing of this system or wait for the United Nations to create new conflict prohibitions—an unlikely eventuality—the time has come to consider the conflict thresholds that might reasonably apply to the nonmilitary domains that escape Article 51 and the treaties based in it.[4] The United States and its allies should define which kinds of nonmilitary attacks rise to the level of major aggression and thereby trigger security guarantees.

Doing so would be in accordance with international law. Though international law may be focused on the prohibition of armed interstate conflict, it does not prevent states and their allies from responding to subconventional attack. Article 2(4) of the UN Charter outlaws "the threat or use of force against the territorial integrity or political independence of any state," without defining force in exclusively military terms. What is prohibited, in other words, is not just armed attack but any threat or use of force that jeopardizes a state's sovereignty—its "assertion of final authority over a given territory."[5] Thus nonmilitary incursions that injure political independence are already illegal under international law. Without drafting new law or amending alliances, then, the United States and its allies can legitimately identify nonmilitary thresholds for collective defense.

The response to a nonmilitary violation need not involve force of arms, and laws and norms of proportionality suggest it should not. Instead allies engaged in collective defense might respond to nonmilitary aggression with economic sanctions, transparency campaigns, intelligence cooperation, and other proportional means.[6] The United States and its allies will surely find that some types of force, such as subconventional conflict and some cyber operations, are amenable to collective deterrence efforts. The allies may also find that other areas, like economic coercion, are too ubiquitous to warrant a coordinated and systematic alliance response in each instance.

To keep Europe, Asia, and the global commons open, and themselves secure and autonomous, the United States and its allies will need to broaden their conception of where and how alliances apply. In so doing, they will find that their alliance logic has changed again. The strategic aims of the present are far less grandiose than those of the immediate post-Cold War period, when America promoted democracy and sought to consolidate its unipolar position. Now the United States and its allies must return to the more basic work of defense and deterrence, adapted to shifting modes of conflict.

Reinforce Asia as China Ascends

Even as China rises and the US-China relationship becomes more competitive, Beijing and Washington need not engage in a new Cold War. Containing China to its current level of power and influence is not a realistic objective, and the United States and its treaty partners all have complex economic relationships with Beijing. They generally want to pursue the benefits of trade with China, not to isolate it. But they can still ensure that China's ascent does not beget an exclusive sphere in Asia.

The greatest military risk to American and allied interests in the Pacific is that China's defense strategy may succeed in preventing US military access to and maneuver within and around the First Island Chain. This would leave US allies undefended and China the sole regional powerbroker. Recall Secretary of State John Foster Dulles's fixation on the First Island Chain as the primary US line of defense in Asia and his concomitant enthusiasm for extending security guarantees to the countries comprising the archipelago. It is no accident that American allies have become uniquely vulnerable as China has developed its anti-access strategy: Beijing recognizes that American regional military power depends on the First Island Chain and expressly aims to undermine it. If the United States and its allies are to deter and defend against China, they will need to turn the tables and again use the First Island Chain to their advantage. They will also benefit by expanding their efforts to include other partners.

A First Island Chain defense strategy would rely on allies' geographic position to restore the military balance that China has upended with its A2/AD activities.[7] Such a strategy, which would likely involve the installation of land- and ship-based missiles, would be controversial among some American allies and would require substantial buy-in to be effective.[8] It could, however, also accommodate nontreaty partners that share similar defense objectives, such as Taiwan or Vietnam, which could develop their own systems. While there is no shortage of political hurdles to constructing a strong defense system in the First Island Chain, US and allied military planners must prioritize the development of a conventional military strategy immediately if they are to keep the Western Pacific open to the United States and its allies.[9]

Beyond conventional military strategy, the allies should work together to increase the costs and reduce the benefits of coercion. Again, it will not be possible to prevent every coercive Chinese move, but the United States and its Asian treaty allies can complicate Beijing's approach. One initiative would be to determine how Article V guarantees apply in cyberspace, setting thresholds for scenarios that warrant kinetic and nonmilitary reprisals. American allies in Asia can strengthen ties and their security by sharing intelligence related to cyber operations and information campaigns and by collaborating to counter foreign influence in their democracies.[10]

Keeping Asia open also calls for sophisticated economic strategy. Since its early 2017 withdrawal from the Trans-Pacific Partnership, the United States has had no regional economic agenda. A new administration seeking economic resilience should rejoin TPP or craft equivalent deals. But a positive trade agenda will not be enough. The United States and its allies must develop a strategy to engage China's use of economic coercion. In doing so, they should be selective. For example, it would not make sense for the United States to present itself as an outright competitor in economic development, because it has neither the resources nor the interests to warrant establishing an alternative to Belt and Road, some of which has no negative impact on US strategy. Indeed, Belt and Road could well pose problems for China in the future, as unsustainable debt will generate political opposition, and Beijing's westward push may raise tensions with Moscow and expose it to political instability.[11]

US and allied governments should instead use policy to encourage their private sectors to lead projects of their own. Japan has quietly permitted some of its companies to participate in Belt and Road while simultaneously announcing development efforts alongside the United States and Australia.[12] If allied initiatives are carried out with higher standards and more transparency than Beijing's, they will naturally provide visible alternatives. Washington and its allies also can play to their strengths. They should allow China to make a broad infrastructure push, while the United States and its partners focus on their comparative advantages in high technology and communications, sustainability, urban planning, and even climate change resilience. Asia's demand for infrastructure and development is real and worth addressing, which is why Belt and Road has had early successes. By staking their claim to the Asian market, however, Washington and its allies can ensure that China does not amass such economic influence and co-opt so much critical infrastructure that it can control a coercive economic sphere.

A third method of standing up to China in Asia involves increased US and allied support to Southeast Asian countries that cannot counter maritime and economic coercion on their own. These include allies such as the Philippines and nontreaty partners such as Vietnam. Because the American foothold in Southeast Asia has never been as strong as in Japan or South Korea, and because its alliances in the region languished after the Cold War, Southeast Asia is a soft strategic underbelly. Southeast Asia may therefore be something of a proving ground for China's efforts to establish an exclusive sphere. But states in the region may also play a role in deterring and defending against China. The United States has begun a worthy capacity-building effort, supplying regional coast guards with retired vessels and comprehensive training. Australia and Japan have engaged in similar activities of their own.[13] Efforts to synchronize these initiatives have slowed, however. The United States could do more to coordinate capacity building through formal agreements, including with nontreaty partners. Washington could also provide more direct aid to Asian countries at risk of Chinese coercion. Currently the overwhelming bulk of resources distributed by the Foreign Military Financing program—a source of grants and loans operated by the State and Defense Departments—are directed to the Middle East. But with Asia now the primary strategic theater, this must change.[14]

One way to enable coordination would be to initiate a defense planning group, akin to NATO's multilateral decision-making institutions. Asian treaty partners lack the shared structure from which their European compatriots benefit: there is no collective venue from which the United States and its Asian allies can develop and direct high-stakes defense strategy. This leaves them dependent on bilateral structures when they could be more efficiently coordinating as a group on everything from A2/AD response to cyber strategy to the deterrence of North Korea. Such coordination would also serve—and benefit from—assurance efforts that would deepen and broaden US alliances and partnerships. For instance, the United States could encourage New Zealand's involvement in nonmilitary efforts to counter coercion. India, though not a treaty partner, also has a role to play in lower-level deterrence initiatives. Delhi need not have a formal alliance to recognize its overlapping interests with US allies in the maritime, economic, and cyber domains.

Hold the Line While Russia Declines

Although Russia does not have the economic and military might to make its claimed sphere of influence a reality, it will for some time retain the ability to disrupt Western institutions, including NATO, and threaten the political independence of its adversaries using coercive means. Moscow's conventional military threat to NATO and European neighbors may attenuate, but its enthusiasm for unsettling Western democracies and institutions may concomitantly spike as it finds itself with fewer means to protect its near abroad.

It will be no simple matter to hold the line while Russia declines. As we have seen, NATO enlargement saddled the alliance with new vulnerabilities. There are many reasons that Moscow should not invade the Baltics—above all the prospect of a major war with NATO. But an overconfident or desperate Putin might also see value in rending the alliance through a fait accompli. If a Russian invasion netted quick wins, would NATO be willing to spill further blood to take back its losses and preserve alliance credibility? That the answer is not a resounding "yes" is well known to Putin. For the United States and its allies, the central high-end military challenge is to close this yawning credibility gap so that they can deter Russia.[15]

NATO aims to address this problem with the Four Thirties readiness plan, which the allies hope to implement by the mid-2020s. The plan calls for thirty land battalions, thirty air squadrons, and thirty warships that stand prepared to deploy to a conflict zone within thirty days.[16] But even if fully implemented, the Four Thirties will not provide sufficient deterrence. In the event of a Russian attack on the Baltics, NATO needs to reach the theater of battle in just a few days to deter further aggression, defend against a rapid seizure, and reduce the risk of serious escalation. European allies can and should help to shorten NATO's response timeline. By streamlining border checks and carefully identifying rail routes and roads that can accommodate heavy military equipment, they could make it easier to access the Baltics and thereby reduce delays.[17] While Europe makes material investments in readiness, the United States should provide support by advising allies and helping to train their forces in rapid-response techniques.

The United States and its allies will not stop all forms of Russian subversion, but they can deter some and diminish the power of others. An important deterrence mechanism, as in Asia, is to define the point at which cyber incursions trigger collective defense. NATO will have to decide, and announce publicly, what sorts of cyber operations would be considered forms of "armed attack" that may warrant military response. The allies would also be wise to identify types of cyber operations that, while not forms of armed attack, still jeopardize members' political independence. In such cases military responses may not be justified, but NATO and its members would be free to retaliate with nonmilitary measures.[18] Like NATO's

Article V, neither of these thresholds would necessitate any particular response. Nonetheless, they would help to establish deterrence by proscribing activity and making reprisal more likely.

NATO's agenda for combating Russian coercion should also include improved coordination of response to disinformation campaigns, especially those that endanger members' political systems. NATO might develop internal procedures for warning allies when evidence of state-backed or state-linked election-subversion campaigns materializes. The alliance could develop practices for issuing public deterrent statements to Russian leaders and warnings to national and international media. Such practices have proven successful in some cases, as when Russia tried and failed to damage the campaign of French President Emmanuel Macron in its final days.[19] Partnerships between allied governments and technology companies will be vital to providing warning and transparency, as private firms are often in the best position to detect, publicize, and rebuff threats in the information domain. Finally, allies should share practices and protocols for resilience planning among populations targeted by Russian information warfare. Estonia has been a model for this type of planning since it suffered Russian cyberattacks in 2007. The Baltic nation now has in place comprehensive strategies for outreach to its Russian-speaking minorities, lest Moscow again exploit them for subversion campaigns.[20]

Countering Russian coercion also requires significant changes to American policy. All of the NATO allies must take steps to deter political disruption and protect against institutional subversion, but the United States lags far behind its European counterparts. Not only has Washington failed to lead alliance deterrence efforts, its inaction has been an invitation for repeat offenses. Indeed, the White House acknowledged America's failure in this respect, admitting in its 2017 National Security Strategy that "US efforts to counter the exploitation of information by rivals have been tepid and fragmented."[21]

Troublingly, the United States lacks a comprehensive strategy to combat coercion. Such a strategy would require close coordination across executive agencies and would have to emerge from the White House. It should also be presented to Congress to ensure a clear and durable national position. This would help to reassure allies, who otherwise worry about America's increasingly turbulent political environment. Operationally, a robust American effort should include a standing coordination cell in the intelligence community that would reconcile counter-disinformation efforts across the Homeland Security, State, Defense, and Treasury Departments. Congress should also institute mandatory reporting requirements so that the White House must notify it of election interference, even if that interference benefits the president or his or her party.[22] Only when the United States is prepared to respond to attacks on its democratic institutions can it lead counter-disinformation efforts within NATO. Until that time, well-meaning partners will try their best, but their efforts may be piecemeal.

Finally, NATO will have to tackle serious antidemocratic tendencies within its own membership, which exacerbate the problem of outside subversion. Recall that post-Cold War NATO enlargement was inspired, at least in part, by a desire to spread and consolidate democracy. There is some evidence to suggest that expansion was successful in this regard.[23] However, several NATO members—including Turkey, a longstanding ally, and Hungary, a newer one—are now experiencing grave democratic backsliding. Democratic decay makes it more likely that NATO will face threats from within. As regimes become less democratic, they may rely on disinformation campaigns of their own, or be more susceptible to external influence, making them particularly untrustworthy partners for sensitive forms of cooperation. The presence of autocrats within NATO ranks also undermines alliance unity, which is critical given that major measures can only be adopted through unanimous vote. Rather than eject undemocratic members, which may be inadvisable over the longer term and difficult to achieve, NATO should institute regular procedures to monitor democratic deficits within the alliance.

When it comes to defending against Russian disinformation campaigns, there is much that individual states can and should do on their own. And many efforts will have to be uniquely tailored to domestic contexts, as each of the allies has its own political system, which may be subject in different ways to Russian subversion. But NATO still has a deterrent role to play. By treating political independence as not just a state concern but rather fit for collective defense, NATO can make Russian leaders think twice about targeting any one member.

Rebalance Collective Defense Responsibilities

A broader interpretation of collective defense—one that includes alliance cooperation both at and below the military threshold—will impose new demands on allies, and the United States should not take them up alone. America's allies in Europe and Asia are far stronger and more stable than they were when the United States extended its security umbrella in the early Cold War, while the United States' once-towering command has diminished in relative terms. It is therefore high time to consider how alliance obligations might be made more symmetric, so long as this is done in the name of collective strategic interest and with collective consent.

Taking on greater responsibility for collective defense may be relatively easy for US allies today, because defensive contributions can come in economic, diplomatic, technological, and intelligence domains. This means that governments can support measures against nonmilitary attack without politically controversial defense-budget hikes. The defense and deterrence projects of the future will be carried out by finance ministries, ministries of foreign affairs, homeland security offices, and intelligence agencies, in addition to militaries. States will still have to make traditional defense outlays but also strategic investments in cybersecurity, intelligence collection and sharing, information campaigns, and election security. Burden-sharing calculations should recognize the contributions these investments make, in addition to a wider range of defense metrics covering research and development, aid to foreign militaries, personnel contributions, pre-crisis military readiness, and willingness to absorb financial and human costs of shared security initiatives.[24]

America's allies are well positioned to take on a broader conception of defense and deterrence because they are leaders in technology, public diplomacy, and counterespionage—key sources of protection from competitive coercion. Although they do not compare to the United States and China in innovation capacity, their wealth and highly educated populations ensure that they will be able to keep pace with changing cyber, AI, and other technological systems that will be central to national security in the decades ahead.[25] And the US alliance network includes some of the world's most sophisticated intelligence services, which can coordinate sustained cross-regional efforts to counter democracy interference and disinformation campaigns.

Indeed, allies in Europe and Asia are proven leaders in nonmilitary counter-coercion initiatives, in many cases demonstrating strategies more sophisticated than America's. Japan may have a relatively paltry defense-budget commitment at just over 1 percent of GDP, but it spends other funds wisely, providing coast guard and development assistance to South China Sea claimants who cannot resist China's advances on their own. Tokyo has also developed a quiet approach to Belt and Road, allowing some of its companies to participate, while also leading higher-standards projects of its own.[26] On matters related to cyber law and security, Estonia has been an entrepreneur, catalyzing international efforts to grapple with the relationship between international law and cyberspace, and hosting NATO's Cyber Defense Center. And several European countries have installed the type of interagency sharing protocols the United States should pursue to halt future election subversion by Russia.[27]

Rebalancing alliance responsibilities to face Chinese and Russian coercion also promises efficiency benefits. The alliance system in Asia is currently a hub-and-spokes network of bilateral treaties, but as China continues to rise, allies will increasingly find they have shared concerns. Australian and Japanese officials have begun working toward defense cooperation that will serve both countries and their allies well in deterring Chinese conventional power.[28] If the alliance aperture is broadened to include cyber cooperation, coast guard training, low intensity–conflict training, and democracy-resilience efforts, the attractiveness of security networking in Asia will rise considerably. Fortunately, in the cyber and information domains, it is not very costly for even far-flung allies to work together.

A novel defense and deterrence logic geared toward competitive coercion will demand rebalancing of domestic budgets, too. The United States needs to reprioritize its national security spending. Congress appropriates as though the primary threat facing the country were kinetic warfare, thus the Defense Department's budget keeps growing, while the State and Treasury Departments, whose activities are vital to contesting coercion, languish. The country grossly underprivileges nonmilitary national security issues such as foreign interference in domestic politics. Washington's budget allocations simply do not mirror the way that conflict will be waged in the coming decades.[29] Today a better defense may come at the Pentagon's expense. While the United States is ramping up its counter-coercion spending, so should its allies. Those on the front lines of maritime security and democracy resilience should take on disproportionally high spending and political burdens. Ultimately, better allied coordination should save money, though. A cooperative counter-coercion strategy will be far cheaper than deploying troops to break open closed spheres of influence.

The United States and its allies will almost certainly find that the challenges of the present are easier to share equitably than were those of the Cold War. During the Cold War, only the United States could effectively deter and defend against the Soviet Union—on behalf of itself and others. While US military remains peerless, the changing nature of competition, and allies' advantages, mean that partners can contribute amply without major hikes in defense spending.

Craft a New Alliance Narrative

As they seek to preserve openness and political independence in Europe, Asia, and elsewhere, US and allied leaders will have extensive foreign policy agendas. Their charge continues at home. Before policymakers can invest in tools that adequately combat competitive coercion, they will need to convince their fellow citizens that military threats and nonmilitary coercion are pressing concerns, and allied action is the fitting countermeasure. With political volatility in the United States and economic and demographic malaise abroad, badly needed alliance renovations will not come easily. Leaders in every allied government will have to cultivate and maintain domestic support.

Creating a new alliance narrative begins with an acknowledgment of the obvious: more than seventy years after the end of the Second World War, the rationale for alliances as a tool of strategy is no longer as intuitive as it once was. Those Americans who lived through the 1930s and 1940s thought it perfectly sensible that the United States should seek forward defense, deterrence, and allied assurance and control in an effort to defend itself from the Soviet Union. Few needed to be convinced that war should be deterred rather than fought at catastrophic cost. Everyday citizens could consult their own memories and readily understand the perils of a world in which America had no allies.

But time passes, and now relative peace and prosperity have changed public perception of alliances. When they are spoken of today, alliances are often maligned as wasteful, useless, and entangling. Alternatively, they are nostalgically extolled: vaunted for their history, their spirit of cooperation, the endurance of shared values.

To hear some American officials' telling, alliances are treasured artifacts to be preserved as ends unto themselves.

Our contemporary alliance debate has been forced into an unacceptable binary: acquiesce to antagonists who prefer to see the system crumble, or else assume that we will be able to restore the system to its post–Cold War zenith. If America continues to follow the first alternative—bludgeoning and coercing allies for underspending while seeking rapprochement with adversaries—the system will crumble. This outcome is all too near. There is no possibility, however, that the second alternative will come about. The hope of complete alliance restoration rests on the faulty assumption that the current president is an anomaly and responsible for hostility that in fact is held on both ends of the political spectrum. Nostalgists, moreover, ignore inexorable shifts in the global balance of power. In doing so they also deny an opportunity to keep pace with a quickly changing strategic landscape.[30]

The Next Alliance Era

Between nostalgia and antagonism lies the promise of change. America cannot recoup its Cold War alliances, but it does need modern ones to confront the world it faces—indeed, it may need them now more than ever. As China continues to ascend, alliance options in Asia will become far more limited. If Washington rests on its laurels, it will miss the chance to protect American security and prosperity on relatively favorable terms and will be doomed to chase vital interests from a position of disadvantage. If it waits until Beijing's military efforts have undercut the credibility of US security guarantees, it will do so without allies, having lost a vital strategic tool.

Reasonable observers will point out that the alliance agenda recommended here is vast. It will take years to complete and budget reallocations within countries combating political chaos. It will also require cooperation across the conflict spectrum among sovereign states. Perhaps this task is too immense, and not worth attempting. Why salvage an architecture whose day has passed? The skeptic will argue that America's alliances should be allowed to die on the vine—or at most relegated to their historical role in the areas of military defense and deterrence. The United States will muddle through other threats unencumbered by thirty-three rowdy partners.

Once again, the counterfactual is revealing. Imagine a world that looks much like ours, but in which the US-centered alliance system is no more. Without NATO on its border, Russia still desires to recoup regional standing, so it continues to fracture Western institutions and democracies where it can. China remains intent on modern forms of hegemony within Asia, an objective close at hand, since the United States has withdrawn its security guarantees and troops from the region. Traditional conflict may not be common, but aggressive cyber operations, information campaigns, and economic coercion abound. In this world the United States waits to act until its vital interests are manifestly in jeopardy and, when they are, cannot count on the effective support of prepared partners. It confronts peacetime cyber intrusions and threats to its democratic system alone. To the extent that geographic barriers remained in the nuclear age, they crumble under the weight of new technology.

Opponents of alliances warn of the risks of partnership and laud the benefits of independence. With no alliance commitments and less emphasis on forward defense, they urge, Washington would be less politically encumbered by chaotic partnerships, less sensitive to the changing threat environment in Europe and Asia, and freer to devote itself to homeland defense. It would face less angst about defending states in the Baltics and the First Island Chain. But these opponents discount the hazards of being an estranged superpower in this world. Policymakers and political observers cannot know precisely what the future holds, but some of these risks are certain.

We know that major-power conflict—the sort of conflict alliances deter—will be far more destructive today than it was seventy-five years ago. Cyber and electronic warfare will exact huge damage before kinetic war has begun. After they do, modern missiles and aircraft will ravage at supersonic speed. In an effort to act before its adversary attacks its sensors and blinds it, the United States and China both have incentives to strike quickly and decisively, leading to rapid conflict escalation.[31] Destruction that once took months to unfold will occur in a matter of hours.

We also know that if the United States withdraws from its alliances and its forward positions, it will lose more than the power of deterrence. It will also lose defensive options that improve its chances of prevailing early in conflict. With a disengaged approach, the United States will face the choice of standing aside or fighting its way back in. The result could be a modern Korean War, replayed with hypercharged speed and destruction.

Without alliances, the United States would still be subject to all manner of nonmilitary coercion. With fewer overseas interests, it would not concern itself with the South China Sea, but it would continue to confront assaults on its elections, cyberattacks on its digital infrastructure and power grids, and major financial havoc. The specter of Russian, North Korean, and Chinese nuclear weapons would hover over these nonmilitary attacks.

In this world America would be a garrison state, turned inward and focused on narrow homeland defense. In exchange for this radical transformation of its grand strategy, the United States might drop its defense budget from just over 3 percent of GDP to 2.5 percent of GDP.[32] But it would lose the trade benefits that followed its alliances, and it would be forced to pay the costs of fighting modern conflict from a homeland posture. Ultimately the budgetary savings could range from modest to nonexistent. Is modest austerity worth the peril?

Instead imagine another possible future. A new administration begins alliance reform efforts in 2021. In its first year in office, it undertakes a review of its strategic objectives and the threats that could place it in jeopardy. It assesses whether it needs to deter and defend against cyberattacks, political interference, and other forms of coercion and meets with allies to discuss how alliances might be used to these ends. In the second year, allies determine the areas in which defense and deterrence are lacking and agree on how they will expand the scope of their partnerships in order to close these gaps. In the third year, each ally outlines its contributions to this new deterrence framework, based on the challenges it faces as well as its comparative advantages. In year four each develops a long-term plan, which incorporates new thresholds for military and nonmilitary response, new institutions to be built, novel forms of cooperation to undertake, and sources of funding for its more holistic strategy. This process takes years to accomplish—one full term of a US president. But once it commences, allies are able to start urgently needed initiatives, such as enhanced cybersecurity coordination and novel cross-regional collaborations. Well before reform is complete, each alliance is steadier and its members safer because the task has begun.

With smaller relative shares of global GDP, Washington and its partners cannot afford to deter and defend against every behavior they consider threatening. But they can engage those that directly imperil their political independence, prosperity, and clear national security interests. With this in mind, alliance leaders pour more resources into intelligence collection, resilience planning, and counter-coercion strategies, and into mechanisms that enable synchronization across the alliance network. The United States reduces its defense spending and increases other foreign policy budgets to do so, while allies increase their spending in defense and nondefense areas to make their contributions more symmetric.

This project is chaotic, even maddening at times, as eclectic democracies struggle to combine strategies and resources. But the result is alliance coordination well before China has transformed the balance of power in Asia. And when an ally's political system comes under attack in the leadup to an election, swift global contributions of intelligence, along with immediate media coverage and diplomatic repudiation, help the ally to limit the damage and preserve its autonomy. The system is not perfect—it never has been—but with reforms underway and eventually solidified, closed spheres of influence become harder to imagine and political independence easier to protect. As modern defense and deterrence take their place in a strategy fit for this world, unseen successes accrue once more.

To be sure, renovated alliance commitments come with some risk of entrapment and abandonment. There is reason to believe that under conditions of waning unipolarity and amidst expanding competition with China, the risk of entanglement will heighten. The logic is straightforward: because China's efforts to change the political status quo put the credibility of US security guarantees at stake, Washington may show its mettle by engaging more actively in regional security.[33] Furthermore, as alliances expand into new domains of deterrence and defense, partners will have more responsibilities and rely on each other in more ways, augmenting the opportunities for both entrapment and abandonment.

As we have seen, however, the result is unlikely to be unwanted war or outright defection. More likely we will see subtle expansion of interests—what I have called alliance dilation—or irksome allied free-riding. The alliance system of the future can emulate the successful policies of the past, including commitments clear enough to facilitate cooperation and deterrence but also vague enough to leave room for maneuver. Entrapment and abandonment will remain alliance shoals to be navigated, but the ability to do so will still be built into the pacts themselves, and attendant costs are unlikely to outweigh the value of alliances that will protect partners more comprehensively than ever before.

When we imagine the costs and benefits of letting alliances waste or revising them to meet the challenges of rising competition, the conclusion is clear. An approach that prioritizes the American homeland only, with a wait-and-see posture toward overseas threats, is untenable in a world where competitors not only have long-range power projection capabilities but also ever-improving capacities to threaten political independence in new domains. America's last disengagement from its allies against a backdrop of rising power competition—in the interwar years—led to cataclysm. Twenty-first-century risks are distinct from those of the prior era, but after the lessons of history were learned at extraordinary expense, why should they be taught again?

We have seen that America's alliances come with greater benefits and far fewer of the costs that some scholars, politicians, and voters assume. Those who prefer to bet on an alliance-free future do so on the basis of error: they forget America's quietly impressive alliance record, they fear forms of abandonment and entanglement that are not borne out in practice, and they fail to recognize that the manifest challenges of a new era cannot be borne alone. Those who would retain alliances untouched despite new threats are no less myopic. Their nostalgia lionizes Washington's alliance successes but fails to account for its strategic purpose in a transformed world.

What has not changed since the Cold War is the fundamental benefit of having allies. Then as now, shared competitors can be bested more efficiently through collective peacetime approaches than through unilateral action in the midst of hostilities. Deterrence remains far preferable to war, and forward defense to conflict on the home front. The choices we face now require us to apply these historically tested axioms to a world in which the terms of conflict have adapted to the success of the US alliance system. It is precisely because of that success that rivals have charted new courses, supplementing conventional and nuclear force with competitive coercion. Their innovation does not obviate this tested network. Rather, it means that the alliance system, too, must adapt, with a new ratio-nale and new strategy.

As Walter Lippmann noted of alliances, "An order of this kind can endure, not forever in a changing world, but for a long and be-neficent period of time."[34] America's shields persisted because they protected security and prosperity. They endured so long that the world changed around them—indeed, changed because of them. They stand ready for renewal, if we have the wisdom to take up the challenge.

NOTES

Introduction

1. Shayna Freisleben, "A Guide to Trump's Past Comments about NATO," CBS News, April 12, 2017, https://www.cbsnews.com/news/trump-nato-past-comments.

2. Moira Fagan, "NATO Is Seen Favorably in Many Member Countries, but Most Americans Say It Does Too Little," Pew Research Center, July 9, 2018, https://www.pewresearch.org/fact-tank/2018/07/09/nato-is-seen-favorably-in -many-member-countries-but-almost-half-of-americans-say-it-does-too-little.

3. See, for example, Nick Wadhams and Jennifer Jacobs, "Trump Said to Seek Huge Premium from Allies Hosting U.S. Troops," *Bloomberg*, March 8, 2019, https://www.bloomberg.com/news/articles/2019-03-08/trump-said-to-seek-huge -premium-from-allies-hosting-u-s-troops.

4. Mira Rapp-Hooper and Matthew C. Waxman, "Presidential Alliance Powers," *Washington Quarterly* 42, no. 2 (2019): 67–83.

5. Hal Brands and Charles Edel, *The Lessons of Tragedy: Statecraft and World Order* (New Haven: Yale University Press, 2019).

6. For discussion of the virtues—and unequal burdens—of US alliances, see, for example, Samuel P. Huntington, "Coping with the Lippmann Gap," *Foreign Affairs* 66, no. 3 (1987): 453–477.

7. Barry R. Posen, *Restraint: A New Foundation for U.S. Grand Strategy* (Ithaca, NY: Cornell University Press, 2015); Christopher A. Preble, *The Power Problem: How American Military Dominance Makes Us Less Prosperous, Less Safe, and Less Free* (Ithaca, NY: Cornell University Press, 2009); Barry R. Posen, "Trump Aside, What's the U.S. Role in NATO?" *New York Times,* March 10, 2019.

8. John J. Mearsheimer and Stephen M. Walt, "The Case for Offshore Balancing: A Superior U.S. Grand Strategy," *Foreign Affairs* 95, no. 4 (2016): 70–83; Barry R. Posen and Andrew L. Ross, "Competing Visions for U.S. Grand Strategy," *International Security* 21, no. 3 (1996): 5–53; Christopher Layne, "From Preponderance to

Offshore Balancing: America's Future Grand Strategy," *International Security* 22, no. 1 (1997): 86–124.

9. Mira Rapp-Hooper, "Trump Will Send Troops to Saudi Arabia. Here's Why It Matters That There's No Formal Defense Alliance," *Washington Post,* September 23, 2019.

10. Notable exceptions include Stephen G. Brooks and William C. Wohlforth, *America Abroad: Why the Sole Superpower Should Not Pull Back from the World* (New York: Oxford University Press, 2016); Mike Beckley, "The Myth of Entangling Alliances: Reassessing the Security Risks of U.S. Defense Pacts," *International Security* 39, no. 4 (2015): 7–48.

11. See, for example, Kenneth N. Waltz, *Theory of International Politics* (Reading, MA: Addison-Wesley, 1979); Stephen M. Walt, *The Origins of Alliance* (Ithaca, NY: Cornell University Press, 1989); John J. Mearsheimer, *The Tragedy of Great Power Politics* (New York: W. W. Norton, 2001); David A. Lake, "Beyond Anarchy: The Importance of Security Institutions," *International Security* 26, no. 1 (2001): 129–160; James D. Morrow, "Alliances, Credibility, and Peacetime Costs," *Journal of Conflict Resolution* 38, no. 2 (1994): 270–297; James D. Morrow, "Alliances: Why Write Them Down?" *Annual Review of Political Science* 3 (2000): 63–83; Glenn Snyder, *Alliance Politics* (Ithaca, NY: Cornell University Press, 1997); Paul W. Schroeder, *Systems, Stability, and Statecraft: Essays on the International History of Modern Europe* (New York: Palgrave Macmillan, 2004), 195–222; Patricia A. Weitzman, *Dangerous Alliances: Proponents of Peace, Weapons of War* (Stanford: Stanford University Press, 2004); Songying Fang, Jesse Johnson, and Brett Ashley Leeds, "To Concede or to Resist? The Restraining Effect of Military Alliances," *International Organization* 68, no. 4 (2014): 775–810; David H. Bearce, Kristen M. Flanagan, and Katharine M. Floros, "Alliances, Internal Information, and Military Conflict among Member-States," *International Organization* 60, no. 3 (2006): 595–625; Brett Ashley Leeds, "Interests, Institutions, and the Reliability of International Commitments," *American Journal of Political Science* 53, no. 2 (2009): 461–476.

12. See, for example, Mark A. Stoler, *Allies in War: Britain and America against Axis Powers 1940–1945* (London: Bloomsbury, 2007); David Reynolds, *The Creation of the Anglo-American Alliance 1937–41* (Chapel Hill: University of North Carolina Press, 1988); Gordon Craig and Gerhart Niemeyer, *Second Chance: America and the Peace* (Princeton: Princeton University Press, 1944; repr. Charleston: Nabu Press, 2011); George F. Kennan, *Fateful Alliance: France, Russia, and the Coming of the First World War* (New York: Pantheon, 1984); Lawrence S. Kaplan, *NATO 1948: The Birth of the Transatlantic Alliance* (New York: Rowman and Littlefield, 2007); Lawrence S. Kaplan, *The United States and NATO: The Formative Years* (Lexington: University of Kentucky Press, 2015); Lawrence S. Kaplan, *NATO Divided, NATO United: The Evo-*

lution of an Alliance (Westport, CT: Greenwood, 2004); James M. Goldgeier, *Not Whether but When: The U.S. Decision to Enlarge NATO* (Washington: Brookings Institution Press, 2010); Marc Trachtenberg, *A Constructed Peace: The Making of the European Settlement, 1945–1963* (Princeton: Princeton University Press, 1999).

13. Rapp-Hooper, "Trump Will Send Troops to Saudi Arabia."

14. Walter Lippmann, *U.S. Foreign Policy: Shield of the Republic* (Boston: Little, Brown, 1943), 6.

1. America's Alliance Logics

1. This definition of grand strategy is adopted from Barry Posen. A similar definition is offered by Paul Kennedy. Barry R. Posen, *Restraint: A New Foundation for U.S. Grand Strategy* (Ithaca, NY: Cornell University Press, 2014), 1; Paul Kennedy, "Grand Strategy in War and Peace: Toward a Broader Definition," in *Grand Strategies in War and Peace*, ed. Paul Kennedy (New Haven: Yale University Press, 1991), 5.

2. Lawrence S. Kaplan, *The United States and NATO: The Formative Years* (Lexington: University of Kentucky Press, 1984), 15–20; Walter A. MacDougall, *Promised Land, Crusader State: The American Encounter with the World since 1776* (Boston: Houghton Mifflin, 1997), 43; John Avlon, *Washington's Farewell: The Founding Father's Warning to Future Generations* (New York: Simon and Schuster, 2017), 190.

3. Avlon, *Washington's Farewell*, 188; Alexander DeConde, "Washington's Farewell, the French Alliance, and the Election of 1796," *Mississippi Valley Historical Review* 43, no. 4 (1957): 648–650.

4. Avlon, *Washington's Farewell*, 184; Washington's Farewell Address, 1796, Avalon Project, Lillian Goldman Law Library, Yale Law School, http://avalon.law .yale.edu/18th_century/washing.asp.

5. Washington's Farewell Address, 1796.

6. Jefferson's First Inaugural, 1801, Avalon Project, Lillian Goldman Law Library, Yale Law School, http://avalon.law.yale.edu/19th_century/jefinau1.asp.

7. Walter Lippmann, *U.S. Foreign Policy: Shield of the Republic* (Boston: Little, Brown, 1943), 63–66; MacDougall, *Promised Land*, 49; Kori Schake, *Safe Passage: The Transition from British to American Hegemony* (Cambridge, MA: Harvard University Press, 2017), 44.

8. Aaron L. Friedberg, *In the Shadow of the Garrison State: America's Anti-Statism and Its Cold War Grand Strategy* (Princeton: Princeton University Press, 2000), 35.

9. MacDougall, *Promised Land*, 51.

10. Friedberg, *In the Shadow of the Garrison State*, 36.

11. MacDougall, *Promised Land*, 123.

12. John Milton Cooper, Jr., *The Warrior and the Priest: Woodrow Wilson and Theodore Roosevelt* (Cambridge, MA: Harvard University Press, 1983), 301; Schake, *Safe Passage,* 223; MacDougall, *Promised Land,* 136–137.

13. Henry Cabot Lodge, "Constitution of the League of Nations," February 28, 1919, Congressional Record, 65th Congress, 3rd session, 4520–4528, reprinted in Robert C. Byrd, *The Senate 1789–1989: Classic Speeches, 1830–1993* (Washington DC: Government Printing Office, 1994), https://www.senate.gov/artandhistory/history /resources/pdf/LodgeLeagueofNations.pdf.

14. Lloyd E. Ambrosius, *Woodrow Wilson and American Internationalism* (New York: Cambridge University Press, 2017), 144–145.

15. David Reynolds, *The Creation of the Anglo-American Alliance, 1937–1941* (Chapel Hill: University of North Carolina Press, 1982), 10. US GDP was three times larger than Britain's, and the British were still deeply indebted to the United States for its supply efforts in World War I. Schake, *Safe Passage,* 256.

16. Schake, *Safe Passage,* 257, 263; Reynolds, *Creation of the Anglo-American Alliance,* 18, 26, 47, 57, 174, 220.

17. Reynolds, *Creation of the Anglo-American Alliance,* 29.

18. Mark A. Stoler, *Allies in War: Britain and America against the Axis Powers* (London: Hodder Arnold, 2005), 30. Along with the outposts it received in the destroyers-for-bases deal, the United States obtained from Britain a pledge that the Royal Navy, if it were defeated, would never give over its US-made destroyers to the enemy. With this promise in hand, Roosevelt could convince Congress and the American people that, if Britain fell, American materiel would not fall into enemy hands.

19. Stacie L. Pettyjohn, *U.S. Global Defense Posture 1783–2011* (Santa Monica, CA: RAND, 2012), 32, 37, 42, 46; Reynolds, *Creation of the Anglo-American Alliance,* 41, 60; Stoler, *Allies in War,* 14, 32.

20. Richard Overy, *Why the Allies Won* (New York: W. W. Norton, 1995), 192.

21. Elliot Converse III, *Circling the Earth: United States Military Plans for a Postwar Overseas Base System, 1942–1948* (Maxwell Air Force Base, AL: Air University Press, 2005); James F. Schnabel, *History of the Joint Chiefs of Staff,* vol. 1: *The Joint Chiefs of Staff and National Policy, 1945–1947* (Washington, DC: Office of the Chairman of the Joint Chiefs of Staff, 1996), 139–160.

22. Harry S. Truman, "Address before a Joint Session of Congress on Universal Military Training," October 23, 1945, in *Public Papers of the President of the United States, 1945* (Washington, DC: Government Printing Office, 1961), 405.

23. Melvyn P. Leffler, *A Preponderance of Power: National Security, the Truman Administration, and the Cold War* (Stanford: Stanford University Press, 1992), 15–16, 56.

24. Lawrence S. Kaplan, *NATO 1948: The Birth of the Transatlantic Alliance* (Lanham, MD: Rowman and Littlefield, 2007), 11.

25. Leffler, *Preponderance of Power*, 10–13, 148, 217; Friedberg, *In the Shadow of the Garrison State*, 39; John Lewis Gaddis, *Strategies of Containment* (Oxford: Oxford University Press, 2005), 62–63.

26. Leffler, *Preponderance of Power*, 211; Kaplan, *United States and NATO*, 41.

27. "Report Prepared by the Policy Planning Staff Concerning Western Union and Related Problems," March 23, 1948, *Foreign Relations of the United States* (hereafter *FRUS*), 1948, vol. 3, doc. 55; "Pentagon Paper (Final Draft)," April 1, 1948, *FRUS*, 1948, vol. 3, doc. 63.

28. "Memorandum of Conversation with Senator Vandenberg," April 27, 1948, *FRUS*, 1948, vol. 3, doc. 83; Kaplan, *NATO 1948*, 94; Leffler, *Preponderance of Power*, 211.

29. Kaplan, *NATO 1948*, 142.

30. Roosevelt's wartime treaty, the Act of Chapultepec, was concluded on March 6, 1945, and later became the Inter-American Treaty of Reciprocal Assistance. Douglas M. Gibler, *International Military Alliances, 1648–2008* (Washington, DC: CQ Press, 2009), 351, 369–371; anonymous former senior Pentagon official, interview with author, April 24, 2014, Washington, DC.

31. Thomas Princen, *Intermediaries in International Conflict* (Princeton: Princeton University Press, 1992), 144.

32. Kaplan, *United States and NATO*, 43–44, 113–116.

33. Matthew C. Waxman, "The Power to Threaten War," *Yale Law Journal* 123, no. 6 (2013): 1626–2133, 1644; Kaplan, *NATO 1948*, 97.

34. Address by Secretary of State Dean Acheson, March 18, 1949, as quoted in Michael J. Glennon, "United States Mutual Security Treaties: The Commitment Myth," *Columbia Journal of Transnational Law* 24, no. 3 (1986): 530–531; North Atlantic Treaty: Hearings before the Senate Committee on Foreign Relations, United States Congress, 81st Congress, 1st Session (Washington, DC: Government Printing Office, 1949), 18.

35. "Military Personnel Historical Reports"; "Military Presence: U.S. Personnel in the Pacific Theater"; "U.S. Military Presence in Europe 1945–2016," U.S. European Command, May 2016, https://www.eucom.mil/doc/35220/u-s-forces-in-europe; Leffler, *Preponderance of Power*, 257, 338; Thomas J. Christensen, *Useful Adversaries: Domestic Mobilization and Sino-American Conflict, 1947–1958* (Princeton: Princeton University Press, 1996), 32.

36. Leffler, *Preponderance of Power*, 252.

37. Kaplan, *United States and NATO*, 164–168; Leffler, *Preponderance of Power*, 386.

38. "Review of Basic National Security Policy," September 30, 1953, *FRUS*, 1952–54, vol. 2, part 1, doc. 93; "Review of Basic National Security Policy," October 30, 1953, *FRUS*, 1952–54, vol. 2, part 1, doc. 101.

39. Michael J. Green, *By More Than Providence: Grand Strategy and American Power in the Asia Pacific since 1783* (New York: Columbia University Press, 2017), 272–274.

40. Robert R. Bowie, *Waging Peace: How Eisenhower Shaped an Enduring Cold War Strategy* (New York: Oxford, 1998), 124, 215.

41. Victor D. Cha, "Powerplay: The Origins of the U.S. Alliance System in Asia," *International Security* 34, no. 3 (2010): 158–196; Victor D. Cha, *Powerplay: The Origins of the American Alliance System in Asia* (Princeton: Princeton University Press, 2016).

42. Bowie, *Waging Peace*, 251.

43. Cha, *Powerplay*, 127, 134; Leffler, *Preponderance of Power*, 255–256, 391–392.

44. Leffler, *Preponderance of Power*, 431.

45. Kimie Hara, *Cold War Frontiers in the Asia-Pacific: Divided Territories in the San Francisco System* (London: Routledge, 2006), 5.

46. Cha, *Powerplay*, 101.

47. Henry W. Brands Jr., "The Dwight D. Eisenhower Administration, Syngman Rhee, and the 'Other' Geneva Conference of 1954," *Pacific Historical Review* 56, no. 1 (1987): 59–85, 63, 66.

48. Cha, *Powerplay*, 108–112.

49. Brands, "The Dwight D. Eisenhower Administration," 70, 87.

50. See Lesek Buszynski, *SEATO: The Failure of an Alliance Strategy* (Singapore: Singapore University Press, 1983), 1–71; Daniel Fineman, *A Special Relationship: The United States and the Military Government in Thailand, 1947–1958* (Honolulu: University of Hawaii Press, 1966), 191, 207–208; "Southeast Asia Treaty Organization (SEATO), 1954," Office of the Historian, Department of State, https://history.state.gov/milestones/1953-1960/seato.

51. US protection in the Taiwan Straits was coupled with an order to Chiang to cease air and sea operations against the mainland. Cha, *Powerplay*, 170.

52. John W. Lewis and Xue Litai, *China Builds the Bomb* (Stanford: Stanford University Press, 1988), 21; "Memorandum by the Assistant Secretary of State for Far Eastern Affairs (Robertson) to the Secretary of State," February 25, 1954, *FRUS*, 1952–54, vol. 14, part 1, doc. 173.

53. "Memorandum by the Assistant Secretary of State for Far Eastern Affairs (Robertson) to the Secretary of State," March 31, 1954, *FRUS*, 1952–54, vol. 14, part 1, doc. 182.

54. "NIE 10-2-54, Communist Courses of Action through Mid-1955," March 15, 1954, *FRUS*, 1952–54, vol. 14, part 1, doc. 179; "Background Paper Prepared in the

Department of State for the United States Delegation to the Geneva Conference," April 6, 1954, *FRUS, 1952–54*, vol. 14, part 1, doc. 183.

55. "Memorandum by the Regional Planning Advisor for Far Eastern Affairs (Ogburn) to the Assistant Secretary of State for Far Eastern Affairs (Robertson)," March 26, 1954, *FRUS, 1952–54*, vol. 14, part 1, doc. 181; Lewis and Xue, *China Builds the Bomb*, 26–27; Christensen, *Useful Adversaries*, 194; John Gittings, *The World and China: 1922–1972* (New York: Harper and Row, 1974), 197.

56. "The Chargé in the Republic of China (Jones) to the Department of State," April 23, 1953, *FRUS, 1952–54*, vol. 14, part 1, doc. 101; "Memorandum by the Secretary of State to the President," November 23, 1954, *FRUS, 1952–1954*, vol. 14, part 1, doc. 403.

57. A prime example of this type of war-specific alliance detail can be found in the Franco-Russian alliance. See George F. Kennan, *The Fateful Alliance: France, Russia, and the Coming of the First World War* (New York: Pantheon, 1984).

58. Oona Hathaway and Scott Shapiro, *The Internationalists: How a Radical Plan to Outlaw War Remade the World* (New York: Simon and Schuster, 2017), 105–106, 131–157; Andrew Holt, "'No More Hoares to Pairs': British Foreign Policymaking and the Abyssinian Crisis, 1935," *Review of International Studies* 37, no. 3 (2011): 1383–1401.

59. Arnold Wolfers, "Collective Defense versus Collective Security," in Wolfers, ed., *Discord and Collaboration: Essays on International Politics* (Baltimore: Johns Hopkins University Press, 1962), 182–186.

60. Ambrosius, *Woodrow Wilson*, 145; Antony Lentin, "'Une Aberration Inexplicable?' Clemenceau and the Abortive Anglo-French Guarantee of 1919," *Diplomacy and Statecraft* 8, no. 2 (2007): 31–49.

61. Keren Yarhi-Milo, *Knowing the Adversary: Leaders, Intelligence, and Assessments of Intentions in International Relations* (Princeton: Princeton University Press, 2014); David M. Edelstein, "Managing Uncertainty: Beliefs about Intentions and the Rise of Great Powers," *Security Studies* 12, no. 1 (2002): 1–40, 31; Randall L. Schweller, *Deadly Imbalances: Tripolarity and Hitler's Strategy of World Conquest* (New York: Columbia University Press, 1998). Schweller emphasizes Hitler's position of structural inferiority, as opposed to his intentions, but the argument nonetheless supports the point.

62. Author's approximation, based on deaths by country in each month of the war. Deaths by country from "The Fallen of World War II," http://www.fallen.io/ww2.

2. Defense and Deterrence in the Cold War

1. Quoted in David Reynolds, *The Origins of the Cold War in Europe: International Perspectives* (New Haven: Yale University Press, 1994), 13.

2. For discussion of alliance dynamics, see Kenneth N. Waltz, *Theory of International Politics* (Reading, MA: Addison-Wesley, 1979); Stephen M. Walt, *Origins of Alliance* (Ithaca, NY: Cornell University Press, 1989); James D. Morrow, "Alliances, Credibility, and Peacetime Costs," *Journal of Conflict Resolution* 38, no. 3 (1994): 270–297; James D. Morrow, "Alliances: Why Write Them Down?" *Annual Review of Political Science* 3 (2000): 63–83; David A. Lake, "Beyond Anarchy: The Importance of Security Institutions," *International Security* 26, no. 1 (2001): 129–160; Brett Ashley Leeds, Andrew G. Long, and Sarah M. Mitchell, "Reevaluating Alliance Reliability: Specific Threats, Specific Promises," *Journal of Conflict Resolution* 44, no. 5 (2000): 686–699; Brett Ashley Leeds, "Alliance Reliability in Times of War: Explaining State Decisions to Violate Treaties," *International Organization* 57, no. 4 (2003): 801–827.

3. Glenn H. Snyder, *Alliance Politics* (Ithaca, NY: Cornell University Press, 1997).

4. Stacie L. Pettyjohn, *U.S. Global Defense Posture: 1783–2011* (Santa Monica, CA: RAND, 2012), 50–60, 78.

5. Bernard Brodie, *Strategy in the Missile Age* (Princeton: Princeton University Press, 1959), 158; Michael J. Lostumbo, Michael J. McNerney, Eric Peltz, Derek Eaton, David R. Frelinger, Victoria A. Greenfield, John Halliday, Patrick Mills, Bruce R. Nardulli, Stacie L. Pettyjohn, Jerry M. Sollinger, and Stephen M. Worman, *Overseas Basing of U.S. Military Forces: An Assessment of Relative Costs and Strategic Benefits* (Santa Monica, CA: RAND, 2013), 74–77; Glenn H. Snyder, *Deterrence and Defense: Toward a Theory of National Security* (Princeton: Princeton University Press, 1961), 24; Thomas C. Schelling, *Arms and Influence* (New Haven: Yale University Press, 1966), 47.

6. Lostumbo et al., *Overseas Basing*, 75–77.

7. Melvyn P. Leffler, *A Preponderance of Power: National Security, the Truman Administration, and the Cold War* (Stanford: Stanford University Press, 1992), 56–58; Pettyjohn, *U.S. Global Defense Posture*, 50–57.

8. "The United States Special Representative in Europe Under the Foreign Assistance Act of 1948 (Harriman) to the Secretary of State," July 14, 1948, *Foreign Relations of the United States* (hereafter *FRUS*), 1948, vol. 3, doc. 120.

9. "Minutes of the Third Meeting of the Washington Exploratory Talks on Security, July 7, 1948, 10 a.m.," *FRUS*, 1948, vol. 3, doc. 114.

10. "Memorandum of the Thirteenth Meeting of the Working Group Participating in the Washington Exploratory Talks on Security," September 2, 1948, *FRUS*, 1948, vol. 3, doc. 144; "Report by the National Security Council," September 3, 1948, *FRUS*, 1948, vol. 3, doc. 146.

11. "Statement of Policy Proposed by the National Security Council," November 9, 1950, *FRUS*, 1950, vol. 6, doc. 851.

12. Michael J. Green, *By More Than Providence: Grand Strategy and American Power in the Asia Pacific since 1783* (New York: Columbia University Press, 2017), 250, 274.

13. "Memorandum of Conversation, by the Deputy to the Consultant (Allison) at the Malacanan Palace, 10:45 a.m.," February 12, 1951, *FRUS*, 1951, vol. 6, part 1, doc. 48; "Draft Position Paper Prepared in the Department of State," December 20, 1951, *FRUS*, 1951, vol. 6, part 1, doc. 121.

14. "Memorandum by the Chief of the Division of Philippine Affairs (Lockhart) to the Secretary of State," April 18, 1945, *FRUS*, 1945, vol. 6, doc. 887; "The Secretary of the Navy (Forrestal) to the Secretary of State," April 30, 1945, *FRUS*, 1945, vol. 6, doc. 888; "The Ambassador in the Philippines (McNutt) to the Secretary of State," December 23, 1946, *FRUS*, 1946, vol. 8, doc. 732; "Memorandum by the Secretary of Defense (Johnson) to the Executive Secretary of the National Security Council (Lay)," September 14, 1950, *FRUS*, 1950, vol. 6, doc. 837.

15. "General of the Army Douglas MacArthur to the Secretary of State," September 1, 1947, *FRUS*, 1947, vol. 6, doc. 413; "The Acting Political Adviser in Japan (Sebald) to the Secretary of State," December 8, 1947, *FRUS*, 1947, vol. 6, doc. 455; "The Secretary of Defense (Marshall) to the Secretary of State," April 19, 1951, *FRUS*, 1951, vol. 6, part 1, doc. 555; "Memorandum by the Central Intelligence Agency," April 20, 1951, *FRUS*, 1951, vol. 6, part 1, doc. 556; "Memorandum by the Consultant to the Secretary (Dulles)," April 12, 1951, *FRUS*, 1951, vol. 6, part 1, doc. 549.

16. Green, *By More Than Providence*, 280; "Memorandum by the Consultant to the Secretary (Dulles) to the Secretary of State," July 7, 1950, *FRUS*, 1950, vol. 6, doc. 720; "Memorandum by the Officer in Charge of Japanese Affairs (Green) to the Director of the Office of Northeast Asian Affairs (Allison)," August 2, 1950, *FRUS*, 1950, vol. 6, doc. 742; "Memorandum by the Secretary of State to the Ambassador at Large (Jessup)," August 22, 1950, *FRUS*, 1950, vol. 6, doc. 752; "The Secretary of State to the Secretary of Defense (Marshall)," December 13, 1950, *FRUS*, 1950, vol. 6, doc. 791; "Report by the Joint Strategic Survey Committee to the Joint Chiefs of Staff," December 28, 1950, *FRUS*, 1950, vol. 6, doc. 797.

17. "Memorandum by the Secretary of State to the President," April 30, 1952, *FRUS*, 1952–54, vol. 15, part 1, doc. 110.

18. "Memorandum of Conversation, by the Assistant Secretary of State for Far Eastern Affairs (Robertson)," April 24, 1953, *FRUS*, 1952–54, vol. 15, part 1, doc. 477.

19. "The President of the Republic of Korea (Rhee) to the Commander in Chief United Nations Command (Clark)," April 30, 1953, *FRUS*, 1952–54, vol. 15, part 1, doc. 487; "The Commanding General, United States Eighth Army (Taylor) to the Commander in Chief, Far East (Clark)," June 9, 1953, *FRUS*, 1952–54, vol. 15, part 2, doc. 586; "Memorandum by the Deputy Assistant Secretary of State for United

Nations Affairs (Sandifer) to the Secretary of State," June 17, 1953, *FRUS*, 1952–54, vol. 15, part 2, doc. 603; "Memorandum by the Joint Chiefs of Staff to the Secretary of Defense," June 30, 1953, *FRUS*, 1952–54, vol. 15, part 2, doc. 648; "Memorandum of Discussion at the 152d Meeting of the National Security Council, Thursday, July 2, 1953," *FRUS*, 1952–54, vol. 15, part 2, doc. 655.

20. Green, *By More Than Providence*, 253–263.

21. "Memorandum by the Assistant Secretary of State for Far Eastern Affairs (Allison) to the Secretary of State," March 25, 1953, *FRUS*, 1952–54, vol. 14, part 1, doc. 85; "The Joint Chiefs of Staff to the Commander in Chief Pacific (Radford)," April 6, 1953, *FRUS*, 1952–54, vol. 14, part 1, doc. 91; "Memorandum of Conversation, by the Acting Officer in Charge of Economic Affairs, Office of Chinese Affairs (Hope)," June 1, 1953, *FRUS*, 1952–54, vol. 14, part 1, doc. 106; "Memorandum by the Regional Planning Adviser for Far Eastern Affairs (Ogburn) to the Director of the Office of Chinese Affairs (McConaughy)," October 30, 1953, *FRUS*, 1952–54, vol. 14, part 1, doc. 144; "Memorandum by the Chairman of the Joint Chiefs of Staff (Radford)," October 29, 1954, *FRUS*, 1952–54, vol. 14, part 1, doc. 369; "The Ambassador in the Republic of China (Rankin) to the Department of State," December 19, 1953, *FRUS*, 1952–54, vol. 14, part 1, doc. 161; "Memorandum for the File by the Director of the Office of Chinese Affairs (McConaughy)," February 27, 1954, *FRUS*, 1952–54, vol. 14, part 1, doc. 174; "Memorandum by the Counselor (MacArthur) to the Acting Secretary of State," October 14, 1954, *FRUS*, 1952–54, vol. 14, part 1, doc. 341.

22. Bernard Brodie, ed., *The Absolute Weapon: Atomic Power and World Order* (New York: Harcourt Brace, 1946), 76.

23. Snyder, *Deterrence and Defense*, 41–43.

24. Paul K. Huth, *Extended Deterrence and the Prevention of War* (New Haven: Yale University, 1988); Patrick M. Morgan, *Deterrence: A Conceptual Analysis* (Beverly Hills, CA: Sage, 1977), 11.

25. Schelling, *Arms and Influence*, 56–60.

26. Snyder, *Deterrence and Defense*, 43.

27. Morrow, "Alliances, Credibility, and Peacetime Costs." For discussions of why alliance formation itself may be an informative signal, see Morrow, "Alliances: Why Write Them Down?"; Alastair Smith, "Alliance Formation and War," *International Studies Quarterly* 39, no. 4 (1995): 405–425; James D. Fearon, "Bargaining, Enforcement, and International Cooperation," *International Organization* 52, no. 2 (1998): 269–305; Brett Ashley Leeds, "Domestic Political Institutions, Credible Commitments, and International Cooperation," *American Journal of Political Science* 43, no. 4 (1999): 979–1002; George W. Downs, David M. Rocke, and Peter N. Barsoom, "Is the Good News about Compliance Good News about Cooperation?" *International Organization* 50, no. 3 (1996): 379–406.

28. See James D. Fearon, "Signaling Foreign Policy Interests: Tying Hands versus Sinking Costs," *Journal of Conflict Resolution* 41, no. 1 (1997): 68–90; Branislav Slantchev, "Military Coercion in Interstate Crises," *American Political Science Review* 99, no. 4 (2005): 533–547, 534; Branislav L. Slantchev, *Military Threats: The Costs of Coercion and the Price of Peace* (Cambridge: Cambridge University Press, 2011), 61, 78–80; Schelling, *Arms and Influence;* Robert Jervis, *The Logic of Images in International Relations* (Princeton: Princeton University Press, 1970); Barry O'Neill, "The Intermediate Nuclear Force Missiles: An Analysis of Coupling and Reassurance," *International Interactions* 15, no. 3–4 (1990): 150; Michael Spence, "Job Market Signaling," *Quarterly Journal of Economics* 87, no. 3 (1973): 355–374.

29. "Memorandum by the Director of the Policy Planning Staff (Kennan)," November 24, 1948, *FRUS*, 1948, vol. 3, doc. 182.

30. "Memorandum by the Joint Chiefs of Staff to the Secretary of Defense (Forrestal)," November 24, 1948, *FRUS*, 1948, vol. 3, doc. 183.

31. "Memorandum of Conversation, by the Director of the Office of European Affairs (Hickerson)," December 31, 1948, *FRUS*, 1948, vol. 3, doc. 203.

32. "The Consultant to the Secretary (Dulles) to the Secretary of Defense (Marshall)," July 10, 1951, *FRUS*, 1951, vol. 6, part 1, doc. 635; "United States–Japanese Draft of a Bilateral Security Treaty," July 31, 1951, *FRUS*, 1951, vol. 6, part 1, doc. 666; "Memorandum by the Consultant to the Secretary (Dulles)," July 15, 1950, *FRUS*, 1950, vol. 6, doc. 723.

33. "Intelligence Estimate Prepared by the Estimates Group, Office of Intelligence Research, Department of State," June 25, 1950, *FRUS*, 1950, vol. 7, doc. 82; "Memorandum of Discussion at the 156th Meeting of the National Security Council, Thursday, July 23, 1953," *FRUS*, 1952–54, vol. 15, part 2, doc. 712.

34. "Memorandum of Conversation, by the Assistant Secretary of State for Far Eastern Affairs (Allison)," March 19, 1953, *FRUS*, 1952–54, vol. 14, part 1, doc. 83; "The Assistant Secretary of State for Far Eastern Affairs (Robertson) to the Department of State," June 26, 1953, *FRUS*, 1952–54, vol. 15, part 2, doc. 639; "Memorandum by the Assistant Secretary of State for Far Eastern Affairs (Robertson) to the Secretary of State," February 25, 1954, *FRUS*, 1952–54, vol. 14, part 1, doc. 173; "Memorandum of Discussion at the 183d Meeting of the National Security Council, Washington, February 4, 1954," *FRUS*, 1952–54, vol. 14, part 1, doc. 167; "Memorandum of Conversation, by the Special Assistant to the President for National Security Affairs (Cutler)," May 22, 1954, *FRUS*, 1952–54, vol. 14, part 1, doc. 196.

35. "Draft Statement of Policy, Prepared by the NSC Planning Board," November 19, 1954, *FRUS*, 1952–54, vol. 14, part 1, doc. 397.

36. "Exploring the Nuclear Posture Implications of Extended Deterrence and Assurance: Workshop Proceedings and Key Takeaways," Center for Strategic and

International Studies, November 2009, 8, https://csis-prod.s3.amazonaws.com /s3fs-public/legacy_files/files/publication/100222_Murdock_NuclearPosture _Print.pdf; Linton Brooks and Mira Rapp-Hooper, "Extended Deterrence, Assurance, and Reassurance in the Pacific during the Second Nuclear Age," in *Strategic Asia 2013–2014: Asia in the Second Nuclear Age*, ed. Ashley J. Tellis, Abraham M. Denmark, and Travis Tanner (Washington, DC: Carnegie Endowment for International Peace, 2013), 268; Jeffrey W. Knopf, "Security Assurances: Initial Hypotheses," in *Security Assurances and Nuclear Nonproliferation*, ed. Jeffrey W. Knopf (Stanford: Stanford University Press, 2012), 14.

37. See Michael Horowitz, *The Diffusion of Military Power: Causes and Consequences for International Politics* (Princeton: Princeton University Press, 2010), 108, for more on how a nuclear alliance strategy can substitute for other defense investments. On nuclear security guarantees as substitutes for indigenous nuclear weapons programs, see Philipp C. Bleek and Eric B. Lorber, "Security Guarantees and Allied Nuclear Proliferation," *Journal of Conflict Resolution* 58, no. 3 (2014): 429–454.

38. Nicholas Miller, "The Secret Success of Nonproliferation Sanctions," *International Organization* 68, no. 4 (2014): 913–944; Gene Gerzhoy, "Allied Coercion and Nuclear Restraint: How the United States Thwarted West Germany's Nuclear Ambitions," *International Security* 39, no. 4 (2015): 91–129. For detailed discussion of weak states' motivation to ally, see Jeremy Pressman, *Warring Friends: Alliance Restraint in International Politics* (Ithaca, NY: Cornell University Press, 2008); Patricia A. Weitsman, *Dangerous Alliances: Proponents of Peace, Weapons of War* (Stanford: Stanford University Press, 2004).

39. See Victor Cha, *Powerplay: The Origins of the American Alliance System in Asia* (Princeton: Princeton University Press, 2016).

40. "Report by the Executive Secretary of the National Security Council (Souers) to the Council," April 13, 1948, *FRUS*, 1948, vol. 3, doc. 71.

41. "The Department of State to the British Embassy," March 13, 1951, *FRUS*, 1951, vol. 6, part 1, doc. 526; "The Secretary of State to the Secretary of Defense (Marshall)," December 13, 1950, *FRUS*, 1950, vol. 6, doc. 790; "Memorandum by the Assistant Secretary of State for European Affairs (Perkins) to Mr. John Foster Dulles, the Consultant to the Secretary," January 15, 1951, *FRUS*, 1951, vol. 6, part 1, doc. 38; "Memorandum by Mr. Robert A. Fearey of the Office of Northeast Asian Affairs," February 16, 1951, *FRUS*, 1951, vol. 6, part 1, doc. 51; "Mr. John Foster Dulles, the Consultant to the Secretary, to the Supreme Commander for Allied Powers," March 2, 1951, *FRUS*, 1951, vol. 6, part 2, doc. 56; "The Ambassador in the Philippines (Cowen) to the Secretary of State," July 17, 1951, *FRUS*, 1951, vol. 6, part 1, doc. 85.

42. "The Secretary of State to the Embassy in the Republic of China," June 30, 1953, *FRUS*, 1952–54, vol. 14, part 1, doc. 117; "Memorandum by the Ambassador in

the Republic of China (Rankin) to the Secretary of State," July 8, 1954, *FRUS*, 1952–54, vol. 14, part 1, doc. 228; "Memorandum by the Assistant Secretary of State for Far Eastern Affairs (Robertson) to the Secretary of State," August 25, 1954, *FRUS*, 1952–54, vol. 14, part 1, doc. 262; "Memorandum by the Ambassador in the Republic of China (Rankin) to the Secretary of State," July 8, 1954, *FRUS*, 1952–54, vol. 14, part 1, doc. 228; "Memorandum of Discussion at the 214th Meeting of the National Security Council, Denver, September 12, 1954," *FRUS*, 1952–54, vol. 14, part 1, doc. 293; "Memorandum of Discussion at the 216th Meeting of the National Security Council, Washington, October 6, 1954," *FRUS*, 1952–54, vol. 14, part 1, doc. 322; "Memorandum by the Secretary of State to the Assistant Secretary of State for Far Eastern Affairs (Robertson)," October 8, 1954, *FRUS*, 1952–54, vol. 14, part 1, doc. 327; "Memorandum of Discussion at the 221st Meeting of the National Security Council, Washington, November 2, 1954," *FRUS*, 1952–54, vol. 14, part 1, doc. 375; "Memorandum by the Acting Director of Central Intelligence (Cabell) to the National Security Council," November 2, 1954, *FRUS*, 1952–54, vol. 14, part 1, doc. 376; "The Secretary of State to the Embassy in the Republic of China," November 3, 1954, *FRUS*, 1952–54, vol. 14, part 1, doc. 381; "Memorandum of Conversation, by the Director of the Office of Chinese Affairs (McConaughy)," November 6, 1954, *FRUS*, 1952–54, vol. 14, part 1, doc. 385; "The Secretary of State to the Embassy in the Republic of China," November 23, 1954, *FRUS*, 1952–54, vol. 14, part 1, doc. 401; "Memorandum by the Secretary of State to the President," November 23, 1954, *FRUS*, 1952–54, vol. 14, part 1, doc. 403.

43. Huth, *Extended Deterrence*; Morgan, *Deterrence*; Jesse C. Johnson and Brett Ashley Leeds, "Defense Pacts: A Prescription for Peace?" *Foreign Policy Analysis* 7, no. 1 (2011): 45–65; Brett Ashley Leeds, "Do Alliances Deter Aggression? The Influence of Military Alliances on the Initiation of Militarized Interstate Disputes," *American Political Science Review* 47, no. 3 (2003): 427–439; Matthew Fuhrman and Todd S. Sechser, "Signaling Alliance Commitments: Hand-Tying and Sunk Costs in Extended Nuclear Deterrence," *American Journal of Political Science* 58, no. 4 (2014): 919–935.

44. Bleek and Lorber, "Security Guarantees and Allied Nuclear Proliferation"; Philipp C. Bleek, "Why Do States Proliferate? Quantitative Analysis of the Exploration, Pursuit, and Acquisition of Nuclear Weapons," in *Forecasting Proliferation in the 21st Century: The Role of Theory*, ed. William Potter and Gaukhar Mukhatzhanova (Stanford: Stanford University Press, 2010); Jeffrey Richelson, *Spying on the Bomb: American Nuclear Intelligence from Nazi Germany to Iran and North Korea* (New York: W. W. Norton, 2006); Gerzhoy, "Allied Coercion and Nuclear Restraint."

45. Hal Brands and Peter Feaver, "What Are America's Alliances Good For?" *Parameters* 47, no. 2 (2017): 15–30.

46. Ronald Krebs, "Perverse Institutionalism: NATO and the Greco-Turkish Conflict," *International Organization* 53, no. 2 (1999): 343–377.

47. Frederic Bozo, *Two Strategies for Europe: De Gaulle, the United States, and the Atlantic Alliance* (New York: Rowman and Littlefield, 2001); Avery Goldstein, *Deterrence and Security in the 21st Century: China, Britain, France, and the Enduring Legacy of the Nuclear Revolution* (Stanford: Stanford University Press, 2000).

48. For the debate over calculations of deterrence effectiveness, see Richard Ned Lebow and Janice Gross Stein, "Deterrence: The Elusive Dependent Variable," *World Politics* 42, no. 3 (1990): 336–369; and Paul Huth and Bruce Russett, "Testing Deterrence Theory: Rigor Makes a Difference," *World Politics* 42, no. 4 (1990): 466–501.

49. James D. Fearon, "Selection Effects and Deterrence," *International Interactions* 28, no. 1 (2002): 5–29.

50. John L. Gaddis, "Elements of Stability in the Postwar International System," *International Security* 10, no. 4 (1986): 99–142.

51. The literature offering "long peace" explanations is voluminous, and the explanations themselves are not mutually exclusive. A sample of seminal works includes Waltz, *Theory of International Politics*, 180–181; Kenneth N. Waltz, "The Spread of Nuclear Weapons: More May Be Better," Adelphi Papers no. 171 (London: International Institute for Strategic Studies, 1981); R. Rosecrance, A. Alexandroff, W. Koehler, J. Kroll, S. Laqueur, and J. Stocker, "Wither Interdependence?" *International Organization* 31, no. 3 (1977): 425–471, 425; Richard Rosecrance, *The Rise of the Trading State: Commerce and Conquest in the Modern World* (New York: Basic Books, 1986); Zeev Maoz and Bruce Russett, "Normative and Structural Causes of the Democratic Peace, 1946–1986," *American Political Science Review* 87, no. 3 (1993): 624–638; Alexander Wendt, *Social Theory of International Politics* (New York: Cambridge University Press, 1999); Mark W. Zacher, "The Territorial Integrity Norm: International Boundaries and the Use of Force," *International Organization* 55, no. 2 (Spring 2001): 215–250; Robert Jervis, "Theories of War in an Era of Leading-Power Peace: Presidential Address, American Political Science Association, 2001," *American Political Science Review* 96, no. 1 (2002): 1–14.

52. Gaddis, "Elements of Stability," 109; Daniel Egel, Adam R. Grissom, John P. Godges, Jennifer Kavanaugh, and Howard J. Shatz, *Estimating the Value of Overseas Commitments* (Santa Monica, CA: RAND, 2016).

53. Marc Trachtenberg, *A Constructed Peace: The Making of the European Settlement 1945–1963* (Princeton: Princeton University Press, 1999), 21–22, 78–81.

54. "JCS to Forrestal," July 22, 1948, in Kenneth Condit, *History of the Joint Chiefs of Staff*, vol. 2: *The Joint Chiefs of Staff and National Policy, 1947–1949* (Washington, DC: Office of the Chairman of the Joint Chiefs of Staff, 1996), 144.

55. Vladislav Zubok, "The Case of Divided Germany, 1953–1964," in *Nikita Khrushchev*, ed. William Taubman, Sergei Khrushchev, and Abbott Gleason (New Haven: Yale University Press, 2000), 276–277; Trachtenberg, *A Constructed Peace*, 66, 102.

56. Hope M. Harrison, *Driving the Soviets Up the Wall: Soviet-East German Relations, 1953–1961* (Princeton: Princeton University Press, 2005), 95–96; Trachtenberg, *A Constructed Peace*, 252–254; Gene Gerzhoy, "Allied Coercion and Nuclear Restraint"; Zubok, "The Case of Divided Germany," 282–288.

57. Frederick Kempe, *Berlin 1961: Kennedy, Khrushchev, and the Most Dangerous Place on Earth* (New York: Putnam, 2011), 21; Harrison, *Driving the Soviets*, 100–101.

58. Kempe, *Berlin 1961*, 130.

59. Trachtenberg, *A Constructed Peace*, 287.

60. Vladislav M. Zubok, *Inside the Kremlin's Cold War: From Stalin to Khrushchev* (Cambridge, MA: Harvard University Press, 1996), 240–243.

61. For an extended discussion of the dynamics between Ulbricht and Khrushchev, see Harrison, *Driving the Soviets*, 125–139.

62. Robert M. Slusser, *The Berlin Crisis of 1961: Soviet-American Relations and the Struggle for Power in the Kremlin* (Baltimore: Johns Hopkins University Press, 1973), x–xi; Kempe, *Berlin 1961*, 243.

63. Kempe, *Berlin 1961*, 245, 247.

64. Kempe, *Berlin 1961*, 247; Jenny Thompson and Sherry Thompson, *The Kremlinologist: Llewellyn E. Thompson, America's Man in Cold War Moscow* (Baltimore: Johns Hopkins University Press, 2018), 255.

65. Slusser, *The Berlin Crisis of 1961*, 28–30; Kempe, *Berlin 1961*, 262.

66. Slusser, *The Berlin Crisis of 1961*, 51, 53, 78.

67. Slusser, *The Berlin Crisis of 1961*, 80.

68. Thompson and Thompson, *The Kremlinologist*, 255.

69. Harrison, *Driving the Soviets*, 165.

70. Zubok, *Inside the Kremlin's Cold War*, 254–256.

71. Zubok, "The Case of Divided Germany," 296; Harrison, *Driving the Soviets*, 184–187.

72. Slusser, *The Berlin Crisis of 1961*, 93; Harrison, *Driving the Soviets*, 166.

73. Slusser, *The Berlin Crisis of 1961*, 113–124, 129.

74. Harrison, *Driving the Soviets*, 180.

75. Harrison, *Driving the Soviets*, 177; Slusser, *The Berlin Crisis of 1961*, 130–131; Kempe, *Berlin 1961*, 84, 473; Bozo, *Two Strategies for Europe*, 69.

76. Harrison, *Driving the Soviets*, 182, 184; Trachtenberg, *A Constructed Peace*, 398–402; Gerzhoy, "Allied Coercion and Nuclear Restraint"; Zubok, "The Case of Divided Germany," 298.

77. John L. Gaddis, *The Cold War: A New History* (New York: Penguin, 2005), 115.

78. Trachtenberg, *A Constructed Peace*, 305–312.

79. See, for example, Van Jackson, *Rival Reputations: Coercion and Credibility in U.S.–North Korea Relations* (Cambridge: Cambridge University Press, 2016); and Thomas Christensen, *Useful Adversaries: Grand Strategy, Domestic Mobilization, and Sino-American Conflict, 1947–1958* (Princeton: Princeton University Press, 1996).

80. Todd S. Sechser and Abigail S. Post, "Hand-Tying versus Muscle Flexing in Crisis Bargaining," unpublished manuscript, April 24, 2017, http://abigailpost.com /docs/post_sechser_handtying.pdf.

81. Steven M. Walt, "Alliance Formation and the Balance of World Power," *International Security* 9, no. 4 (1985): 3–43.

3. At What Cost, Alliance?

1. Kennedy's warning was also directed at nontreaty partners. John F. Kennedy's Inaugural Address, January 20, 1961, John F. Kennedy Presidential Library, https://www.jfklibrary.org/Research/Research-Aids/Ready-Reference/JFK -Quotations/Inaugural-Address.aspx.

2. Hal Brands and Peter Feaver, "What Are America's Alliances Good For?" *Parameters* 47, no. 2 (2017): 15–30, 18.

3. Kathleen H. Hicks, Jeffrey Rathke, Seamus P. Daniels, Michael Matlaga, Laura Daniels, and Andrew Linder, "Counting Dollars or Measuring Value: Assessing NATO and Partner Burden Sharing," Center for Strategic and International Studies, July 2018, https://csis-prod.s3.amazonaws.com/s3fs-public/publication /180703_Hicks_CountingDollars.pdf?ODJoCMVuu4utZMU.R1Y14EFdp.ma7JEc.

4. Stacie L. Pettyjohn, *U.S. Global Defense Posture: 1783–2011* (Santa Monica, CA: RAND, 2012), 133–135.

5. See "Allied Contributions to the Common Defense," annual reports from the Department of Defense to Congress, 1981–1990.

6. Barry R. Posen, *Restraint: A New Foundation for U.S. Grand Strategy* (Ithaca, NY: Cornell University Press, 2014), 35; Christopher A. Preble, *How American Military Dominance Makes Us Less Prosperous, Less Safe, and Less Free* (Ithaca, NY: Cornell University Press, 2009), 95, 106.

7. Stephen G. Brooks and William C. Wohlforth, *America Abroad: The United States Global Role in the 21st Century* (Oxford: Oxford University Press, 2016), 131–133.

8. Pettyjohn, *U.S. Global Defense Posture*, 200–235.

9. Glenn H. Snyder, "The Security Dilemma in Alliance Politics," *World Politics* 36, no. 4 (1984): 461–495, 467; Tongfi Kim, "Why Alliances Entangle but Seldom Entrap States," *Security Studies* 20, no. 3 (2011): 350–377.

10. Kenneth N. Waltz, *Theory of International Politics* (Reading, MA: Addison-Wesley, 1979), 165–170.

11. Snyder, "Security Dilemma," 483–484.

12. Posen, *Restraint*, 54, 63, 67, 80, 84, 85; Stephen M. Walt, "How to Tell If You're in a Good Alliance," *Foreign Policy*, October 28, 2019, https://foreignpolicy.com /2019/10/28/kurds-turkey-israel-saudi-arabia-good-alliance; Mike Beckley, "The Myth of Entangling Alliances: Reassessing the Security Risks of U.S. Defense Pacts," *International Security* 39, no. 4 (2015): 7–48.

13. Beckley, "Myth of Entangling Alliances"; Neil Narang and Rupal Mehta, "The Unforeseen Consequences of Extended Deterrence: Moral Hazard in a Nuclear Client State," *Journal of Conflict Resolution* 63, no. 1 (2019): 218–250.

14. Beckley, "Myth of Entangling Alliances," 10, 32; Francis J. Gavin, "Choosing Tragedy in Vietnam," *Orbis* 45, no. 1 (Winter 2001); 137; Lawrence S. Kaplan, *The United States and NATO: The Formative Years* (Lexington: University of Kentucky Press, 1984), 27.

15. Beckley, "Myth of Entangling Alliances," 36.

16. Beckley, "Myth of Entangling Alliances," 39–40.

17. Kim, "Why Alliances Entangle."

18. Glenn H. Snyder, *Alliance Politics* (Ithaca, NY: Cornell University Press, 1997), 169.

19. "Memorandum by the Regional Planning Adviser in the Bureau of Far Eastern Affairs (Green)," September 18, 1958, *FRUS, 1958–1960*, vol. 19, doc. 106; Nancy Bernkopf Tucker, *Taiwan, Hong Kong, and the United States, 1945–1992: Uncertain Friendships* (New York: Twayne, 1994), 22, 32.

20. Philip Zelikow, *Suez Deconstructed: An Interactive Study in Crisis, War, and Peacemaking* (Washington, DC: Brookings Institution Press, 2018), "Part Two, What to Do about the Crisis": Washington (133–152), and "Part Three, What to Do about the War": Washington (271–292).

21. Walt, "How to Tell If You're in a Good Alliance."

22. Kaplan, *The United States and NATO,* 28–29.

23. Lesek Buszynski, *SEATO: The Failure of an Alliance Strategy* (Singapore: Singapore University Press, 1983), 2, 72–181; Amy Searight, "Southeast Asian Alliances and Partnerships," in *Ironclad: Forging a New Future for America's Alliances,* ed. Michael J. Green (Washington, DC: Center for Strategic and International Studies, 2019); Richard M. Nixon, "Asia after Vietnam," *Foreign Affairs* 46, no. 1 (October 1967).

24. "The Central Committee Politburo's Report on the Sino-American Meetings" (drafted by Chou Enlai), May 26, 1971, as excerpted in Chen Jian, *Mao's China after the Cold War* (Chapel Hill: University of North Carolina Press, 2002), 264–265.

25. Memorandum of Conversation, "Taiwan," October 21, 1971, NSC Box 846, Richard Nixon Library.

26. Shirley A. Kan, "China / Taiwan: Evolution of the 'One China' Policy—Key Statements from Washington, Beijing and Taipei," Congressional Research Service Report RL 30341, December 13, 2007; James Mann, *About Face: A History of America's Curious Relationship with China from Nixon to Clinton* (New York: Vintage, 2000), 96–98.

27. David Edelstein and Joshua Shifrinson, "It's a Trap! Security Commitments and the Risk of Entrapment," in *US Grand Strategy in the 21st Century: The Case for Restraint,* ed. A. Trevor Thrall and Benjamin H. Friedman (London: Routledge, 2018).

28. Snyder, "Security Dilemma," 466.

29. Frederic Bozo, *Two Strategies for Europe: De Gaulle, the United States, and the Atlantic Alliance* (Lanham, MD: Rowman, Littlefield, 2001), 168.

30. Helga Haftendorn, *NATO and the Nuclear Revolution: A Crisis of Credibility* (Oxford: Clarendon, 1996), 1.

31. Garrett Martin, "1967 Withdrawal from NATO: The Cornerstone of de Gaulle's Grand Strategy?" *Journal of Transatlantic Studies* 9, no. 3 (2011): 232–243; Frederic Bozo, "Détente versus Alliance: France, the United States, and the Politics of the Harmel Report (1964–1968)," *Contemporary European History* 7, no. 3 (1998): 343–360.

32. Martin, "1967 Withdrawal from NATO," 236; Bozo, *Two Strategies for Europe,* 85–123.

33. Bozo, *Two Strategies for Europe,* 131, 154–156; Thomas A. Schwartz, *Lyndon Johnson and Europe in the Shadow of Vietnam* (Cambridge, MA: Harvard University Press, 2003), 96–97.

34. Martin, "1967 Withdrawal from NATO," 239; Schwartz, *Lyndon Johnson and Europe,* 102; Bozo, *Two Strategies for Europe,* 170.

35. "Memorandum from President Johnson to Secretary of State Rusk and Secretary of Defense McNamara," May 4, 1966, *FRUS,* 1964–68, vol. 13, doc. 161.

36. "Report of the Special Committee Visiting American Military Installations and NATO Bases in France," House of Representatives Committee on Armed Services, September 12, 1966, 10381, 10384, 10387; Bozo, *Two Strategies for Europe,* 165, 172, 174.

37. There is a wide range of estimated losses because officials incorporated estimates of the residual value of lost property. "The Crisis in NATO," report of the Sub-

committee on Europe of the Committee of Foreign Affairs, House of Representatives, August 1966, 4; Staff Memorandum on United States Investment of Military Assistance Funds in Military Installations Located in France, House Committee on Foreign Affairs, March 1, 1967.

38. Memorandum from Johnson to Rusk and McNamara, May 4, 1966; "National Security Action Memorandum No. 345," April 22, 1966, *FRUS, 1964–68*, vol. 13, doc. 159; Bozo, *Two Strategies for Europe*, 189.

39. Report of the Council, "Future Tasks of the Alliance (The Harmel Report)," December 13–14, 1967, NATO, https://www.nato.int/cps/en/natohq/official_texts _26700.htm; Bozo, "Détente versus Alliance," 343–360; Andreas Wenger, "Crisis and Opportunity: NATO's Transformation and Multilateralization of Détente 1966–1968," *Journal of Cold War Studies* 6, no. 1 (2004): 22–74.

40. Stephen Daggett, "Costs of Major U.S. Wars," Congressional Research Service, June 29, 2010, 2. Report archived by the Federation of American Scientists at https://fas.org/sgp/crs/natsec/RS22926.pdf.

41. Posen, *Restraint*, 90, 100, 107, 135–155; Brands and Feaver, "What Are America's Alliances Good For?," 18.

42. Zack Cooper, "Pacific Power: America's Asian Alliances beyond Burden-Sharing," *War on the Rocks*, December 14, 2016, https://warontherocks.com/2016 /12/pacific-power-americas-asian-alliances-beyond-burden-sharing.

43. Daggett, "Cost of Major U.S. Wars"; "Fact Sheet: America's Wars," U.S. Department of Veterans Affairs, https://www.va.gov/opa/publications/factsheets/fs _americas_wars.pdf.

44. Michael J. Lostumbo, Michael J. McNerney, Eric Peltz, Derek Eaton, David R. Frelinger, Victoria A. Greenfield, John Halliday, Patrick Mills, Bruce R. Nardulli, Stacie L. Pettyjohn, Jerry M. Sollinger, and Stephen M. Worman, *Overseas Basing of U.S. Military Forces: An Assessment of Relative Costs and Strategic Benefits* (Santa Monica, CA: RAND, 2013), 139.

45. Daniel Egel, Adam R. Grissom, John P. Godges, Jennifer Kavanaugh, and Howard J. Shatz, *Estimating the Value of Overseas Security Commitments* (Santa Monica, CA: RAND, 2016), 63, 71, 73.

4. Alliances after the Cold War

1. See, for example, John Mearsheimer, "The False Promise of International Institutions," *International Security* 19, no. 3 (1994–95): 5–49; Kenneth N. Waltz, "NATO Expansion: A Realist's View," *Contemporary Security Policy* 21, no. 2 (2000): 25–38.

2. Ronald D. Asmus, *Opening NATO's Door: How the Alliance Remade Itself for a New Era* (New York: Columbia University Press, 2002), 59.

3. Asmus, *Opening NATO's Door*, xxv.

4. James Goldgeier, *Not Whether but When: The US Decision to Enlarge NATO* (Washington, DC: Brookings Institution, 1999), 3.

5. Quoted in Goldgeier, *Not Whether but When*, 71.

6. James Steinberg, interview with author, July 25, 2018, New York; Goldgeier, *Not Whether but When*, 17.

7. Ronald D. Asmus, Richard L. Kugler, F. Stephen Larrabee, "Building a New NATO," *Foreign Affairs*, September / October 1993.

8. Asmus, *Opening NATO's Door*, 15–16, 23–25, 42.

9. Dimitrii Trenin, *Post-Imperium: A Eurasian Story* (Washington, DC: Carnegie Endowment for International Peace, 2011), 4; Joshua R. Shifrinson, "Deal or No Deal? The End of the Cold War and the US Offer to Limit NATO Expansion," *International Security* 40, no. 4 (2016): 7–44; Asmus, *Opening NATO's Door*, 5.

10. Strobe Talbott, *The Russia Hand* (New York: Random House, 2003), 31; Goldgeier, *Not Whether but When*, 21.

11. Asmus, Kugler, and Larrabee, "Building a New NATO."

12. Asmus, *Opening NATO's Door*, 261.

13. As quoted in Goldgeier, *Not Whether but When*, 38.

14. Steinberg interview. For evidence that the alliance may have facilitated some democratic reforms, see Rachel A. Epstein, "NATO Enlargement and the Spread of Democracy: Evidence and Expectations," *Security Studies* 14, no. 1 (2005): 63–105.

15. Asmus, *Opening NATO's Door*, 23, 124, 127–128; Goldgeier, *Not Whether but When*, 86; Talbott, *Russia Hand*, 92.

16. "FY 1994–1999 Defense Planning Guidance Sections for Comment," Department of Defense, February 18, 1992, https://nsarchive2.gwu.edu/nukevault/ebb245/doc03_extract_nytedit.pdf.

17. Goldgeier, *Not Whether but When*, 4; Talbott, *Russia Hand*, 218.

18. Asmus, *Opening NATO's Door*, 20–26; Talbott, *Russia Hand*, 38, 44, 47, 52; Goldgeier, *Not Whether but When*, 37.

19. Asmus, *Opening NATO's Door*, 37, 48; Talbott, *Russia Hand*, 131; Steinberg interview; Goldgeier, *Not Whether but When*, 37.

20. Goldgeier, *Not Whether but When*, 22–24; Talbott, *Russia Hand*, 115, 137; Asmus, *Opening NATO's Door*, 54–67.

21. Asmus, *Opening NATO's Door*, 35, 63, 97–98; Goldgeier, *Not Whether but When*, 50–51.

22. Steinberg interview; Kimberley Marten, "Reconsidering NATO Expansion: A Counterfactual Analysis of Russia and the West in the 1990s," *European Journal of International Security* 3, no. 2 (2018): 135–161; Asmus, *Opening NATO's Door*, 78, 110, 191, 187; Talbott, *Russia Hand*, 217.

23. Asmus, *Opening NATO's Door*, 103, 195; Goldgeier, *Not Whether but When*, 90, 173; Talbott, *Russia Hand*, 245–247; Marianne Hanson, "Russia and NATO Expansion: The Uneasy Basis of the Founding Act," *European Security* 7, no. 2 (1998): 13–29.

24. Asmus, *Opening NATO's Door*, 121; Goldgeier, *Not Whether but When*, 113; Talbott, *Russia Hand*, 220; George Kennan, "A Fateful Error," *New York Times*, February 5, 1997.

25. Talbott, *Russia Hand*, 247; Asmus, *Opening NATO's Door*, 86, 119, 254; Goldgeier, *Not Whether but When*, 127, 132; Ronald D. Asmus, Richard L. Kugler, and F. Stephen Larrabee, "What Will NATO Enlargement Cost?" *Survival* 38, no. 3 (1996): 5–26; "NATO Expansion: Cost Issues," Congressional Research Service, February 26, 1998, http://www.congressionalresearch.com/97-668/document.php ?study=NATO+EXPANSION+COST+ISSUES.

26. Steinberg interview.

27. Mark Kramer, "NATO, the Baltic States, and Russia: A Framework for Sustainable Enlargement," *International Affairs* 78, no. 4 (2002): 731–756.

28. Michael J. Green, *By More Than Providence: Grand Strategy and American Power in the Asia Pacific since 1783* (New York: Columbia University Press, 2017), 459.

29. Kurt Campbell, interview with author, May 23, 2018, Washington, DC; Michael J. Green, interview with author, June 26, 2018, Washington, DC.

30. Green, *By More Than Providence*, 432; Joseph S. Nye, interview with author, October 4, 2018, Cambridge, MA.

31. James L. Schoff, *Uncommon Alliance for the Common Good: The United States and Japan after the Cold War* (Washington, DC: Carnegie Endowment for International Peace, 2017), 41; "Issues in the Policy and Strategy Section," April 14, 1992; "Prevent the Reemergence of a New Rival: The Making of the Cheney Regional Defense Strategy, 1991–1992," document 10, National Security Archive, February 26, 2008, http://nsarchive.gwu.edu/nukevault/ebb245.

32. Campbell interview.

33. Green, *By More Than Providence*, 442.

34. "The United States and Japan: Advancing Toward a Mature Partnership," Institute for National Strategic Studies, National Defense University, October 11, 2000, 3, https://permanent.access.gpo.gov/websites/nduedu/www.ndu.edu/inss /press/Spelreprts/sr_01/sfjapan.pdf; Nye interview.

35. "Korea: U.S.-South Korean Relations," Congressional Research Service, July 20, 1998, 4, 10; Nigel R. Thalakada, *Unipolarity and the Evolution of America's Cold War Alliances* (New York: Palgrave, 2012), 97–98.

36. Campbell interview; Nye interview. On the strategic review prepared by the Higuchi Commission, see Green, *By More Than Providence*, 467–468.

37. Richard J. Samuels, *Securing Japan: Tokyo's Grand Strategy and the Future of East Asia* (Ithaca, NY: Cornell University Press, 2007), 66–68.

38. Green, *By More Than Providence*, 443; Schoff, *Uncommon Alliance*, 6.

39. Scott A. Snyder, *South Korea at the Crossroads* (New York: Columbia University Press, 2018), 11, 13.

40. Yoichi Funabashi, *Alliance Adrift* (New York: Council on Foreign Relations, 1999), 68, 173; James J. Przystup, "U.S.–Japan Relations: Progress toward a Mature Partnership," Institute for National Strategic Studies, 2005, 14; Katharine Moon, *Sex among Allies: Military Prostitution in U.S.-ROK Relations* (New York: Columbia University Press, 1997), 57–83.

41. Snyder, *South Korea at the Crossroads*, 14, 74; "Korea: U.S.-South Korean Relations."

42. Samuels, *Securing Japan*, 92; Thalakada, *Unipolarity*, 68–69; Green, *By More Than Providence*, 467–68; Nye interview; Funabashi, *Alliance Adrift*, 288.

43. Green, *By More Than Providence*, 465, 468; Funabashi, *Alliance Adrift*, 249, 293; Nye interview.

44. Campbell interview; Green interview; anonymous former Pentagon official, interview with author, February 5, 2019, Washington, DC.

45. "Withdrawal of US Forces from Thailand: Ways to Improve Future Withdrawal Operations," General Accounting Office Report to Congress, June 3, 1977.

46. Amy Searight, "Southeast Asian Alliances and Partnerships," in *Ironclad: Forging a New Future for America's Alliances*, ed. Michael J. Green (Washington, DC: Center for Strategic and International Studies, 2019); Andrew Yeo, *Activists, Alliances and Anti-U.S. Base Protests* (Cambridge: Cambridge University Press: 2011), 44–49; Renato de Castro, "Adjusting to the Post-U.S. Bases Era: The Ordeal of the Philippine Military's Modernization Program," *Armed Forces and Society* 26, no. 1 (1999): 119–137.

47. James Curran, *Fighting with America* (Sydney: Penguin Random House, 2016), 50, 54–55.

48. Thalakada, *Unipolarity*, 68.

49. Funabashi, *Alliance Adrift*, 161; Green, *By More Than Providence*, 457.

50. On the pitfalls of this approach, see Kurt Campbell and Richard Weitz, "The Limits of U.S.-China Military Cooperation: Lessons from 1995–1999," *Washington Quarterly* 29, no. 1 (2005): 169–186.

51. Funabashi, *Alliance Adrift*, 161, 354–355; Green interview.

52. Funabashi, *Alliance Adrift*, 368.

53. Campbell interview; Green interview.

54. Rushabh Doshi, "The Long Game: Chinese Grand Strategy after the Cold War" (Ph.D. diss., Harvard University, 2019).

55. Campbell interview; Nye interview.

56. Michael O'Hanlon, "Why China Cannot Conquer Taiwan," *International Security* 25, no. 2 (2000): 51–86; Joseph S. Nye, "As China Rises, Must Others Bow?" *Economist*, June 25, 1998.

57. Ivo H. Daalder and Michael E. O'Hanlon, *Winning Ugly: NATO's War to Save Kosovo* (Washington, DC: Brookings Institution, 2000) 17, 69.

58. Derek Chollet and James Goldgeier, *America between the Wars: From 11/9 to 9/11* (New York: Public Affairs, 2008), 215, 222; Daalder and O'Hanlon, *Winning Ugly*, 9.

59. Daalder and O'Hanlon, *Winning Ugly*, 36–37.

60. Daalder and O'Hanlon, *Winning Ugly*, 30.

61. Chollet and Goldgeier, *America between the Wars*, 224.

62. "The Kosovo Report," Independent International Commission on Kosovo, October 23, 2000, https://reliefweb.int/report/albania/kosovo-report.

63. Daniel L. Byman, Matthew C. Waxman, and Jeremy Shapiro, "The Future of U.S. Coercive Air Power," in *Strategic Appraisal: United States Air and Space Power in the 21st Century*, ed. Zalmay Khalilzad and Jeremy Shapiro (Santa Monica, CA: RAND Corporation, 2002), 65; Daalder and O'Hanlon, *Winning Ugly*, 74.

64. Daalder and O'Hanlon, *Winning Ugly*, 26, 74, 83.

65. Byman, Waxman, and Shapiro, "Future of U.S. Coercive Air Power," 67; Judith Matloff, "Russia's Tough Talk Unsettles West," *Christian Science Monitor*, April 12, 1999; Daalder and O'Hanlon, *Winning Ugly*, 140; Chollet and Goldgeier, *America between the Wars*, 231.

66. Vicktor Chernomyrdin, "Bombs Rule Out Talk of Peace," *Washington Post*, May 27, 1999.

67. Byman, Waxman, and Shapiro, "Future of U.S. Coercive Air Power," 67; Daniel Byman and Matthew Waxman, *The Dynamics of Coercion: American Foreign Policy and the Limits of Military Might* (Cambridge: Cambridge University Press, 2002), 36; Chollet and Goldgeier, *America between the Wars*, 232; Daalder and O'Hanlon, *Winning Ugly*, 140–141, 173; Celeste Bohlen, "Accord Is Reached on Integrating Russian Troops to Kosovo Force," *New York Times*, June 19, 1999.

68. Andrew Gilligan, "Russia, Not Bombs, Brought an End to the War, Says Jackson," *London Sunday Telegraph*, August 1, 1999.

69. Schoff, *Uncommon Alliance*, 41; Funabashi, *Alliance Adrift*, 275; Thalakada, *Unipolarity*, 67, 81–82; Samuels, *Securing Japan*, 94, 172.

70. NATO, "NATO's Assistance to Iraq," September 1, 2015, https://www.nato.int/cps/en/natohq/topics_51978.htm; John Springford, "'Old' and 'New' Europe United: Public Attitudes towards the Iraq War and US Foreign Policy," Centre for European Reform, December 11, 2003, https://www.cer.eu/publications/archive/briefing-note

/2003/old-and-new-europeans-united-public-attitudes-towards-iraq-w; Przystup, "U.S.–Japan Relations," 1–15; Katsumi Ishizuka, "Japan's Policy towards the War on Terror in Afghanistan," Working Paper 3, Afrasian Research Centre, Ryukoku University, 2012, https://afrasia.ryukoku.ac.jp/english/publication/upfile/WP003.pdf; Thalakada, *Unipolarity*, 97; Balbina Hwang, "South Korean Troops to Iraq: A Boost for U.S.-ROK Relations," Heritage Foundation, February 13, 2004, https://www .heritage.org/asia/report/south-korean-troops-iraq-boost-us-rok-relations; "South Korea to Send Troops to Afghanistan," Reuters, October 30, 2009; "Australia in Iraq: A Brief History of Australia's Involvement from 1991–2014," ABC News, September 15, 2014, http://www.abc.net.au/news/2014-09-15/mark-corcoran27s-iraq-backgrounder /5743020.

71. Searight, "Southeast Asian Alliances and Partnerships."

72. Green interview.

73. John J. Mearsheimer, "Why the Ukraine Crisis Is the West's Fault," *Foreign Affairs*, September / October 2014; Thom Shanker and Mark Landler, "Putin Says U.S. Is Undermining Global Stability," *New York Times*, February 11, 2007.

74. Adam P. Liff, "China and the U.S. Alliance System," *China Quarterly* 233 (2018): 137–165.

75. Marten, "Reconsidering NATO Expansion," 149–152, 160; Andrew C. Kuchins and Igor A. Zevelev, "Russian Foreign Policy: Continuity in Change," *Washington Quarterly* 35, no. 1 (2012): 147–161, 150–154; Steinberg interview.

76. Asmus, *Opening NATO's Door*, 285; Trenin, *Post-Imperium*, 106; Marten, "Reconsidering NATO Expansion," 149–152, 160.

77. Trenin, *Post-Imperium*, 33–34.

78. Goldgeier, *Not Whether but When*, 116.

79. Chernomyrdin, "Bombs Rule Out Talk of Peace."

80. Michael Mandelbaum, "A Perfect Failure: NATO's War against Yugoslavia," *Foreign Affairs*, September / October 1999.

81. Stephen Blank, "NATO Enlargement and the Baltic States," *World Affairs* 160, no. 3 (1998): 115–125; Ronald D. Asmus and Robert C. Nurick, "NATO Enlargement and the Baltic States," *Survival* 38, no. 2 (1996): 121–142; Kramer, "NATO, the Baltic States, and Russia," 731–756.

5. The Dawn of Modern Competition

1. Dmitri V. Trenin, *Post-Imperium: A Eurasian Story* (Washington, DC: Carnegie Endowment for International Peace, 2011).

2. Andrew C. Kuchins and Igor A. Zevelev, "Russian Foreign Policy: Continuity in Change," *Washington Quarterly* 35, no. 1 (2012): 147–161; Brian D. Taylor, *The Code of Putinism* (Oxford: Oxford University Press, 2018), 39.

3. Olga Malinova, "Obsession with Status and *Ressentiment:* Historical Backgrounds of the Russian Discursive Identity Construction," *Communist and Post-Communist Studies* 47, no. 3–4 (2014): 291–303, 303; Kuchins and Zevelev, "Russian Foreign Policy," 152.

4. Trenin, *Post-Imperium,* introduction, 33; Olga Oliker, Keith Crane, Lowell H. Schwartz, and Catherine Yusupov, *Russian Foreign Policy: Sources and Implications* (Santa Monica, CA: RAND, 2009), 93.

5. Dmitry Gorenburg, "Circumstances Have Changed since 1991, but Russia's Core Foreign Policy Goals Have Not," PONARS Eurasia Policy Memo No. 560, George Washington University, January 2019, 1, http://www.ponarseurasia.org/sites /default/files/policy-memos-pdf/Pepm560_Gorenburg_Jan2019_0.pdf; Andrew Radin and Clint Reach, *Russian Views of the International Order* (Santa Monica, CA: RAND, 2015), 13.

6. Trenin, *Post-Imperium,* 107; Radin and Reach, *Russian Views,* 11, 13.

7. Trenin, *Post-Imperium,* 66, 131–132.

8. Taylor, *Code of Putinism,* 2.

9. In retrospect, analysts believe the Kosovo intervention may have marked a downturn in US-Russia relations. Nadezhda K. Arbatova and Alexander A. Dynkin, "World Order after Ukraine," *Survival* 58, no. 1 (2016): 71–90, 84.

10. Kuchins and Zevelev, "Russian Foreign Policy," 156; Taylor, *Code of Putinism,* 12; Radin and Reach, *Russian Views,* 10; Anthony Cordesman, "Russia and the 'Color Revolution': A Russian Military View of a World Destabilized by the US and the West," Center for Strategic and International Studies, May 28, 2014, https://www.csis.org/analysis/russia-and-"color-revolution"; Trenin, *Post-Imperium,* 28–30.

11. Taylor, *Code of Putinism,* 177; Russian Federation, National Security Strategy, December 2015, available in English translation at http://www.ieee.es/Galerias /fichero/OtrasPublicaciones/Internacional/2016/Russian-National-Security -Strategy-31Dec2015.pdf.

12. "US-Russia Relations: 'Reset' Fact Sheet," Obama White House press release, June 24, 2010, https://obamawhitehouse.archives.gov/realitycheck/the-press-office /us-russia-relations-reset-fact-sheet.

13. Kuchins and Zevelev, "Russian Foreign Policy," 152–155.

14. Celeste Wallander, "Russian Transimperialism and Its Implications," *Washington Quarterly* 30, no. 2 (2007): 107–122.

15. Taylor, *Code of Putinism,* 182; Robert Coalson, "Top General Lays Bare Putin's Plan for Ukraine," *Huffington Post,* November 2, 2014, https://www.huffpost .com/entry/valery-gerasimov-putin-ukraine_b_5748480; Radin and Reach, *Russian Views,* 69.

16. Dmitri V. Trenin, "Russia Leaves the West," *Foreign Affairs*, July / August 2006; Trenin, *Post-Imperium*, 80; Taylor, *Code of Putinism*, 5, 20; Wallander, "Russian Transimperialism," 117.

17. Vladimir Putin, Speech to the 70th UN General Assembly, September 28, 2015, http://en.kremlin.ru/events/president/news/50385; Vladimir Putin, "Speech and the Following Discussion at the Munich Conference on Security Policy," February 10, 2007, http://en.kremlin.ru/events/president/transcripts/24034; Steve LeVine, "Why Xi and Putin Think the West Is in Free Fall," *Axios*, June 10, 2018, https://www.axios.com/xi-jinping-vladimir-putin-new-world-order-west-g7 -summit-4119f4f5-f531-49c2-a382-23574fb739b3.html.

18. Trenin, *Post-Imperium*, 176, 183; Taylor, *Code of Putinism*, 169–170. The World Bank estimates oil prices will hover around $70 per barrel by 2030. World Bank, *Commodity Markets Outlook*, April 2018.

19. Wallander, "Russian Transimperialism," 115–116; Taylor, *Code of Putinism*, 5, 76–77, 105.

20. Trenin, *Post-Imperium*, 75.

21. "Russian Military Spending," Federation of American Scientists, n.d., https://fas.org/nuke/guide/russia/agency/mo-budget.htm.

22. Richard Connolly and Matthieu Boulègue, "Russia's New State Armament Programme: Implications for the Russian Armed Forces and Military Capabilities to 2027," Chatham House, May 2018, 15, https://www.chathamhouse.org/sites/default /files/publications/research/2018-05-10-russia-state-armament-programme -connolly-boulegue-final.pdf.

23. Taylor, *Code of Putinism*, 142, 193.

24. Trenin, *Post-Imperium*, 179.

25. David A. Shlapak and Michael W. Johnson, *Reinforcing Deterrence on NATO's Eastern Flank: Wargaming the Defense of the Baltics* (Santa Monica, CA: RAND, 2016). On the precise scenarios and escalation risks entailed in a Baltic conflict, see Ulrich Kuhn, *Preventing Escalation in the Baltics: A NATO Playbook* (Washington, DC: Carnegie Endowment for International Peace, 2018). On Enhanced Forward Presence, see "NATO's Enhanced Forward Presence," Factsheet, North Atlantic Treaty Organization, December 2018, https://www.nato.int/nato _static_fl2014/assets/pdf/pdf_2018_12/20181205_1812-factsheet_efp_en.pdf.

26. Joshua Shifrinson, "Time to Consolidate NATO?" *Washington Quarterly* 40, no. 1 (2017): 109–123; Shlapak and Johnson, "Reinforcing Deterrence," 10; Michael Birnbaum, "If They Needed to Fend Off War with Russia, US Military Leaders Worry They May Not Get There in Time," *Washington Post*, June 24, 2018.

27. Trenin, *Post-Imperium*, 100.

28. Radin and Reach, *Russian Views*, 28.

29. Aaron L. Friedberg, "Globalisation and Chinese Grand Strategy," *Survival* 60, no. 1 (2018): 7–40, 7; Aaron L. Friedberg, "Competing with China," *Survival* 60, no. 3 (2018): 7–64, 19.

30. Robert Zoellick, "Wither China? From Membership to Responsibility," Remarks to the National Committee on U.S.-China Relations, September 21, 2005.

31. Friedberg, "Competing with China," 11, 12; Joseph S. Nye, interview with author, Cambridge, MA, October 4, 2018; Ely Ratner and Kurt Campbell, "The China Reckoning," *Foreign Affairs*, April / May 2018; James Mann, *The China Fantasy: How Our Leaders Explain Away Chinese Repression* (New York: Viking, 2007); Elizabeth Economy, "Is American Policy toward China Due for a Reckoning?" *China File*, February 15, 2018, http://www.chinafile.com/conversation/american-policy-toward -china-due-reckoning.

32. Andrew J. Nathan, "The Chinese World Order," *New York Review of Books*, October 12, 2017; Elizabeth C. Economy, *The Third Revolution: Xi Jinping and the New Chinese State* (Oxford: Oxford University Press, 2018), 2–32.

33. Andrew J. Nathan, "Authoritarian Resilience," *Journal of Democracy* 14, no. 1 (2003): 6–17.

34. Friedberg, "Competing with China," 16.

35. Friedberg, "Competing with China," 20.

36. Andrew Nathan and Andrew Scobell, "How China Sees America: The Sum of Beijing's Fears," *Foreign Affairs*, September / October 2012.

37. "Counter-Coercion Series: The Scarborough Shoal Standoff," Asia Maritime Transparency Initiative, Center for Strategic and International Studies, May 22, 2017, https://amti.csis.org/counter-co-scarborough-standoff.

38. Economy, *The Third Revolution;* Zheng Wang, "The Chinese Dream: Concept and Context," *Journal of Chinese Politics* 19, no. 1 (2014): 1–13; Christopher K. Johnson, *Decoding China's Emerging 'Great Power' Strategy in Asia* (Washington, DC: Center for Strategic and International Studies, 2014); Rush Doshi, "Xi Jinping Just Made It Clear Where China's Foreign Policy Is Headed," *Washington Post*, October 25, 2017.

39. Nadège Rolland, "Reports of Belt and Road's Death Are Greatly Exaggerated," *Foreign Affairs*, January 29, 2019; Nathan and Scobell, "How China Sees America"; Economy, *Third Revolution*, 65. The Chinese government reports 125 participating countries but has not released a list. The World Bank has substantiated the participation of seventy-one countries. Estimates of Chinese investment can be as high as $8 trillion, but the World Bank puts the number at $575 billion. "Belt and Road

Economics: Opportunities and Risks of Transport Corridors," World Bank, June 18, 2019, https://www.worldbank.org/en/topic/regional-integration/publication/belt-and-road-economics-opportunities-and-risks-of-transport-corridors.

40. Nadège Rolland, *China's Eurasian Century? Political and Strategic Implications of the Belt and Road Initiative* (Washington, DC: National Bureau of Asian Research, 2017); Friedberg, "Globalisation and Chinese Grand Strategy," 26.

41. Andrew J. Nathan, "China's Rise and International Regimes: Does China Seek to Overthrow Global Norms?" in *China in the Era of Xi Jinping: Domestic and Foreign Policy Challenges,* ed. Robert S. Ross and Jo Inge Bekkevold (Washington, DC: Georgetown University Press, 2016), 171; Alastair Ian Johnston, *Social States: China in International Institutions* (Princeton: Princeton University Press, 2007).

42. Elizabeth C. Economy, "Why China Is No Climate Leader," *Politico,* June 12, 2017; Christina Nuñez, "China Poised for Leadership on Climate Change after U.S. Reversal," *National Geographic,* March 28, 2017.

43. Michael J. Mazarr, Timothy R. Heath, and Astrid Stuth Cevallos, *China and the International Order* (Santa Monica, CA: RAND, 2018), 29–31.

44. Evan Feigenbaum, "Reluctant Stakeholder: Why China's Highly Strategic Brand of Revisionism Is More Challenging than Washington Thinks," Carnegie Endowment for International Peace, April 27, 2018, https://carnegieendowment.org/2018/04/27/reluctant-stakeholder-why-china-s-highly-strategic-brand-of-revisionism-is-more-challenging-than-washington-thinks-pub-76213.

45. Nathan, "Chinese World Order"; Toshi Yoshihara and James Holmes, *Red Star over the Pacific: China's Rise and Challenges to U.S. Maritime Strategy* (Annapolis: Naval Institute Press, 2011); Oriana Skyler Mastro, "Why Chinese Assertiveness Is Here to Stay," *Washington Quarterly* 37, no. 4 (2014): 151–170; Andrew Erickson, ed., *China's Naval Shipbuilding: An Ambitious and Uncertain Course* (Annapolis: Naval Institute Press, 2017).

46. Thomas G. Mahnken, "Weapons: The Growth and Spread of the Precision-Strike Regime," *Daedalus* 140, no. 3 (Summer 2011): 45.

47. Aaron Friedberg, *Beyond Air-Sea Battle: The Debate over US Military Strategy in Asia* (London: International Institute for Strategic Studies, 2014); Eric Heginbotham, Michael Nixon, Forrest E. Morgan, et al., *The US-China Military Scorecard* (Santa Monica, CA: RAND, 2015).

48. Evan B. Montgomery, "Contested Primacy in the Western Pacific: China's Rise and the Future of US Power Projection," *International Security* 38, no. 4 (2014): 115–149.

49. Zack Cooper and Darren Lim, "Reassessing Hedging: The Logic of Alignment in East Asia," *Security Studies* 24, no. 5 (2015): 696–727; Adam P. Liff, "China and the US Alliance System," *China Quarterly* 233 (2018): 137–168; Nathan and Scobell, "How China Sees America"; Mazarr et al., *China and the International Order,* 29.

50. Ben Blanchard, "With One Eye on Washington, China Plots Its Own 'Asia Pivot,'" Reuters, July 3, 2014; Friedberg, "Competing with China," 31.

51. As quoted in Linda Robinson, Todd C. Helmus, Raphael S. Cohen, et al., *Modern Political Warfare: Current Practices and Possible Responses* (Santa Monica, CA: RAND, 2018), xiii.

52. Hal Brands, "Paradoxes of the Gray Zones," Foreign Policy Research Institute, February 5, 2016, https://www.fpri.org/article/2016/02/paradoxes-gray-zone.

53. Tom G. Mahnken, Ross Babbage, and Toshi Yoshihara, "Countering Comprehensive Coercion: Competitive Strategies against Authoritarian Political Warfare," Center for Strategic and Budgetary Assessments, May 30, 2018, 7, https://csbaonline.org/research/publications/countering-comprehensive-coercion-competitive-strategies-against-authoritar.

54. Tanisha M. Fazal, "Why States No Longer Declare War," *Security Studies* 21, no. 4 (2012): 557–593.

55. Peter Mattis, "Contrasting China's and Russia's Influence Operations," *War on the Rocks,* January 16, 2018, https://warontherocks.com/2018/01/contrasting-chinas-russias-influence-operations.

56. Valery Gerasimov, "The Value of Science in Prediction," Military-Industrial Kurier, February 27, 2013, https://www.ies.be/files/Gerasimov%20HW%20ENG.pdf; Robinson et al., *Modern Political Warfare,* 51–53.

57. Sam Jones, "Ukraine: Russia's New Art of War," *Financial Times,* August 28, 2014.

58. Roy Allison, "Russia's 'Deniable' Intervention in Ukraine: How and Why Russia Broke the Rules," *International Affairs* 90, no. 6 (2014): 1255–1297; Mahnken, Babbage, and Yoshihara, "Countering Comprehensive Coercion," 17; Clint Watts, *Messing with the Enemy: Surviving in a Social Media World of Hackers, Terrorists, Russians, and Fake News* (New York: Harper Collins, 2018); James N. Miller and Richard Fontaine, "Cyber and Space Weapons Are Making Nuclear Deterrence Trickier," Center for a New American Security, November 26, 2017, https://www.cnas.org/publications/commentary/cyber-and-space-weapons-are-making-nuclear-deterrence-trickier.

59. Robinson et al., *Modern Political Warfare,* 85–100; Mahnken, Babbage, and Yoshihara, "Countering Comprehensive Coercion," 25; Kuhn, *Preventing Escalation in the Baltics.*

60. David M. Edelstein, *Over the Horizon: Time, Uncertainty, and the Rise of Great Powers* (Ithaca, NY: Cornell University Press, 2017).

61. David Shambaugh, ed., *The China Reader: Rising Power* (Oxford: Oxford University Press, 2016), 376; Christopher Yung and Patrick McNulty, "An Empirical Analysis of Claimant Tactics in the South China Sea," *Strategic Forum,* National Defense University, August 2015, https://inss.ndu.edu/Portals/68/Documents

/stratforum/SF-289.pdf; Alastair Ian Johnson, "How New and Assertive Is China's New Assertiveness?" *International Security* 37, no. 4 (2013): 7–48; M. Taylor Fravel, "Regime Insecurity and International Cooperation: Explaining China's Compromises in Territorial Disputes," *International Security* 30, no. 2 (2005): 46–83.

62. Christopher K. Johnson, *Decoding China's;* Robert D. Blackwill and Kurt M. Campbell, *Xi Jinping on the Global Stage: Chinese Foreign Policy under a Powerful but Exposed Leader* (New York: Council on Foreign Relations, 2016); Adam Liff and G. John Ikenberry, "Racing towards Tragedy? China's Rise, Military Competition in the Asia-Pacific, and the Security Dilemma," *International Security* 39, no. 2 (2014): 52–91; Ronald O'Rourke, "Coast Guard Cutter Procurement: Background and Issues for Congress," Congressional Research Service.

63. Michael Green, Kathleen Hicks, Zack Cooper, John Schaus, and Jake Douglas, *Countering Coercion in Maritime Asia* (Washington, DC: Center for Strategic and International Studies, 2017), 12–13; James Kraska and Brian Wilson, "China Wages Maritime 'Lawfare,'" *Foreign Policy,* March 12, 2009; Peter Harrell, Elizabeth Rosenberg, and Edoardo Saravalle, "China's Use of Coercive Economic Measures," Center for a New American Security, June 2018, https://www.cnas.org/publications/reports/chinas-use-of-coercive-economic-measures; Mahnken, Babbage, and Yoshihara, "Countering Comprehensive Coercion," 40; Joe Uchill, "China's 'Influence' vs. 'Interference' in the Midterms," *Axios,* October 11, 2018, https://www.axios.com/2018-midterm-elections-china-interference-john-brennan-8538f44b-ee2e-40dc-b731-2c4958b460ee.html; Rush Doshi and Robert D. Williams, "Is China Interfering in American Politics?" Brookings Institution, October 2, 2018, https://www.brookings.edu/blog/order-from-chaos/2018/10/02/is-china-interfering-in-american-politics; Amy Remeikis, "Sam Dastyari Quits as Labor Senator over China Connections," *Guardian,* December 11, 2017.

64. LeVine, "Why Xi and Putin Think the West Is in Free Fall."

65. Dimitri Trenin, "Common Interests Drive Sino-Russian Ties," *China Daily,* September 12, 2018; Alexander Gabuev, "Why Russia and China Are Strengthening Security Ties," *Foreign Affairs,* September 24, 2018; Alexander Gabuev, "Russia and China's Dangerous Entente," *Wall Street Journal,* October 4, 2017.

6. The Shields Wear from Within

1. See, for example, Donald J. Trump, "Remarks at the KI Convention Center in Green Bay, Wisconsin," August 5, 2016, available via UCSB American Presidency Project, https://www.presidency.ucsb.edu/documents/remarks-the-ki-convention-center-green-bay-wisconsin.

2. James Goldgeier and Elizabeth N. Saunders, "The Unconstrained Presidency," *Foreign Affairs,* September / October 2018; Mira Rapp-Hooper and Matthew C. Waxman, "Presidential Alliance Powers," *Washington Quarterly* 42, no. 2 (2019): 67–83.

3. Ilan Ben Meier, "That Time Trump Spent Nearly $100,000 on an Ad Criticizing U.S. Foreign Policy in 1987," *Buzzfeed,* July 10, 2015, https://www.buzzfeednews.com/article/ilanbenmeir/that-time-trump-spent-nearly-100000-on-an-ad-criticizing-us; Glenn Plaskin, "The 1990 Playboy Interview with Donald Trump," *Playboy,* March 1, 1990, https://www.playboy.com/read/playboy-interview-donald-trump-1990.

4. Michael Flynn, Michael Allen, and Carla Martinez Maichan, "Trump Wants South Korea and Japan to Pay More for Defense," *Washington Post,* November 26, 2019.

5. Mark Landler, "Trump Orders Pentagon to Consider Reducing U.S. Forces in South Korea," *New York Times,* May 3, 2018; Paula Hancocks, "Japan and South Korea Hit Back at Trump's Nuclear Comments," March 31, 2016, CNN, https://www.cnn.com/2016/03/31/politics/trump-view-from-south-korea-japan.

6. Tara Copp, "President Trump Has Ordered the Pentagon to Cancel Military Exercises with South Korea—What Happens Next?" *Military Times,* June 12, 2018, https://www.militarytimes.com/news/your-military/2018/06/12/pentagon-assessing-trump-directive-to-cancel-korea-military-exercises.

7. Mark S. Sheetz, "Exit Strategies: American Grand Designs for Postwar European Security," *Security Studies* 8, no. 4 (1999): 1–43; Richard Nixon, "Informal Remarks at Guam with Newsmen," July 25, 1969, available via UCSB American Presidency Project, https://www.presidency.ucsb.edu/documents/informal-remarks-guam-with-newsmen; "Trump Is Pushing NATO Allies to Spend More on Defense. But So Did Obama and Bush," CNBC, July 11, 2018, https://www.cnbc.com/2018/07/11/obama-and-bush-also-pressed-nato-allies-to-spend-more-on-defense.html; Michael Birnbaum and Philip Rucker, "At NATO, Trump Claims Allies Make New Defense Spending Commitments after He Upends Summit," *Washington Post,* July 12, 2018.

8. Josh Rogin, "Trump Still Holds Jimmy Carter's Views on Withdrawing Troops from South Korea," *Washington Post,* June 7, 2018; Choe Sang-Hun, "Allies for 67 Years, U.S. and South Korea Split Over North Korea," *New York Times,* September 4, 2017; Uri Friedman, "Trump versus NATO: It's Not Just about the Money," *Atlantic,* July 12, 2018; Julie Hirschfeld Davis, "Trump Warns NATO Allies to Spend More on Defense, Or Else," *New York Times,* July 2, 2018; Sophie Tatum, "Trump Seems to Question U.S. Commitment to Defending All NATO Allies," CNN, July 18, 2018, https://edition.cnn.com/2018/07/17/politics/trump-nato-fox/index.html.

9. Colin Kahl and Hal Brands, "Trump's Grand Strategic Train Wreck," *Foreign Policy*, January 31, 2017, https://foreignpolicy.com/2017/01/31/trumps-grand-strategic -train-wreck.

10. Alina Polyakova, "Putin Didn't Have to Push the Kremlin's Narrative. Trump Did It for Him," Brookings Institution, July 20, 2018, https://www.brookings.edu /blog/order-from-chaos/2018/07/20/putin-didnt-have-to-push-the-kremlins -narrative-trump-did-it-for-him; "Donald Trump Still Has No Proper Asia Policy," *Economist*, September 13, 2018; "National Security Strategy of the United States of America," The White House, December 2017, https://www.whitehouse.gov/wp -content/uploads/2017/12/NSS-Final-12-18-2017-0905.pdf; "Summary of the National Defense Strategy of the United States of America," Department of Defense, 2018, https://dod.defense.gov/Portals/1/Documents/pubs/2018-National-Defense -Strategy-Summary.pdf.

11. Rapp-Hooper and Waxman, "Presidential Alliance Powers."

12. Glenn H. Snyder, "The Security Dilemma in Alliance Politics," *World Politics* 36, no. 4 (1984): 461–495, 467–468.

13. Jonathan Stearns, "NATO Members Post New Defense Spending Increase," *Bloomberg*, March 15, 2018; Katherine Zeising, "Defence Budget 2018 at a Glance," *Australian Defence Magazine*, May 8, 2018, http://www.australiandefence.com.au /budget-policy/defence-budget-2018-at-a-glance; Crystal Prior and Tom Le, "Looking beyond One Percent: Japan's Security Expenditures," *The Diplomat*, April 3, 2018, https://thediplomat.com/2018/04/looking-beyond-1-percent-japans-security -expenditures; "South Korea Has 7% Increase in Defense Budget for 2018 with $40.5 Billion," *Army Recognition*, January 4, 2018, https://www.armyrecognition.com /january_2018_global_defense_security_army_news_industry/south_korea_increase _of_7_for_defense_budget_2018_with_$40.5_billion.html.

14. David Wemer, "NATO's Stoltenberg Credits Trump as Allies Increase Defense Spending," Atlantic Council, July 11, 2018, http://www.atlanticcouncil.org /blogs/new-atlanticist/stoltenberg-nato-engages.

15. Birnbaum and Rucker, "At NATO, Trump Claims"; Nick Wadhams and Jennifer Jacobs, "Trump Seeks Huge Premium from Allies for Hosting US Troops," *Bloomberg News*, March 8, 2019.

16. Arne Delfs and Gregory Viscusi, "Merkel Says Europe Can't Count on U.S. Military Umbrella Anymore," *Bloomberg*, May 1, 2018; "Emmanuel Macron Warns Europe: NATO Is Becoming Brain-Dead," *Economist*, November 7, 2019; Robert E. Kelly, "It's All Up to Moon Now," Lowy Institute, June 19, 2018, https://www .lowyinstitute.org/the-interpreter/its-all-moon-now.

17. Zack Cooper, "Pacific Power: America's Asian Alliances beyond Burden-Sharing," *War on the Rocks*, December 14, 2016, https://warontherocks.com/2016 /12/pacific-power-americas-asian-alliances-beyond-burden-sharing.

18. Joshua Shifrinson, "Sound and Fury, Signifying Something? NATO and the Trump Administration's Second Year," H-Diplo / International Security Studies Forum, July 12, 2018.

19. Robert Kagan, "Trump's America Does Not Care," *Washington Post,* June 14, 2018; Rebecca Friedman Lissner and Mira Rapp-Hooper, "The Day after Trump: American Strategy for a New International Order," *Washington Quarterly* 41, no. 1 (2018): 7–25.

20. G. John Ikenberry, "The Rise of China and the Future of the West," *Foreign Affairs,* January / February 2008.

21. Dina Smeltz, Ivo H. Daalder, Karl Friedhoff, and Craig Kafura, "What Americans Think about America First: Results of the 2017 Chicago Council Survey of American Public Opinion and U.S. Foreign Policy," Chicago Council on Global Affairs, October 2, 2017; Dina Smeltz, Ivo H. Daalder, Karl Friedhoff, Craig Kafura, and Brendan Helm, "Rejecting Retreat: Americans Support US Engagement in Global Affairs," Chicago Council on Global Affairs, September 6, 2019, https://www.thechicagocouncil.org/publication/rejecting-retreat.

22. Jake Sullivan, "The World after Trump: How the System Can Endure," *Foreign Affairs,* March / April 2018; Robert Kagan, *The Jungle Grows Back: America and Our Imperiled World Order* (New York: Knopf, 2018).

23. For an extended version of this argument see Rebecca R. Lissner and Mira Rapp-Hooper, *An Open World: How America Can Win the Contest for 21st Century Order* (New Haven, CT: Yale University Press, 2020).

24. Kenneth Schultz, "The Perils of Polarization for U.S. Foreign Policy," *Washington Quarterly* 40, no. 4 (2018): 7–28; Tom Nichols, *The Death of Expertise: The Campaign against Established Knowledge and Why It Matters* (Oxford: Oxford University Press, 2017).

25. John Voorheis, Nolan McCarty, and Boris Shor, "Unequal Incomes, Ideology and Gridlock: How Rising Inequality Increases Political Polarization," unpublished manuscript, August 21, 2015, http://ssrn.com/abstract=2649215; Nat O'Connor, "Three Connections between Rising Economic Inequality and the Rise of Populism," *Irish Studies in International Affairs* 28 (2017): 29–43.

26. Robert J. Blendon, Logan S. Casey, and John M. Benson, "Public Opinion and Trump's Jobs and Trade Policies," *Challenge* 60, no. 3 (2017): 228–244.

27. Pew Global Attitudes Survey, Spring 2017, https://www.pewresearch.org/global/dataset/spring-2017-survey-data; Moira Fagan, "NATO Seen Favorably in Almost Half of Member Countries, but Most Americans Say It Does Too Little," Pew Global Attitudes, July 9, 2018, https://www.pewresearch.org/fact-tank/2018/07/09/nato-is-seen-favorably-in-many-member-countries-but-almost-half-of-americans-say-it-does-too-little.

28. Schultz, "Perils of Polarization."

29. Richard Wike, Bruce Stokes, Jacob Poushter, and Janell Fetterolf, "U.S. Image Suffers as Publics around the World Question Trump's Leadership," Pew Research Center, June 26, 2017, http://www.pewglobal.org/2017/06/26/u-s-image-suffers-as-publics-around-world-question-trumps-leadership; Bruce Stokes, "New Crisis of Confidence in US Leadership," Australian Institute of International Affairs, July 19, 2017, https://www.internationalaffairs.org.au/australianoutlook/ausrtralia-crisis-of-confidence-us-leadership.

30. "The Long View: How Will the Global Economic Order Change by 2050?" PricewaterhouseCoopers, February 2017, https://www.pwc.com/gx/en/world-2050/assets/pwc-world-in-2050-summary-report-feb-2017.pdf; Howard Shatz, *U.S. International Economic Strategy in a Turbulent World* (Santa Monica, CA: RAND, 2016); Jonathan Caverly, "America's Arms Sales Policy: Security Abroad, Not Jobs at Home," *War on the Rocks*, April 6, 2018, https://warontherocks.com/2018/04/americas-arms-sales-policy-security-abroad-not-jobs-at-home.

31. See GDP data provided by the Organisation for Economic Cooperation and Development (OECD), https://data.oecd.org/gdp/gross-domestic-product-gdp.htm, accessed December 9, 2019; "World Trade Statistical Review 2017," World Trade Organization, 2017, https://www.wto.org/english/res_e/statis_e/wts2017_e/wts2017_e.pdf; Malcom Scott and Cedric Sam, "Here's How Fast China's Economy Is Catching up to the US," *Bloomberg*, May 12, 2016.

32. Kevin Zraik, "China Will Feel One-Child Policy's Effects for Decades, Experts Say," *New York Times*, October 30, 2015; David Shambaugh, "The Coming Chinese Crackup," *Wall Street Journal*, March 6, 2015; Michael Auslin, *The End of the Asian Century: War, Stagnation, and Risks to the World's Most Dynamic Region* (New Haven, CT: Yale University Press, 2017); Duncan Clark, "China Is Shaping the Future of Global Tech," *Financial Times*, January 12, 2018.

33. Eric Heginbotham, Michael Nixon, Forrest E. Morgan, et al., *The US-China Military Scorecard* (Santa Monica, CA: RAND, 2015).

34. Kenneth Rapoza, "Russia Tries Rebranding Itself as a Digital Economy," *Forbes,* June 11, 2018; see OECD GDP data.

35. World Bank Data, Population Growth (annual %), https://databank.worldbank.org/home.aspx; OECD, Gross Domestic Product Data, https://data.oecd.org/gdp/gross-domestic-product-gdp.htm; Choi He-suk, "South Korea 2030—A New Society with New Challenges," *Korea Herald,* August 16, 2017; "Population Estimates and Projections," Infrastructure Australia, April 2015, https://www.infrastructureaustralia.gov.au/sites/default/files/2019-07/Background-paper-on-demographic-projections.pdf; "The 2018 Ageing Report," European Economy Institutional Paper 065, European Commission, November 2017, https://ec.europa.eu/info/sites/info/files/economy-finance/ip065_en.pdf.

36. Hal Brands, "Dealing with Allies in Decline: Alliance Management and US Strategy in an Era of Global Power Shifts," Center for Strategic and Budgetary Assessments, 2017, 14; Charles Krauthammer, "The Unipolar Moment," *Foreign Affairs*, Winter 1991; "GDP Long-term Forecast," OECD, https://data.oecd.org/gdp/gdp-long-term-forecast.htm.

37. Military Expenditures Database, Stockholm International Peace Research Institute, 2018, https://www.sipri.org/databases/milex; Erik Brattberg and Jamie Fly, "Two Cheers for European Defense Cooperation," *Foreign Policy*, March 9, 2018; David A. Shlapak and Michael W. Johnson, "Reinforcing Deterrence on NATO's Eastern Flank: Wargaming the Defense of the Baltics," RR-1253-A, RAND research reports, 2016, https://www.rand.org/pubs/research_reports/RR1253.html; Prior and Le, "Looking beyond One Percent"; Brands, "Dealing with Allies in Decline."

38. PricewaterhouseCoopers, "Long View"; M. Mas, J. Fernández de Guevara, J. C. Robledo, M. Cardona, M. López-Cobo, R. Righe, and S. Samoili, "The 2018 PREDICT Key Facts Report: An Analysis of ICT R&D in the EU and Beyond," European Commission Joint Research Center Technical Report, 2018, http://dx.doi.org/10.2760/984658.

39. Curtis Bradley and Jack Goldsmith, "Constitutional Issues Relating to the NATO Support Act," *Lawfare*, January 28, 2019, https://www.lawfareblog.com/constitutional-issues-relating-nato-support-act; Scott R. Anderson, "Saving NATO," *Lawfare*, July 25, 2018, https://www.lawfareblog.com/saving-nato; Ashley Deeks, "Can Congress Constitutionally Restrict the President's Troop Withdrawals?" *Lawfare*, February 6, 2019, https://www.lawfareblog.com/can-congress-constitutionally-restrict-presidents-troop-withdrawals.

40. Rapp-Hooper and Waxman, "Presidential Alliance Powers."

7. Defense and Deterrence for a New Era

1. Aaron L. Friedberg, "Competing with China," *Survival* 60, no. 3 (2018): 7–64, 26; Michael J. Green, *By More Than Providence: Grand Strategy and American Power in the Pacific since 1873* (New York: Columbia University Press, 2017).

2. UN Charter, art. 51.

3. Thomas M. Franck, "Who Killed Article 2(4)? Or: Changing Norms Governing the Use of Force by States," *American Journal of International Law* 64, no. 5 (October 1970): 809–837; Michael J. Glennon, "How International Rules Die," *Georgetown Law Journal* 93, no. 3 (2005): 931–999, 993.

4. Kristen E. Eichensehr, "The Cyber Law of Nations," *Georgetown Law Journal* 103, no. 2 (2015): 317–380, 335–338.

5. Stephen D. Krasner, "Sovereignty: An Institutional Perspective," *Comparative Political Studies* 21, no. 66 (1988): 66–94.

6. See, for example, John Schaus, Michael Matlaga, Kathleen H. Hicks, Heather A. Conley, and Jeff Rathke, "What Works: Countering Gray Zone Coercion," Center for Strategic and International Studies, July 2018, https://www.csis.org/analysis/what-works-countering-gray-zone-coercion; Kathleen H. Hicks, Alice Hunt Friend, et al., "By Other Means: Part I—Campaigning in the Gray Zone," Center for Strategic and International Studies, July 2019, https://www.csis.org/analysis/other-means-part-i-campaigning-gray-zone.

7. Evan Braden Montgomery, "Managing China's Missile Threat: Future Options to Preserve Forward Defense," Testimony before the U.S.-China Economic and Security Review Commission, April 1, 2015.

8. Charles Edel and Dougal Robinson, "Reading the Tea Leaves in Canberra," *The American Interest*, August 29, 2018, https://www.the-american-interest.com/2018/08/29/reading-the-tea-leaves-in-canberra.

9. David E. Sanger and William J. Broad, "U.S. to Tell Russia It Is Leaving the Landmark INF Treaty," *New York Times*, October 19, 2018; Eric Sayers, "The Intermediate-Range Nuclear Forces Treaty and the Future of the Indo-Pacific Military Balance," *War on the Rocks*, February 13, 2018, https://warontherocks.com/2018/02/asia-inf; Kori Schake, "Trump's Defensible Decision to Withdraw from a Nuclear Treaty," *Atlantic*, October 23, 2018.

10. Peter Mattis, "Contrasting China's and Russia's Influence Operations," *War on the Rocks*, January 16, 2018, https://warontherocks.com/2018/01/contrasting-chinas-russias-influence-operations.

11. Paul Stronski and Nicole Ng, "Cooperation and Competition: Russia and China in Central Asia, the Russian Far East, and the Arctic," Carnegie Endowment for International Peace, February 28, 2018, https://carnegieendowment.org/2018/02/28/cooperation-and-competition-russia-and-china-in-central-asia-russian-far-east-and-arctic-pub-75673.

12. Ralph Jennings, "Japan Is Committing to China's Belt and Road Initiative, but What's in It for Them?" *Forbes*, April 17, 2018; Stephen Dzeidzic, "Why Australia Wants to Build Its Own Belt and Road Scheme with Japan and the US to Rival China's Investment," *ABC News*, July 31, 2018, http://www.abc.net.au/news/2018-07-31/australia-japan-us-alternative-to-china-belt-and-road-initiative/10055060.

13. Aaron Mehta, "Carter Announces $425 Million in Pacific Partnership Funding," *Defense News*, May 30, 2015, https://www.defensenews.com/home/2015/05/30/carter-announces-425m-in-pacific-partnership-funding; Mina Pollman, "US-Japan-Australia Security Cooperation: Beyond Containment," *The Diplomat*, April 21, 2015, https://thediplomat.com/2015/04/us-japan-australia-security-cooperation-beyond-containment.

14. For data on disbursements through the Foreign Military Financing program, see Security Assistance Monitor, https://www.securityassistance.org/data/country /military/Foreign%20Military%20Financing; Eric Sayers, "Assessing America's Indo-Pacific Budget Shortfall," *War on the Rocks*, November 15, 2018, https:// warontherocks.com/2018/11/assessing-americas-indo-pacific-budget-shortfall.

15. Joshua Shifrinson, "Time to Consolidate NATO?" *Washington Quarterly* 40, no. 1 (2017): 109–123.

16. David A. Shlapak and Michael W. Johnson, "Reinforcing Deterrence on NATO's Eastern Flank: Wargaming the Defense of the Baltics," RR-1253-A, RAND research report, 2016, https://www.rand.org/pubs/research_reports/RR1253.html.

17. Jen Judson, "Outgoing US Army Europe Commander Pushes for 'Military Schengen Zone,'" *Defense News*, July 28, 2017, https://www.defensenews.com/smr /european-balance-of-power/2017/07/28/outgoing-us-army-europe-commander -pushes-for-military-schengen-zone.

18. For a similar recommendation see Laura Rosenberger, Jamie Fly, and David Salvo, "Policy Blueprint for Countering Authoritarian Interference in Democracies," German Marshall Fund of the United States, 2018, 22, http://www.gmfus.org/sites /default/files/publications/pdf/Policy-Blueprint.pdf.

19. Heather A. Conley, "Successfully Countering Russian Electoral Interference," Centre for Strategic and International Studies, June 21, 2018, https://www.csis.org /analysis/successfully-countering-russian-electoral-interference.

20. "Putin's Asymmetric Assault on Democracy in Russia and Europe: Implications for U.S. National Security," a minority staff report prepared for the Committee on Foreign Relations, United States Senate, January 10, 2018, 99–133; Elizabeth Dwoskin and Craig Timberg, "Microsoft Says It Has Found a Russian Operation Targeting U.S. Political Institutions," *Washington Post*, August 21, 2018; Linda Robinson, Todd C. Helmus, Raphael S. Cohen, et al., *Modern Political Warfare: Current Practices and Possible Responses* (Santa Monica, CA: RAND, 2018), 295.

21. Philip Ewing, "Mueller on Russian Election Interference: They're Doing It 'As We Sit Here,'" NPR, July 24, 2019; White House, National Security Strategy of the United States of America, December 2017, 35, https://www.whitehouse.gov/wp -content/uploads/2017/12/NSS-Final-12-18-2017-0905.pdf.

22. Rosenberger, Fly, and Salvo, "Policy Blueprint," 21–23.

23. Rachel A. Epstein, "NATO Enlargement and the Spread of Democracy: Evidence and Expectations," *Security Studies* 14, no. 1 (2005): 63–105.

24. Michael Green, Kathleen Hicks, Zack Cooper, John Schaus, and Jake Douglas, *Countering Coercion in Maritime Asia* (Washington, DC: Center for Strategic and International Studies, 2017), 1–45.

25. Michael C. Horowitz, "Artificial Intelligence, International Competition, and the Balance of Power," *Texas National Security Review* 1, no. 3 (May 2018); Michael C. Horowitz, "The Algorithms of August," *Foreign Policy,* September 12, 2018.

26. Michael J. Green, "Japan's Free and Open Indo-Pacific Strategy as Grand Strategy," *Tomodachi* (magazine of the Japanese Ministry of Foreign Affairs), 2018, https://www.japan.go.jp/tomodachi/_userdata/pdf/2018/spring2018/28_29.pdf; Walter Sim, "Japan Vows Quality Infrastructure in Mekong Region in Push for Free and Open Indo-Pacific," *Straits Times,* October 9, 2018, https://www.straitstimes.com/asia/east-asia/japan-vows-quality-infrastructure-in-mekong-region-in-push-for-free-and-open-indo.

27. Andrew Radin, *Hybrid Warfare in the Baltics: Threats and Potential Responses* (Santa Monica, CA: RAND, 2017); Rick Noak, "Everything We Know So Far about Russian Election Meddling in Europe," *Washington Post,* January 10, 2018.

28. Richard Fontaine, Patrick M. Cronin, Mira Rapp-Hooper, and Harry Krejsa, "Networking Asian Security: An Integrated Approach to Order in the Pacific," Center for a New American Security, June 2017, https://www.cnas.org/publications/reports/networking-asian-security; Michael Heazel and Andrew O'Neill, eds., *China's Rise and US-Japan-Australia Relations: Primacy and Leadership in East Asia* (London: Edward Elgar, 2018).

29. Rosa Brooks, *How Everything Became War and the Military Became Everything* (New York: Simon and Schuster, 2016); Jessica Tuchman Matthews, "America's Indefensible Defense Budget," *New York Review of Books,* July 28, 2018; Matthew Armstrong, "No We Do Not Need to Revive the US Information Agency," *War on the Rocks,* November 12, 2015, https://warontherocks.com/2015/11/no-we-do-not-need-to-revive-the-u-s-information-agency; Alex Stamos, "How the U.S. Has Failed to Protect the 2018 Election—And Four Ways to Protect 2020," *Lawfare,* August 22, 2018, https://www.lawfareblog.com/how-us-has-failed-protect-2018-election-and-four-ways-protect-2020; see also *The Budget and Economic Outlook, 2018–2028,* Congressional Budget Office, 2018, Table 2.4, "Discretionary Spending Projected in CBO's Baseline," 58.

30. Robert Kagan, *The Jungle Grows Back: America and Our Imperiled World* (New York: Knopf, 2018); Hal Brands and Eric Edelman, "Avoiding a Strategy of Bluff: The Crisis of American Military Primacy," Center for Strategic and Budgetary Assessments, 2017, http://csbaonline.org/uploads/documents/Strategic_Solvency_FINAL.pdf.

31. Forrest E. Morgan, Karl P. Mueller, Evan S. Medeiros, Kevin L. Pollpeter, and Roger Cliff, *Dangerous Thresholds: Managing Escalation in the 21st Century* (Santa Monica, CA: RAND, 2008); Caitlin Talmadge, "Would China Go Nuclear? Assessing

the Risk of Chinese Nuclear Escalation in a Conventional War with the United States," *International Security* 41, no. 4 (2017): 50–92.

32. Barry Posen's restraint strategy seeks to end or amend most US alliances and reduce its overseas posture to bring the annual defense budget down to 2.5% of GDP. The World Bank estimates 2017 US defense spending as a percentage of GDP at 3.1%. Barry R. Posen, *Restraint: A New Foundation for U.S. Grand Strategy* (Ithaca, NY: Cornell University Press, 2014), 135; World Bank Data, Military Expenditure (% GDP), 1960–2017, https://data.worldbank.org/indicator/ms.mil.xpnd.gd.zs.

33. David Edelstein and Joshua Shifrinson, "It's a Trap! Security Commitments and the Risk of Entrapment," in *US Grand Strategy in the 21st Century: The Case for Restraint,* ed. A. Trevor Thrall and Benjamin H. Friedman (London: Routledge, 2018), 35–37.

34. Walter Lippmann, *US Foreign Policy: Shield of the Republic* (Boston: Little Brown, 1943), 174.

ACKNOWLEDGMENTS

Nuclear weapons were my first intellectual love; alliances my second. While studying the former, I found my enthusiasm for the latter encouraged beyond my wildest dreams. This book owes so much to the support of incomparable academic mentors: Richard Betts, Page Fortna, Robert Jervis, and Andrew Nathan. Bob Jervis is an immense source of inspiration to this day. I also had the great fortune of serving as Ken Waltz's final research assistant. I had the opportunity to discuss with him some of the ideas in these pages when they were barely embryonic. Ken's friendship will remain one of my life's privileges. He is much missed.

My decision to pursue a career in the policy world and to deepen my expertise in Asia has been no less supported. I am especially indebted to Kurt Campbell, Mike Green, and Jim Steinberg, all of whom provided thoughtful guidance as I repurposed my academic research for a policy-facing audience. All three are consummate scholar-practitioners with deep expertise. My work has benefited from the wisdom they have earned through service, and from their scholarship. I am also grateful to Joe Nye for his support.

This book would have been impossible if not for my affiliation with some remarkable institutions and the people comprising them. The project began at the Center for a New American Security, and I am particularly indebted to Richard Fontaine for his counsel. I am also grateful to Anthony Cho for excellent research assistance and to Hannah Suh for stalwart support of all kinds. I wrote the book at the China Center at Yale Law School, and it would not have materialized without the support and enthusiasm of Paul Gewirtz and Robert Williams. Dylan Kolhoff and Josh Hochman lent superb research assistance at Yale. Now, at the Council on Foreign Relations, I continue to rely on fine colleagues. I am grateful to Richard Haass, Jim Lindsay, Liz Economy, the CFR communications teams, and many others who have helped me share my ideas with the world. My role as a volunteer advisor to Hillary Clinton's 2016 presidential campaign was formative and demonstrated to me the urgency of using scholarly findings to defend America's most remarkable and underappreciated tool of statecraft. It was an enormous privilege to work for Jake Sullivan, Laura Rosenberger, and Dan Kurtz-Phelan.

Shields of the Republic is a far stronger book because of feedback I received from wonderful scholars. Tarun Chhabra and the Brookings Institution generously hosted a manuscript workshop, where I benefited from suggestions offered by Rush Doshi, Jim Goldgeier, Brian Hahs, Ryan Hass, David Shear, Tom Wright, Tarun, and others. I am especially grateful for regular exchanges with David Edelstein and Elizabeth Saunders, from whom I learn so much. Anonymous reviewers offered thoughtful comments that buttressed my work.

At Harvard University Press, I am grateful to Thomas LeBien for seeing promise in my work and finding it a home. The manuscript benefited immensely from Simon Waxman's thoughtful editing and Heather Hughes's guidance. I am particularly indebted to Sharmila Sen, whose strong leadership is matched by her compassion for her authors and their ideas.

I am all the more fortunate to have colleagues who are also dear friends. Charles Edel has been a fount of wisdom and encouragement from this project's inception. I am a better foreign policy scholar for Zack Cooper's constructive camaraderie. Rebecca Lissner's intellectual partnership extends far beyond the bounds of our work together; this book would not be here without her.

My deepest appreciation is owed to my family. My grandparents, Will and Clara, nourished my love of history. They encouraged me to consider counterfactual worlds, by virtue of the lives they lived. They will be with me always. My brother Teo has been a tremendous source of intellectual and emotional support at moments of difficulty as well as triumph. My husband, Matt, is a partner and champion in work and life, and my love and appreciation for him has only grown. Our little wonder, Emilie, timed her debut and masterminded her earliest months in a manner that allowed me to finish this project with a fuller heart than I had ever imagined. Finally, through her counsel and her example, my remarkable mother, Rayna Rapp, taught me that one could make a rich and exciting career in the world of ideas—and could make those ideas matter beyond the bounds of any discipline. In my younger years, she read every paper I wrote with affection and care. I publish my first book with love for, and gratitude to, these extraordinary supporters.

INDEX

Page numbers followed by *f* or *n* indicate figures or notes.